Redesigning Petroleum Taxation

Since its inception some 40 years ago, petroleum-specific taxation in the UK has been subject to numerous modifications. Often these modifications were brought into place not only to sufficiently incentivise the investors but also to capture a fair share for the government. However, it is evident from the frequency of changes that finding the right balance between these two aims is no easy matter. Such a balance, and the consequent fiscal stability, is necessary for the long-term relationship between the parties to endure to their mutual benefit. Still, it does not take much for one or other party to feel that they are out of balance. As a consequence, one party feels that the other party is taking an undue proportion of the value generated and that they are losing out.

Yet achieving that balance and fiscal stability is possible. To understand this possibility, this book first clarifies what is meant by sufficient incentivisation and fair share before developing a new fiscal system that manages this balance and stability. Such clarification yields objective criteria against which to assess not only the existing regime, but also the newly proposed regime. This approach is further complemented by the critical analysis of the fiscal legislative framework and the evaluation of the legal positions of specific contractual elements and mechanisms found within that framework. This latter analysis is important in order to reduce the legal uncertainty such elements may create, which can otherwise lead to further reactive amendments and revisions to the fiscal regime in the future.

Emre Üşenmez is a petroleum economist and a legal expert in the upstream oil and gas sector. He is a Senior Lecturer in Finance at the University of Aberdeen's AFG College and a Senior Lecturer in Law at the University of Aberdeen Law School. Until August 2018 he also served as Dean for Internationalisation focussing on China and East Asia at the University of Aberdeen. He is also an associate at the Aberdeen Energy Institute and Aberdeen University Centre for Energy Law (AUCEL). Prior to joining the University of Aberdeen, he worked in the natural resources sector in Azerbaijan and has significant experience working with the staff of national ministries, and state and private oil companies around the world.

He is a Fellow of the Higher Education Academy and holds a PhD in Economics, Finance and Law, an MSc in Petroleum, Energy Economics and Finance, and an LLM in Oil & Gas Law from the University of Aberdeen. He also holds a BSc in Economics and a BA in Political Science from North Carolina State University.

Routledge Explorations in Environmental Economics
Edited by **Nick Hanley**, *University of Stirling, UK*

48 The Impact of Climate Policy on Environmental and Economic Performance
Evidence from Sweden
Rolf Färe, Shawna Grosskopf, Tommy Lundgren, Per-Olov Marklund and Wenchao Zhou

49 Economics of International Environmental Agreements
A Critical Approach
Edited by M. Özgür Kayalıca, Selim Çağatay and Hakan Mıhçı

50 Environmental and Economic Impacts of Decarbonization
Input-Output Studies on the Consequences of the 2015 Paris Agreements
Edited by Óscar Dejuán, Manfred Lenzen and María-Ángeles Cadarso

51 Advances in Fisheries Bioeconomics
Theory and Policy
Edited by Juan Carlos Seijo and Jon G. Sutinen

52 Redesigning Petroleum Taxation
Aligning Government and Investors in the UK
Emre Üşenmez

53 National Pathways to Low Carbon-Emission Economies
Innovation Policies for Decarbonizing and Unlocking
Edited by Kurt Hübner

54 The Economics of Renewable Energy in the Gulf
Edited by Hisham M. Akhonbay

For more information about this series, please visit www.routledge.com/series/REEE

Redesigning Petroleum Taxation

Aligning Government and Investors in the UK

Emre Üşenmez

Routledge
Taylor & Francis Group
LONDON AND NEW YORK

First published 2019
by Routledge
2 Park Square, Milton Park, Abingdon, Oxon OX14 4RN

and by Routledge
711 Third Avenue, New York, NY 10017

Routledge is an imprint of the Taylor & Francis Group, an informa business

British Library Cataloguing-in-Publication Data
A catalogue record for this book is available from the British Library

Library of Congress Cataloging-in-Publication Data
A catalog record has been requested for this book

ISBN: 978-1-138-21996-0 (hbk)
ISBN: 978-1-315-41409-6 (ebk)

Typeset in Times New Roman
by Integra Software Services Pvt. Ltd.

Visit the eResources: https://www.routledge.com/9781138219960

MIX
Paper from responsible sources
FSC® C013056

Printed and bound in Great Britain by
TJ International Ltd, Padstow, Cornwall

Contents

Charts

Tables

Abbreviations

ACE	Allowance for Corporate Equity
ATL	Above the Line (Credit)
BOE	Barrel of Oil Equivalent
BT	Brown Tax
CA	Court of Appeals
CAA	Cluster Area Allowance
CAPEX	Capital Expenditures
CBIT	Comprehensive Business Income Tax
CFD	Contract for Differences
CGT	Capital Gains Tax
CIT	Corporate Income Tax
CT	Corporation Tax
DCF	Discounted Cash Flow
DECC	Department of Energy and Climate Change
DRD	Decommissioning Relief Deed
E&A	Exploration and Appraisal
E&P	Exploration and Production
ECJ	European Court of Justice
EES	Exploration Expenditure Supplement
EMV	Expected Monetary Value
EMV/I	Expected Monetary Value/Investment Ratio
EOR	Enhanced Oil Recovery
FOB	Free on Board
FPSO	Floating Production Storage and Offloading
FV	Future Value
HMRC	Her Majesty's Revenue and Customs
HP/HT	High Pressure/High Temperature oil field
HRIT	Higher Rate of Income Tax
IA	Investment Allowance
IASB	International Accounting Standards Board
IOR	Improved Oil Recovery
IRR	Internal Rate of Return
IT	Income Tax

MEA	Mineral Extraction Allowance
MER UK	Maximum Economic Recovery from the UK
MER	Maximum Economic Recovery
MOD	Money of the Day
NPV	Net Present Value
OGA	Oil and Gas Authority
OPEX	Operating Expenditures
P/I	Profit/Investment Ratio
PPT	Progressive Profits Tax
PRT	Petroleum Revenue Tax
PSA	Production Sharing Agreement
PV	Present Value
R&D	Research and Development
RFCT	Ring Fence Corporation Tax
RFES	Ring Fence Expenditure Supplement
ROI	Return on Investment
RRT	Resource Rent Tax
SC	Supplementary Charge
TRA	Tariff Receipt Allowance
Ts&Cs	Terms and Conditions
uH	Ultra-heavy oil field
uHP/HT	Ultra-high pressure/high temperature
UK	United Kingdom
UKCS	United Kingdom Continental Shelf
USD	United States Dollar
VAT	Value Added Tax
WACC	Weighted Average Cost of Capital

Cases

K cases

A-G v Great Southern and Western Rly Co of Ireland (1925) AC 754
Amerada Hess Ltd v Inland Revenue Commissioners (2000) STC (SCD) 397
Atherton (HM Inspector of Taxes) v British Insulated and Helsby Cables, Limited [1925] KB 421, 10 TC 155 (CA)
Auckland Harbour Board v The King (1924) AC 318
Benson (Inspector of Taxes) v Yard Arm Club Ltd [1979] 1 WLR 347 (CA)
BP Oil Development Ltd v Commissioners of Inland Revenue [1992] STC 28, 64 TC 498 (Ch D)
British Insulated and Helsby Cables Ltd v Atherton [1926] AC 205 (HL)
Churchward v R (1865) LR 1 QB 173 (pre-SCJA 1873)
Commercial Cable Co v Government of Newfoundland (1916) 2 AC 610
ECC Quarries Ltd v Watkins (Inspector of Taxes) [1975] 3 All ER 843 (Ch D), (1977) 1 WLR 1386
Gaspet Ltd v Elliss (Inspector of Taxes) [1985] 1 WLR 1214 (Ch D)
H.T.V. Ltd v Price Commission [1976] ICR 170 (CA)
Hinton (Inspector of Taxes) v. Madden & Ireland Ltd [1959] 3 ALL ER 356, [1959] 1 WLR 875, 38 TC 391 (HL)
IRC v Mobil North Sea Ltd [1986] 1 WLR 296, [1986] STC 45 at 60–61, 60 TC 310 (Ch D)
Macbeth v Haldimand (1786) 1 Term Rep 172, 99 ER 1036 (KB)
Mackay v A-G for British Columbia (1922) 1 AC 457
Mobil North Sea Ltd v IRC [1987] 1 WLR 1065, [1987] STC 458, 60 TC 310 (HL)
Phillips v Eyre (1870) LR 6 QB 1
Preston, Re sub nom R v IRC, ex p Preston [1985] AC 835, [1985] 2 All ER 327, [1985] 2 WLR 836 (HL)
Pyrah (Inspector of Taxes) v Annis & Co Ltd [1957] 1 All ER 196, [1957] 1 WLR 190, 37 TC 163
R v IRC, ex p Preston [1983] 2 All ER 300 (QB)
Rederiaktiebolaget Amphitrite v R [1921] 3 KB 500 (KBD)
Robertson v Minister of Pensions [1949] 1 KB 227 at 237 (KB)

RTZ Oil and Gas v. Elliss (Inspector of Taxes) [1987] 1 WLR 1442, [1987] STC 512 (Ch D)
Strick (Inspector of Taxes) v Regent Oil Co Ltd [1966] AC 295 (CA)
Test Claimants in the Thin Cap Group Litigation v Commissioners of Inland Revenue (C-524/04) [2007] ECR I-02107
Town Investments Ltd v Department of the Environment [1978] AC 359 (HL)
Tucker (Inspector of Taxes) v. Granada Motorway Services Ltd [1979] 2 All ER 801, [1979] STC 393 (HL)
Yarmouth v France (1887) 19 QBD 647, 57 LJQB 7 (QBD)

Australian cases

Woodside Energy Ltd v Commissioner of Taxation for the Commonwealth of Australia [2006] FCA 1303 (4 October 2006) [52]

USA cases

Exxon Corporation and Affiliated Companies v Commissioner of Internal Revenue 113 US TC 24 (1999)

Arbitration tribunals

AGIP Company v Popular Republic of the Congo (International Centre for Settlement of Investment Disputes, 30 November 1979) 21 ILM 726–739
Amoco International Finance Corporation v Islamic Republic of Iran (1988) 27 ILM 1314 (United States Claims Tribunal, Partial Award)
Revere Copper and Brass, Incorporated v Overseas Private Investment Corporation (American Arbitration Association, 24 August 1978) 17 ILM 1321–1383
Saudi Arabia v Arabian American Oil Company (Aramco) Arbitration Tribunal (23 August 1958) 27 ILR 117–233
Texaco Overseas Petroleum Company/California Asiatic Oil Company v Government of the Libyan Arab Republic (1978) 17 ILM 1–37
The Government of the State of Kuwait v The American Independent Oil Company (Aminoil) (The Arbitration Tribunal, 24 March 1982) 21 ILM 976–1052

Legislations

K legislation

Capital Allowances Act 1968
Capital Allowances Act 2001
Capital Gains Tax Act 1979
Companies Act 2006
Corporation Tax Act 2009
Corporation Tax Act 2010
Crown Proceedings Act 1947
Energy HL Bill (2015–16)
Energy Act 2016
Finance (No.2) Act 1979
Finance (No.2) Act 1992
Finance Act 1973
Finance Act 1980
Finance Act 1981
Finance Act 1983
Finance Act 1984
Finance Act 1985
Finance Act 1987
Finance Act 1988
Finance Act 1991
Finance Act 1993
Finance Act 1994
Finance Act 2000
Finance Act 2001
Finance Act 2002
Finance Act 2006
Finance Act 2007
Finance Act 2008
Finance Act 2009
Finance Act 2011
Finance Act 2012

Finance Act 2013
Finance Act 2014
Finance Act 2015
Finance Act 2016
Income and Corporation Taxes Act 1988
Infrastructure Act 2015
Oil Taxation Act 1975
Oil Taxation Act 1983
Petroleum Act 1998
Petroleum and Submarine Pipe-lines Act 1975
Petroleum Royalties (Relief) Act 1983
Taxation (International and Other Provisions) Act 2010
Taxation of Chargeable Gains Act 1992

UK statutory instruments

Additionally-developed Oil Fields Order 2013, SI 2910
Oil Taxation (Market Value of Oil) Regulations 2006, SI 3313
Oil Taxation (Nomination Scheme for Disposals) (Amendment) Regulations 2007, SI 1454
Petroleum (Production) Regulations 1982, SI 1982/1000
Qualifying Oil Fields Order 2012, SI 3153
The Investment Allowance and Cluster Area Allowance (Investment Expenditure) Regulations 2016

USA legislation

26 US Code § 901–989

EU legislation

Treaty Establishing the European Community – Consolidated Version [2002] OJ C 340/0173
European Convention of Human Rights and Fundamental Freedoms [1953]

Australian legislation

Petroleum Resource Rent Tax Assessment Act 1987
Tax Laws Amendment (2013 Measures No. 2) Act 2013
Trade Practices Act 1974

Parliamentary debates, official documents and policy papers

Parliamentary debates

HC Deb 5 December 2005, vol 440, col 612
HC Deb 9 May 2002, vol 385, vols 359–361
HC Deb 23 March 2011 vol 525, cols 964–965
HC Deb 5 July 2011, vol 530, col 82WS
HC Deb 6 November 2014 vol 587, cols 52–53WS

Official documents and policy papers

Australian Taxation Office, 'Guide to Depreciating Assets 2013' (Guide 1996–06, ATO 2013)

Australian Tax Office, 'Petroleum Resource Rent Tax' (Guide, ATO 2016)

Davey, E, 'Written Ministerial Statement by Edward Davey: Review of UK Offshore Oil & Gas Recovery' (Written Statement, DECC 10 June 2013)

Department for Business, Innovation & Skills, 'Guidelines on the Meaning of Research and Development for Tax Purposes' (Guidelines, DBIS 2010)

Department for Trade and Industry, 'Outcome of Consultation Paper on Appropriate Timing of Abolition of North Sea Royalty' (Consultation, DTI 2002)

Department of Energy & Climate Change and Oil and Gas Authority, 'Maximising Economic Recovery of UK Petroleum: the MER UK strategy' (Strategy, DECC and OGA 18 March 2016)

Department of Energy & Climate Change and Oil and Gas Authority, 'OGA Decommissioning Strategy' (Strategy, DECC and OGA 30 June 2016)

Department of Energy & Climate Change, 'Government Response to Sir Ian Wood's UKCS: Maximising Economic Recovery Review' (Report, DECC July 2014)

Department of Energy & Climate Change, 'Maximising Economic Recovery of Offshore UK Petroleum: Draft Strategy For Consultation' (Consultation, DECC November 2015)

Department of Energy & Climate Change, 'Oil and Gas – Guidance: Oil and Gas: Fields and Field Development: Brown Field Allowances: Guidance' (Guidance, DECC 22 January 2013, as updated on 29 December 2014)

Department of Energy & Climate Change, 'Wood Sets Out £200 billion Roadmap for Future of Offshore Oil and Gas Industry & World's First Gas CCS Plant Planned' (Press Release, DECC 24 February 2014)

Department of Energy & Climate Change, 'Digest of United Kingdom Energy Statistics 2015' (Report, National Statistics July 2015)

Department of Energy & Climate Change, 'Oil and Gas: Field Data' (Guidance, DECC 22 January 2013, as updated on 10 September 2015)

Department of Energy & Climate Change, 'Outcome of Consultation Paper on Appropriate Timing of Abolition of North Sea Royalty Consultation' (DECC April 2002)

Department of Energy and Climate Change, 'UKCS Field Information' (DECC, 20 April 2015) <https://www.og.decc.gov.uk/fields/fields_index.htm> accessed 22 April 2015

Henry K, Harmer J, Piggott J, Ridout H, and Smith G, 'Australia's Future Tax System: Report to the Treasurer' (Commonwealth of Australia The Treasury, December 2009).

HM Revenue & Customs, '"Above the Line" credit for Research and Development: response to consultation' (Consultation, HMRC 27 March 2012)

HM Revenue & Customs, 'Capital Allowances Manual' (Manual, HMRC 11 February 2015)

HM Revenue & Customs, 'Finance Bill 2015: Corporation Tax: Oil and Gas Taxation and the Reduction in Supplementary Charge' (Policy Paper, HMRC 10 December 2014)

HM Revenue & Customs, 'International Manual' (Manual, HMRC 14 May 2015)

HM Revenue & Customs, 'Number of oil and gas fields with different PRT liabilities' (Table, HMRC 30 June 2014)

HM Revenue & Customs, 'Oil and Gas Taxation: Reduction in Petroleum Revenue Tax and Supplementary Charge' (Policy Paper, HMRC 16 March 2016)

HM Revenue & Customs, 'LBS Oil and Gas Market Values for Category 1 crudes 2015' (List, HMRC Large Business Service 2 June 2015)

HM Revenue & Customs, 'Oil Taxation Manual' (Manual, HMRC 12 November 2014)

HM Revenue & Customs, 'Thin Capitalisation: Practical guidance – comparison of lending in the UK with other countries: Thin capitalisation rules in different jurisdictions' (INTM – International Manual, HMRC 14 May 2015)

HM Treasury, 'Budget 2002: The Strength to make long-term decisions: Investing in an enterprising, fairer Britain' (Report, HM Treasury 17 April 2002)

HM Treasury, 'Budget 2016' (Report, HM Treasury 16 March 2016)

HM Treasury, 'Fiscal reform of the UK Continental Shelf: response to the consultation on an investment allowance' (Consultation, HM Treasury March 2015)

HM Treasury, 'Maximising economic recovery – consultation on a cluster area allowance: summary of responses' (Consultation, HM Treasury December 2014)

HM Treasury, 'Maximising economic recovery: consultation on a cluster allowance' (Consultation, HM Treasury July 2014)

HM Treasury, 'Tax certainty for oil and gas decommissioning will lead to extra £13 billion North Sea investment' (Press Release, HM Treasury 17 October 2013)

HM Treasury, 'Autumn Statement 2014' (Statement, HM Treasury December 2014)

HM Treasury, Britain meeting the global challenge: Enterprise, fairness and responsibility (Pre-Budget Report, HM Treasury 5 December 2005)

HM Treasury, 'Budget 2011' (Report, HM Treasury 23 March 2011)

HM Treasury, 'Budget 2012' (Report, HM Treasury 21 March 2012)

HM Treasury, 'Budget 2014' (Report, HM Treasury 19 March 2014)

HM Treasury, 'Budget 2015' (Report, HM Treasury 18 March 2015)

HM Treasury, 'Decommissioning Relief Deeds: increasing tax certainty for oil and gas investment in the UK continental shelf' (Consultation, HM Treasury 9 July 2012)

HM Treasury, 'Driving Investment: a plan to reform the oil and gas fiscal regime' (Report, HM Treasury December 2014)

IFRS, 'Conceptual Framework for Financial Reporting: Chapter 1: The Objective of Financial Reporting' (Agenda Paper 7A, IASB Meeting September 2007)

IFRS, 'International Accounting Standards: IAS 16 – Property, Plant and Equipment' (Standards, IFRS 2003)

International Accounting Standards Board (IASB), A Review of Conceptual Framework for Financial Reporting (Discussion Paper DP/2013/1, IFRS Foundation 2013)

International Accounting Standards Board (IASB), Conceptual Framework for Financial Reporting: The Objective of Financial Reporting and Qualitative Characteristics and Constraints of Decision-Useful Financial Reporting Information (Exposure draft issued on 29 May 2008, IFRS Foundation 2008)

International Organization of Securities Commissions, 'Oil Price Reporting Agencies – Report by IEA, IEF, OPEC and IOSCO to G20 Finance Ministers' (Report, IOSCO 14 November 2011)

IRS, 'Foreign Tax Credit' (2013) <http://www.irs.gov/Individuals/International-Taxpayers/Foreign-Tax-Credit> accessed 01 October 2014

Norges Offentlige Utredninger, 'Skattlegging av petroleumsvirksomhet' (Report No 18, Ministry of Finance Norway June 2000)

North West Shelf Gas, 'North West Shelf Project: Overview' (2014) < http://www.nwsg.com.au/projects/overview> accessed 26 March 2017

Norwegian Ministry of Finance, 'Riktige beregninger fra Finansdepartementet' (Norwegian Ministry of Finance 2013)

Norwegian Ministry of Finance, 'Skattlegging av petroleumsvirksomhet' (Norwegian Official Report 2000:18 Norwegian Ministry of Finance 2000)

Oil & Gas Authority, 'Call to Action: The Oil and Gas Authority Commission 2015' (Report, the OGA Commission 25 February 2015)

Oil & Gas UK, 'Budget Lays Strong Foundations for Regeneration of the UK North Sea' (Press Release, Oil & Gas UK 18 March 2015)

Oil & Gas UK, 'Oil & Gas UK meeting with Chancellor George Osborne' (Press Release, Oil & Gas UK 25 February 2015)

Oil & Gas UK, 'Report paints bleak picture of high-potential industry but the solution is clear, says Oil & Gas UK' (Press Release, Oil & Gas UK 24 February 2015)

Oil & Gas UK, 'Tax Changes Vital for the Future of the UK's North Sea Oil and Gas Industry' (Press Release, Oil & Gas UK 19 March 2015)

Oil & Gas UK, 'Wood Review Final Recommendations Can Be Game Changers for UK Continental Shelf' (Press Release, Oil & Gas UK 24 February 2014)

Oil & Gas UK, 'Activity Survey 2014' (Report, Oil & Gas UK 2014)

Oil & Gas UK, 'Activity Survey 2015' (Report, Oil & Gas UK 2015)

Oil & Gas UK, 'Activity Survey 2016' (Report, Oil & Gas UK 2016)

Oil & Gas UK, Decommissioning Insight 2014 (Report, Oil & Gas UK 2014)

Oil & Gas UK, 'Economic Report 2013' (Report, Oil & Gas UK 2013)

Oil & Gas UK, 'Economic Report 2014' (Report, Oil & Gas UK 2014)

Oil and Gas Authority, 'Summary of UK Estimated Remaining Recoverable Hydrocarbon Resources 2015' (Report, OGA 2016)

Osborne G, 'Chancellor George Osborne's Budget 2014 Speech' (Speech, HM Treasury, 2014)

Parliament of Australia, 'Budget 2010-11: Taxation – Resource Super Profits Tax' (Budget Review, Parliament of Australia May 2010)

Parliament of Australia, 'Budget Measures: Budget Paper No.2: 2010–2011' (Budget Paper, Commonwealth of Australia 2010)

Parliament of Australia, 'Taxation – Resource super profits tax' (Budget Review, Commonwealth of Australia 2010)

PILOT Progressive Partnership Work Group, 'The Work of the Progressive Partnership Group' (PILOT 2002)

PILOT, 'About PILOT: What is PILOT?' (2010) < http://www.pilottaskforce.co.uk/data/aboutpilot.cfm> accessed 16 January 2015

PILOT, 'Maximising Economic Recovery of the UK's Oil and Gas Reserves: Context for the Brownfields Challenge' (Report, PILOT March 2005)

PILOT, 'Priority Areas' (2010) <http://pilottaskforce.co.uk> accessed 08 April 2015

Rudd K and Swan W, 'Stronger, fairer, simpler: a tax plan for the future' (Commonwealth of Australia the Treasury Media Release 2 May 2010) <http://ministers.treasury.gov.au/DisplayDocs.aspx?doc=pressreleases/2010/028.htm&pageID=003&min=wms&Year> accessed 26 March 2017

The Treasury, 'The Resource Super Profits Tax: a Fair Return to the Nation' (Commonwealth of Australia The Treasury 2010)

United Nations Centre on Transnational Corporations (UNCTC), 'Financial and Fiscal Aspects of Petroleum Exploitation' (UNCTC Advisory Studies, Series B No 3, ST/CTC/SER.B/3, 1987)

US Department of Treasury, Integration of the Individual and Corporate Tax Systems: Taxing Business Income Once (US Government Printing Office, Washington 1992)

US Energy Information Agency, 'Petroleum & Other Liquids: Europe Brent Spot Price FOB' (US EIA 13 December 2015)

Wood, Sir I, 'UKCS Maximising Recovery Review: Final Report' (Report, 25 February 2014)

Wood, Sir I, 'UKCS Maximising Recovery Review: Interim Report' (Report, 11 November 2013)

1 Introduction

Since the enactment of the Continental Shelf Act 1964 the UK sector of the North Sea has developed into one of the major hydrocarbon jurisdictions in the world.[1] The period from 1965 to the present has been marked with successive changes to the fiscal regime,[2] particularly since 1975 when any notable production began. In that year, all extant licences were retrospectively amended[3] to include a 12½% royalty payment on semi-annual production.[4] The same year also witnessed the introduction of two petroleum-specific tax instruments,[5] the Ring Fence Corporation Tax (RFCT)[6] and the Petroleum Revenue Tax (PRT).[7] The former instrument effectively isolated, or ring-fenced, petroleum exploitation activities from other activities a company may also be engaged in[8] and applied the corporation tax as if it were a 'separate trade'.[9]

Since its introduction the headline rate of the RFCT has changed 12 times under 9 different pieces of legislation, ranging from 52% to 30%.[10] Also in this period, the relevant RFCT rules regarding the treatment of losses and expenditures changed even more frequently, with the most recent changes introduced in 2015.[11]

The second petroleum-specific tax instrument, PRT, also ring-fenced petroleum exploitation activities, albeit with a tighter ring isolating the companies' petroliferous trades[12] at a field level.[13] That is, whereas RFCT applied to a company's profits arising from all its upstream activities in the UK, PRT was levied on the profits arising from individual fields.[14] Like RFCT, the headline rate for PRT also changed over time. Since its introduction the PRT rate has changed 7 times in the same number of pieces of legislation with the most recent change brought about in 2016.[15] It should, however, be noted that these most recent changes applied only to pre-1993 fields because the PRT had been abolished for the fields that received a development consent from the regulator after 15 March 1993.[16] Also, as was the case under the RFCT mechanism, the rules governing the calculation of the PRT liability were also subject to frequent changes.[17]

This period also witnessed the gradual abolition of the royalty mechanism first in 1982 for those fields that received a development consent after 31 March 1982,[18] and then in its entirety from 1 January 2003.[19]

The fiscal changes were not limited to above, however. In 2002, the government introduced a new imposition called the Supplementary Charge (SC).[20] The SC behaved almost identically to the RFCT but it was only an additional charge and not a corporation tax.[21] Continuing the fiscal tradition, the government changed the SC headline rate 6 times in its 14 years of existence with the most recent three changes taking place within a 15-month period.[22] These changes were, of course, in addition to a number of changes brought about to the way in which the losses and the expenditures were treated under the SC as well.[23]

It is against this considerably unstable fiscal background that this work has been prepared with the overarching objective of developing a policy framework for a fiscal regime that is not only stable enough to avoid future alterations but also sufficiently fair to balance the unaligned imperatives of the investors and the government.

Most of the changes to the fiscal mechanisms discussed above have been introduced in order to incentivise the investors to explore for and get petroleum, all the while 'aiming to ensure that an appropriate share of the benefits accrues to the UK economy as a whole'.[24]

These two aims of petroleum taxation – of incentivising investors to conduct petroleum operations and collecting an *appropriate share* of the proceeds – have been officially reiterated by the UK government a number of times over the years with the latest iteration in December 2014[25] In response to the publication of the Wood Report.[26] The Wood Report was the product of the review conducted by Sir Ian Wood examining the governance and stewardship of the UK's hydrocarbon sector. At that time the Treasury published its most recent Fiscal Review setting the objective of petroleum taxation again as 'maximising economic recovery of hydrocarbon resources whilst ensuring a fair return on those resources for the nation'.[27]

It is therefore clear that the taxation of petroleum exploitation in the UK consistently and officially has had a dual purpose. One, for the tax to be accommodating enough to entice investors, and two, for it to be robust enough to collect an appropriate level of revenue for the UK from the upstream activities.

However, it is evident from the frequency of the changes to the fiscal regime that finding the right balance between these two aims is no easy matter. Even the most recent changes introduced by the Treasury have fallen short of its own stated aims. Still, attaining such a balance – and, consequently fiscal stability – is necessary for the long-term relationship between the parties to endure to their mutual benefit. Unfortunately, it does not take much for one or the other party to feel that they are out of balance. As a consequence, one party feels that the other party is taking an undue proportion of the value generated and that they are losing out.

Yet achieving that balance and fiscal stability is possible. This is the fundamental objective of this work, developing a policy framework that satisfies such possibility. To understand this possibility, it is important to first understand the joint purposes of petroleum taxation stated by the Treasury. Therefore initially this work discusses in Chapter 2 the government's rationale for reform that led to the Treasury's Fiscal Review. This discussion provides the parameters to analyse the conditions under which both the investors are incentivised and the 'maximum economic recovery of hydrocarbon resources' are attained, and ascertain what is meant by *appropriate share* or by *fair return* for the state.

Based on that understanding this work subsequently evaluates the Treasury's most recent reforms in terms of the extent of their deviation from the stated aim of petroleum taxation. To do so, however, it is necessary to first understand what is being reformed. Chapter 3 therefore discusses the fiscal regime in place prior to the Fiscal Review reforms. It sets the then existing regime against the Treasury's joint purposes of taxation to evaluate where the regime stood with respect to the Fiscal Review objective. Such an evaluation, in turn, aids not only in understanding the shortcomings of the ensuing reforms discussed in Chapter 4 but also in developing the new policy framework that successfully balances the joint aims of the Treasury.

Accordingly this work, in Chapter 5, advocates the abolition of both RFCT and SC and proposes a new fiscal regime that is based on project-level cash flows. This proposal builds on some specific elements of PRT as well as on the theoretical tax system put forward in 1948 by E C Brown[28] although uniquely modifying them to adopt to the realities of the petroliferous trade in the UK. A contractual mechanism is subsequently proposed to underpin this new fiscal system in its entirety. It posits that such a contractual arrangement will not only create the necessary stability without jeopardising the parliamentary sovereignty but will also ensure robust and tailored tax returns for the government without significantly compromising on simplicity.

A number of fiscal mechanisms aimed at establishing such a balance by building on Brown's theoretical model have been proposed since the turn of the millennium, notably in Norway[29] and Australia.[30] Although this is not a comparative study, this work nonetheless also aims to understand the reasons behind the failure of those proposals in these respective jurisdictions. That understanding also informs the new policy framework developed in this work.

The principal findings of the study are subsequently highlighted in Chapter 6.

Notes

1 The historical account of the development of oil sector in the UK is beyond the scope of this work. For an excellent account see Alex Kemp, *The Official History of North Sea Oil and Gas* (Routledge 2012)

2 Throughout the work the terms fiscal regime and fiscal system are used interchangeably.

3 Petroleum and Submarine Pipe-lines Act 1975, s 18

4 Petroleum and Submarine Pipe-lines Act 1975, s 2 and Sch 2

5 Throughout the work the term instruments, mechanisms, and tools are used interchangeably to refer to individual fiscal pillars.
6 Oil Taxation Act 1975, s 13
7 Oil Taxation Act 1975, Pt I
8 Such as refining
9 Oil Taxation Act 1975, s 13
10 See Emre Usenmez, *'The UKCS Fiscal Regime*' in G Gordon, J Paterson and E Usenmez (eds), *Oil and Gas Law: Current Practice and Emerging Trends* (2nd Ed, DUP 2011) 6.7–6.8 for the details of the changes and the relevant legislations.
11 The most recent changes will be discussed in Section 4.1 below. For an account of the historical changes see Usenmez (n 10)
12 Please note that 'petroliferous trade' is a term employed by the HM Revenue & Customs, the oil and gas industry and the petroleum tax experts both in academia and in the professions to refer to upstream activities. See for example, HM Revenue & Customs, '*Oil Taxation Manual'* (Manual, HMRC 1 September 2016) OT20250-4; Oil & Gas Authorit, *Call to Action: The Oil and Gas Authority Commission 2015* (25 February 2015 Report OGA); Pinsent Masons LLP, *'Shale Gas Toolkit: Tax and Incentives for the Shale Gas Industry Part 2'* (2015 Report Pinsent Masons LLP); Deloitte LLP, *'Oil and gas taxation in the UK: Deloitte taxation and investment guides'* (2013 Report Deloitte LLP); and Alex G Kemp, *The Official History of North Sea Oil and Gas: Volume II* (Routledge 2012). Due to this wide spread use of the term, the same convention is adopted throughout this work.
13 Oil Taxation Act 1975, s 1
14 Note that the definition and the determination of a field are given in Oil Taxation Act 1975, s 1
15 Most recent at the time of writing. Finance Act 2016, s 140. Section 4.1 below discusses the changes in detail. Also see Usenmez (n 10) 6.27–6.28 for the discussion of the changes to the PRT rate and of the relevant legislations.
16 Finance Act 1993, ss 185–186
17 See Usenmez (n 10) for a discussion on the historical changes.
18 Petroleum Royalties (Relief) Act 1983 s 1 read together with Finance Act 1983 s 36(2).
19 See the announcement at Department of Energy and Climate Change, '*Outcome of Consultation Paper on Appropriate Timing of Abolition of North Sea Royalty'* (Consultation, DECC April 2002).
20 Finance Act 2002, ss 91–92
21 HM Revenue & Customs, '*Oil Taxation Manual'* (Manual, HMRC 1 September 2016) OT21219
22 Section 4.1 below discusses these most recent changes in detail. For a discussion on the historical account see Usenmez (n 10) and Emre Usenmez, '*The Stability of the UK Tax Regime for Offshore Oil and Gas: Positive Developments and Potential Threats'* (2010) ICCLR 16
23 Section 3.3 discusses the treatments of the losses and expenditures.
24 HM Revenue & Customs (n 21) OT00010
25 HM Treasury, '*Driving Investment: a plan to reform the oil and gas fiscal regime'* (Report, HM Treasury December 2014)
26 Sir Ian Wood, '*UKCS Maximising Recovery Review: Final Report'* (Report, 24 February 2014)
27 HM Treasury (n 25) Box 4.A

28 E Carry Brown, '*Business-Income Taxation and Investment Incentives*' in L A Metzler (ed), *Income, Employment and Public Policy: Essay in Honor of Alvin H. Hansen* (New York, W W Norton & Co, Inc 1948)
29 Norges Offentlige Utredninger, 'Skattlegging av petroleumsvirksomhet' (Report No 18, Ministry of Finance Norway June 2000)
30 Parliament of Australia, 'Budget 2010–11: Taxation – Resource Super Profits Tax' (Budget Review, Parliament of Australia May 2010)

2 Government's rationale for fiscal reform

2.1. Government's rationale for reform: the Wood Review & its aftermath

On 4 December 2014, the Treasury published its review of the oil and gas fiscal regime (the Fiscal Review).[1] It was commissioned by the then Chancellor George Osborne that previous March[2] in response to the publication of the final report by Sir Ian Wood (the Wood Report).[3]

The Wood Report was one of the most influential documents in recent times to shape oil and gas governance in the UK. It was the product of another review commissioned that preceding June by the then Secretary of State for Energy Edward Davey, looking into the governance and stewardship of the UK's hydrocarbon sector.[4] This latter review was carried out in response to the maturity of the UK Continental Shelf (UKCS) as this maturity continued to pose certain unique challenges that were deemed to be significant enough to warrant a review.[5]

The UKCS is a mature province. More than 42 billion barrels of oil equivalent (boe) has been extracted to date,[6] and the production has been in a steady decline since the turn of the millennium. Chart 2.1 illustrates the total annual petroleum production in the UK.

Yet the UKCS is not a hopeless case. The current regulator of the oil and gas industry, the Oil and Gas Authority (OGA), estimates that there are still somewhere between 10 and 20 billion boe oil and gas reserves available.[7] This estimate includes those discoveries where there are ongoing discussions with the regulator on the development plans, and of those fields that are either in development or already producing.[8] On top of these estimates, there is also potential for additional oil and gas resources estimated to be between 1.5 and 7.2 billion boe.[9] This latter estimate, though, consists of those discoveries that are currently neither commercially nor technically viable to develop.[10] Nonetheless, regardless of the extent of their current viability, the realisation of the possibility of recovering these estimated reserves require a two-step process. First, identifying the challenges posed by the maturity and then reforming the governance of the industry in order to overcome those challenges.[11]

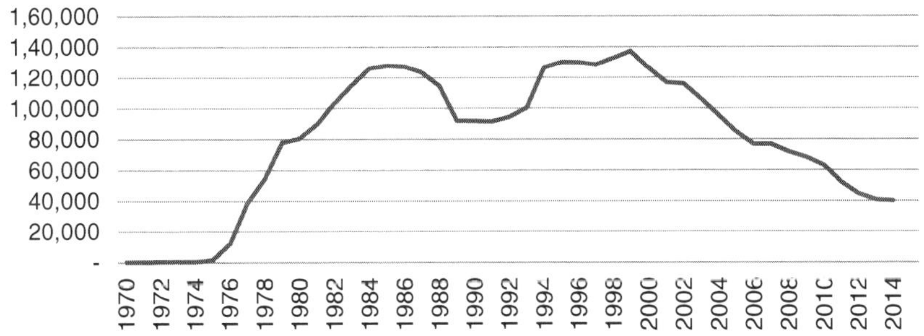

Chart 2.1 UK annual petroleum production (thousand tonnes)

Source: Department of Energy & Climate Change, *Digest of United Kingdom Energy Statistics* 2016 (Report, National Statistics July 2016)

It was for these reasons that the Secretary of State invited Sir Ian Wood, a recently retired chairman of the oil services company Wood Group[12] and a veteran of the UK's oil industry, to lead this review.[13] He was mandated with examining the existing licensing and other regulatory rules, the industry stewardship, and the collaboration between the operators and the government in their robustness of creating sufficient incentives to recover these resources.[14]

Subsequently in his final report, the Wood Report, and previously in his interim report (the Wood Interim Report),[15] Sir Ian established the goal of Maximising Economic Recovery from the UKCS, or MER UK for short, and highlighted six key issues that required immediate attention. The report then provided four recommendations to address these issues and six key specific areas for which a set of strategies needed in addressing these issues. These will be briefly discussed in turn.

2.1.1. Six issues of the Wood Report

According to Sir Ian, the first issue resided with the operators, who have been too individualistic in their commercial objectives without 'appropriate' consideration to infrastructure sharing.[16] The situation was exacerbated given that the new infrastructures were also being built without due consideration to a 'wider potential demand'.[17] This meant those fields that might be economical to develop if they could share an infrastructure were either not being developed at all, or being developed at significantly higher costs and poorer recovery rates.[18]

The second issue partially attributed the investor's less-than-optimal performance in the UKCS to the instability of the applicable tax regime.[19] The problem was that this fiscal instability was increasing the riskiness of the province for investors as they were unsure as to which tax was applicable when. As will be discussed in the next Chapter in detail, the applicable regime has been subject to all too frequent modifications, particularly in the last decade and a half. Although some of these changes were 'well received',[20] the instability of the fiscal regime as a whole naturally posed additional difficulties for the investment decisions. This, therefore, potentially resulted in investment levels lower than it would have otherwise been under a more stable fiscal regime as the investors were allowing for this fiscal risk in their decision processes.

The third issue Sir Ian reported emphasised the inadequateness of the 'light touch' approach of the under-resourced Department of Energy and Climate Change (DECC) in managing the maturation of the UKCS.[21] Interestingly, this is the only issue Sir Ian did not provide an explanation for, but was rather content with using adjectives. The DECC, according to Sir Ian, was 'too thinly spread to respond effectively to many of the demands of managing an increasingly complex business and operating environment'.[22]

The fourth issue turned the focus back on the industry. It was deemed to be equally inadequate in its stewardship as evidenced by the decline in the production efficiency and by the under-investment in Improved Oil Recovery (IOR) and Enhanced Oil Recovery (EOR) techniques.[23] Despite acknowledging the high costs of these techniques, the Wood Report expressed that these commercial decisions had to be incentivised by the Regulator.[24] It is important to note that the encouragement was not to come from the Treasury in the form of fiscal reforms but instead from the Regulator. Effectively, Sir Ian was acknowledging that basing business and investment decisions on commercial imperatives was an insufficient approach for this industry and such important decisions, at least partially, would be better served by the bureaucrats and the technocrats of the Regulator, who would have a better understanding of the 'big picture'. The fact that this was not happening, was an issue according to Sir Ian.

The fifth issue expanded on the first issue and regards access to infrastructure. Wood underlined the difficulties created by the legal and commercial barriers put up by the operators of those infrastructures to which access for processing and transport of production from small, marginal fields were vital.[25] This meant, as emphasised in the first issue, that the developments of assets were either not happening, or if they were, then only either at higher costs or at lower recovery rates. Therefore at least some of the reserves that could be recovered were being left *in situ*.

Although the sixth issue Sir Ian highlighted is not directly relevant for the purposes of this work, it is nonetheless important to briefly mention in order to provide a complete picture of the rationale of the changes that followed. This final issue pointed out that the implementations of the PILOT[26] initiatives were inadequate, regardless of how high the quality of the initiatives have been.[27] PILOT is a joint government-industry initiative chaired by the Secretary of State that succeeded the Oil and Gas Industry Task Force in 2000.[28] Since its establishment, it put forward a number of initiatives ranging from prevention of helicopter accidents to offshore safety, from the development of relevant skills for the industry to cross-border cooperation between Norway and the UK.[29] The issue highlighted by Sir Ian, however, wasn't the quality of the PILOT's work but rather its implementation by the industry and the regulator. Though specifically which aspects regarding the implementation of the initiatives were not elaborated on in the Wood Report. PILOT's work, for example, successfully led to the more tailored licences since 2002 aimed at addressing certain difficulties faced by smaller investors.[30] Certain other successful initiatives, including the fallow areas initiatives and stewardship, aimed at alleviating the problems unique to maturity were also the direct results of PILOT's work.[31] Therefore, it would have been useful to know the specific implementation issues pertaining to PILOT's work in order to have a better understanding of the ensuing recommendations put forward by Sir Ian. Unfortunately, as it stands, the public had to take Sir Ian's word for it.

2.1.2. Recommendations and the six strategies of the Wood Report

In the same report Sir Ian put forward four recommendations to address the foregoing six issues.[32] The first recommendation focussed on a new strategy for Maximum Economic Recovery from the UK (MER UK)[33] with a holistic approach that views exploration, development and production in unison.[34] It also required the Treasury, the Regulator and the industry to further collaborate, to ensure that the challenges posed by both mature and the frontier plays would be adequately addressed by the fiscal and regulatory regime.[35]

Accordingly, this tripartite group were required, both in the first and fourth recommendations concurrently,[36] to develop six specific strategies in addressing the challenge of MER UK. The first of these, the exploration strategy, was to address the declining exploration activity by focussing on the fiscal and licensing treatment. The intent of this strategy would be to 'stimulate exploration' by specifically focussing on a number of aspects including the cost drivers – particularly the drilling costs, emphasising 'regional exploration plans', incentivising seismic surveys, providing current geological data and the Regulator facilitating 'appropriate sharing of information within current portfolios'.[37]

The second specific MER UK strategy then was to address the issues surrounding asset stewardship with the requirements of the operators providing accurate and timely data for evaluation by the Regulator, which was to have powers to 'facilitate an appropriate change in operatorship or ownership of the assets'.[38]

The third strategy was mandated with moving the focus away from individual fields towards a regional approach with the *obligation* on operators to cooperate with the Regulator and other licensees.[39]

The fourth strategy was then required to develop plans to extend the life of existing assets and resolve the access to infrastructure issues while promoting investment into new infrastructure.[40]

The fifth strategy was required to focus on the utilisation of existing technology efficiently to maximise recovery while incentivising the development of new technology in achieving this aim.[41]

The final specific strategy was then required to focus on reducing the decommissioning costs, while avoiding premature abandonment under a 'single decommissioning forum…jointly led by the new Regulator and the Industry'.[42]

Sir Ian's second recommendation was complementary to the first in that the regulatory party to the tripartite collaboration could no longer be the 'under-resourced and under-powered' DECC, which was deemed as inadequate in managing the UKCS,[43] but instead a new 'arm's length' regulator financed by the industry,[44] and empowered to manage the operational aspects of the sector, namely the licensing and stewardship.[45] Such a regulator, according to Sir Ian, was not to replace DECC but work closely with it.[46] With its specific focus on MER, and with the 'autonomy from ministers and their department' and from the government salary structures, it was expected that the new Regulator could attract the required talent and signal to the industry that it was 'serious in its management of the UKCS'.[47]

Interestingly, it was never made clear in the Wood Report as to what specific issues the new Regulator could address that the existing one was either unable to or was doing so insufficiently. It was true that Sir Ian's recommendation was specific in that the new Regulator was expected to focus on the operational aspects of the sector governance. Yet it was unclear, at least within the Wood Report, what the evidence was against the DECC in its operational management. The Wood Report only stated that the DECC's problems emanated from inadequate funding and resourcing.[48] However, the solution Sir Ian recommended seems to repeat the over-recommended and proven-not-to-work remedies of creating a new regulator, or throwing money to the problem or both.[49] Even if the DECC, or the new regulator, could be sufficiently funded and resourced,[50] there would be no guarantee that such resourcing would continue to be adequate in the face of future developments. Thus far, time and time again, it proved that the Regulator was *almost always* under-resourced and under-funded.[51] A better approach would have been to move away from an interventionist stance to accepting the current position of the existing regulator as the default, and then develop solutions within the given constraints.[52]

In fact, it is the position of this work that the solution lies instead in fiscal reform. Specifically, this work argues in Chapter 5 that the reformed fiscal regime ought to adopt the new system being put forward in this book[53] which, by building upon the theoretical Brown Tax[54] mechanism and modifying it to the realities of the UK's petroleum exploitation sector, aims to fiscally align the interests of the government and the investor in order to assist in achieving the MER UK objective. It is posited that such an approach would see most, if not all, of Sir Ian's recommendations satisfied.

Notwithstanding the issues surrounding the recommendation of a new Regulator, Sir Ian's final recommendation further provided for the real possibility of implementing the new fiscal regime advocated in this work. To date a number of countries, notably Australia and Norway, proposed loosely similar mechanisms – though, certainly with large and distinct differences – to the one proposed in this book. These proposals were in the end either not implemented at all or adopted with significant changes in these countries because of both political pressures and the possibility of disincentivising investors.[55] Yet this final recommendation of Sir Ian's could actually provide the possibility of overcoming such barriers in the UK. This recommendation stated that in order to collaborate with the Treasury and the industry, and to implement the strategies laid out in the first and fourth recommendations, the new Regulator was recommended to have new, additional powers.[56] Specifically, the new Regulator was recommended to have powers that would require the licensees to 'act in such a way that is consistent with MER UK',[57] including the power to resolve disputes and make recommendations to the parties in dispute.[58] It was also to be able to oblige, in the licence terms, the sharing of data with powers for sanctions and incentives.[59] Finally, it was recommended that the licence terms could allow for the Regulator to attend the Operating Committees and the Technical Management Committees of the licence consortia.[60]

Based on the foregoing it may not be immediately obvious why this recommendation might create the environment for the implementation of the proposed tax system in this work. This recommendation introduces the possibility for the UK government, through the new Regulator, to have a more active role over the management of upstream assets, albeit indirectly. It will be shown in Chapter 5 that the new fiscal system proposed in this work puts the government into a position similar to an equity partner, albeit indirectly, thus aligning its fiscal and financial position with its new role under this recommendation.[61]

2.1.3. The response to the Wood Report and its implementation

Looking at the proposed heavy government involvement, recommendation for additional powers for the Regulator and the industry financing of the new Regulator, it would have been expected that the industry would strongly argue against being micromanaged by the new Regulator. In the least, the strategy to give the Regulator the powers to 'facilitate an appropriate change in operatorship or ownership of the assets'[62] had to be enough to raise the alarm bells that assets can be lost not due to commercial decisions but due to the Regulator's command. Similarly, the fact that not only was the industry now heading towards having yet another entity to report to in addition to the DECC, or, since July 2016, the Department for Business, Energy & Industrial Strategy (DBEIS),[63] the Treasury, and the Health and Safety Executive, but also the new Regulator could be sitting at the decision-making committees of the private commercial enterprises, would have been more than sufficient to raise significant concerns among the investors. Yet the industry instead welcomed the report and praised the recommendations. This may have presumably been because the industry was involved in the process from the outset.[64] Somewhat less surprisingly, the DECC also welcomed the Wood Report and pledged to implement the recommendations immediately.[65]

Accordingly, the UK Government accepted Sir Ian's recommendations[66] and swiftly initiated the creation of a new regulator, the Oil and Gas Authority (OGA),[67] and opened a public consultation on how this new regulator could be a competent entity in line with the Wood Report.[68] By 1 July 2015, the new regulator was incorporated as a limited company[69] under the Companies Act 2006,[70] effectively making it a Government Company[71] with a right under the Energy Act 2016[72] to 'participate' in the meetings of the licensees without a vote.[73]

In addition to this, the government also separately legislated the MER UK as a 'principal objective' to be achieved through 'development, construction, deployment and use of equipment used in the petroleum industry (including upstream infrastructure)', and through 'collaboration' between licence holders, operators, asset owners and contractors.[74]

The government also granted powers to the Secretary of State to produce and revise strategies in attaining this principal objective.[75] Although it is important to note that the strategies are not limited only to these matters above and can be broader as long as it is for 'enabling the principal objective to be met'.[76]

Within a year, as obligated,[77] the Secretary produced the first strategy.[78] This strategy expresses that as a result of complying with the strategy, the companies may not be individually better off if it meant that the UK benefits overall. It states that

> compliance with the Strategy may oblige individual companies to reallocate value between them, matching risk to reward. However, while the net result should deliver greater value overall, it will not be the case that all the companies will always be individually better off.[79]

This can, therefore, possibly mean that a company may gain values at lower levels – or, loose value outright – than it would otherwise have in the absence of the Strategy due to its compliance with the Strategy. However, to minimise the impact of this the Strategy provides a number of safeguards for investors. Accordingly, investors are not obligated to carry out an investment of funding activity 'where they will not make a satisfactory expected commercial return on that investment or activity'.[80] In this case the 'satisfactory commercial return' is defined as an 'expected *post-tax* return that is *reasonable* having regard to all the circumstances including the risk and nature of investment (or other funding as the case may be) and the particular circumstances affecting the person'.[81]

The Strategy also provides for a more specific safeguard whereby if an investor is either planning to delay investment or not invest at all, despite an obligation arising from the Strategy to undertake such investment, then 'the OGA must discuss the situation' with the investor 'before taking any enforcement action in relation to that decision'.[82]

Unfortunately, though, lack of elaborations both on how the 'post-tax return that is reasonable' would be determined and by whom, and on what is meant by 'discuss the situation' reduces the strength of these safeguards. One could imagine a circumstance where after a discussion with the investor following the claims by that investor that actions emanating from this Strategy are to result in less-than-satisfactory expected commercial returns, the OGA can still enforce the same actions. The only possible limitation to this may come from a secondary claim by the investor that such actions would undermine the investor confidence more than the potential benefits to the UK.[83] Yet this latter claim would be harder to demonstrate than 'satisfactory return' since it would be a very difficult task to tease out the magnitude of the causality of the actions on the confidence of the investors.

This Strategy also introduces a 'Central Obligation'[84] which is similar to, though broader than, the MER UK definition. It is given as

> [r]elevant persons must, in the exercise of their relevant functions, take the steps necessary to secure that the maximum value of economically recoverable petroleum is recovered from the strata beneath relevant UK waters.[85]

This broad Central Obligation aligns itself closer to the MER UK objective through the 'Supporting Obligations' which are set out to 'clarify how the Central Obligation' applies in exploration, development, asset stewardship, technology, decommissioning and the OGA plans.[86] In performing these obligations, the Strategy then provides a set of 'Required Actions and Behaviours' for the relevant parties which relate to timing, collaboration and cost reduction, and 'actions where relevant parties decide not to ensure maximum economic recovery'.[87] These latter actions include obligation of divestment of assets to 'other financially and technically competent persons' or relinquishment.[88]

There is a statutory obligation on the licence holders, the operators and the infrastructure owners to comply with this strategy and the other strategies that are to follow.[89] Such compliance is to be monitored and assessed in annual reports[90] by the Secretary of State with powers to propose actions to be taken.[91] Such reports are then to be shared with the House of Parliament.[92]

In addition to the foregoing, the Secretary is also granted with the authority to promulgate regulations with respect to charging a levy to finance the OGA,[93] although no regulations in this regard have been made at the time of writing. However, the OGA is not without a budget. £7m was set aside for the staffing costs of the new Regulator.[94] Moreover, from 2016 onwards the Government is contributing £3m annually to the operating cost of the Regulator.[95]

2.1.4. Government's rationale for reform: the Fiscal Review

It is against this background and in direct response to the Wood Report that the Chancellor Osborne announced a review of the UK's petroleum tax regime in 2014.[96] The review was to ascertain how the regime could adapt to the 'changing economics of the UKCS, create fiscal stability, help the UKCS compete for investment, simplify the regime and ultimately use the regime to help' with the

MER UK strategy established in the Wood Report.[97] Although a review of the fiscal regime was not directly within the scope of the Wood Report,[98] it nonetheless referred to the need for adjustments to the fiscal regime when discussing the six key issues and the subsequent recommendations.[99] In response, the Treasury produced the Fiscal Review following a public consultation.[100]

The case for reforming the tax treatment of the UKCS was clear. Compared to other mature and politically stable jurisdictions the returns to the investors were noticeably less. In fact, the consultations leading to the Fiscal Review revealed that on average the investors were obtaining around 5% to 10% lower rates of return in the UKCS than other jurisdictions.[101] The differential was worse when compared to the rates of return obtainable in onshore North America.[102] These lower returns were not being helped by the relatively higher costs. In 2013, an exploration well was costing an investor in the UKCS approximately £70 million on average, compared to £20 million or less per well in most of the 2000s.[103]

Furthermore, the modifications and series of allowances introduced during the last 15-year period of frequent fiscal tinkering not only increased the complexity of the applicable regime, but also made it less certain as it became less clear to the investors at the time of making investment decisions whether any or some of the available allowances would apply, let alone, how.[104] The problems were not only related to uncertainties either. By incentivising investments into assets with specific qualities such allowances created distortions in the investment decisions in favour of those assets over others.[105] Thus it was clear that these additional complexities also introduced inefficiencies into the investor decision-making by championing certain upstream asset categories over others.

Therefore, with these comparatively lower potential returns, higher costs and increased complexities and inefficiencies in the regime, the fiscal treatment of the UKCS certainly needed to be reformed. In view of this, the Fiscal Review set the objectives and principles within which the reform was to take place.

As an objective, the Fiscal Review emphasised that the new, reformed fiscal regime had to support the MER UK strategy while ensuring a 'fair return' for the UK in the form of economic 'rent'.[106] To achieve this objective, it provided three principles to guide the fiscal reform policy. First, the overall tax burden had to fall in tandem as the UKCS continued to mature.[107] Second, in echo of the Wood Review, the government had to be guided not only by revenues in developing fiscal policies but also by 'wider economic benefits of oil & gas production'.[108] Third, the concept of 'fair return' had to consider the 'competitiveness of commercial opportunities' and 'take account of both prices and costs'.[109]

This objective, established by the Treasury, is therefore also the goal of this work. Accordingly the subsequent analysis and discussions will also be guided by these Fiscal Review principles in developing the new fiscal regime proposed in Chapter 5. However, it should be noted that the Fiscal Review's second principle seems more of a platitude than a guiding principle. Had it been prioritising 'wider economic benefits of oil & gas production' over *short-term* revenues it would have not only created a clearer-direction for the policymakers but also would have addressed the important trade-off in fiscal policy between gains in short-term tax income and 'supporting the near-term investment that will generate higher production, revenues and wider economic benefits in the future'.[110] Unfortunately, despite identifying this trade-off as a problem in the Fiscal Review, this particular principle expressed by the Treasury falls short of providing a robust guidance. As such, this work will focus only on the first and third principles and will not consider the second principle any further.

Although these principles are provided as guides to the fiscal reforms, the Fiscal Review, unfortunately, does not elaborate neither on these guiding principles nor on the objective of ensuring 'fair return' in the form of 'rent'. Fortunately, though, these can be deduced both from petroleum tax theory and from the ways in which investors consider opportunities. Therefore, in order to clarify these concepts the next two sections discuss first the purpose of petroleum taxation in the form of rents, and then subsequently the methodologies employed by investors in evaluating potential investments in the upstream petroleum sector. Understanding of these will then aid in developing the criteria to assess the reforms introduced by the Government following the Fiscal Review and the new fiscal regime proposed in this book.

2.2. The Fiscal Review objective and the purpose of petroleum taxation

The central objective of the Fiscal Review is to ensure returns equivalent to 'rents' arising from petroleum extraction projects in support of the MER UK imperatives.[111] As such, this objective recognises that the natural resources sector has certain unique features like high front-end costs, long lead times to the commencement of production, and a number of uncertainties along the way that present particular challenges. Although individually these may not necessarily be unique to natural resources, the scale of these features together certainly poses unique difficulties.

These unique features are not the same for every project either. Oil fields vary significantly in their sizes and shapes, and accordingly the associated costs also differ. This in turn means that the fields that cost the same to develop may yield different amounts of hydrocarbons and *vice versa*. This is analogous to the agricultural land rent that David Ricardo advanced in the 19th century[112] which suggests that even if the same capital and labour are to be employed on two otherwise identical fields, their harvest yields would be different due to the inherent variations in nature. That difference between the two yields would be the *rent*. Therefore, by reapplying this insight of Ricardo the technical definition of economic rents can be derived as those returns over and above the 'supply price of investment'[113] or, those revenues 'accruing to a factor of production in excess of its transfer earnings'.[114]

This classical Ricardian analysis suggests that an economic rent is the difference between what a factor of production[115] actually earns and what is required at the minimum to lure it from its alternative use and bring it to employment for this particular purpose instead. More recently the concept of economic rent has been described as 'the difference between the price that is actually paid and the price that would have to be paid in order for the good or service to be produced',[116] or simply 'the difference between existing market price for a commodity or input factor and its opportunity cost'.[117] Thus it can be seen that the concept of economic rent put forward by David Ricardo 200 years ago is still used in the taxation literature as a fundamental objective.[118]

Insofar as the petroleum sector is concerned, therefore, this concept means the revenues received from the petroleum exploitation can be divided into two sections.[119] The first section consists of all the necessary costs, often referred to as the total economic costs, to incentivise capital, labour and other factors of production away from their alternative use and instead employ them in exploring for, appraising, developing and producing hydrocarbons. This can simply be interpreted as the necessary returns to cover the costs and the minimum profits required to incentivise an investor to invest its resources in hydrocarbon exploitation. The second section is those profits over and above that total economic cost, which is the economic rent.

This first section of the revenues, or the *supply price of investment*, varies in the upstream hydrocarbon sector depending on whether it refers to short-, medium- or long-run. The fundamental differences between these three time references lie in whether the fields are currently producing, or just been discovered but not developed yet, or yet to be explored for and discovered, respectively.[120] Chart 2.2 below displays these differences.

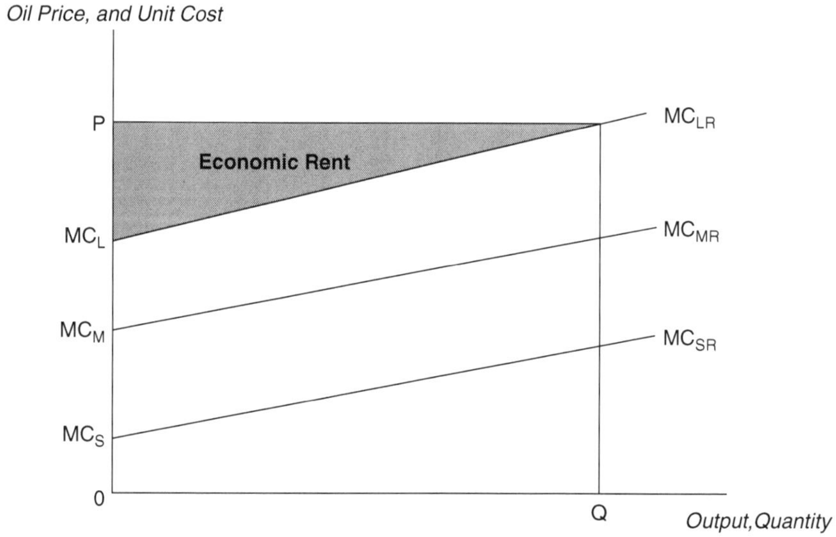

Chart 2.2 Economic rent and different supply prices of investment in the upstream sector
Source: Kemp (n 113) Ch 2

The marginal costs of continuing production – i.e. the cost of producing one more barrel of oil[121] – from an already developed field is represented by the MC_S-MC_{SR} curve.[122] By definition, the marginal cost is dependent on the output, depicted as 0-Q, and the oil price, depicted as 0-P.[123] The MC_S-MC_{SR} curve effectively shows the supply price of investment for each additional barrel to be produced from an existing and developed field. As such, the marginal cost curve increases with the output. From the perspective of tax theory, this implies that should the government collect all the revenue[124] above this total economic cost curve – depicted as the trapezoid MC_s-P-MC_{LR}-MC_{SR} – the investor would still continue to produce from the existing developed field. However, there would not be any incentives to develop any discoveries nor to explore for new fields,[125] as the money that could have been spent on these activities would be taxed away.

Similarly, the curve MC_M-MC_{MR} represents the combined marginal costs of continuing production from already developed fields *and* of developing existing discoveries. Should the revenues above this area be collected by the government, the investor would continue to both develop the discoveries and produce from the existing fields, but would not have the incentive to explore for new fields. This is the issue the term *quasi-rent* refers to. By definition, the collection of the quasi-rents by the government does not create any disincentives in the short and medium run. However, they do discourage investments into exploration in the long-run as the money that could have been used on exploration is taken away as tax. This issue is especially pronounced since at this stage there is a noticeable risk that the exploration would not result in an economic discovery – a risk, the investor would need to be compensated for if the investor is to part with its money. Taxation of quasi-rents prevents such investments from taking place. This disincentivisation, in turn, results in reduction in potential production in the future, and consequently, in economic rents.[126] In Chart 2.2, the quasi-rent refers to the area between MC_L-MC_M-MC_{MR}-MC_{LR}. That area of revenue would go towards investing for exploration if not taxed.

The real economic rent therefore is the shaded area of revenue above the MC_L-MC_{LR} curve. Theoretically this is the share of revenue resource taxation tries, or at least ought to try, to capture. This is because in the absence of this section of revenue, an investor still has the incentive to explore for new fields in addition to the incentives for developing the discoveries and continuing to produce from the existing fields. This means losing this share would not alter the investment decisions. This is exactly why capturing economic rents is the purpose of petroleum taxation since that is precisely the point at which the government can maximise its revenue without distorting investment decisions. This therefore, in a sense, is the elusive quest of resource taxation. This also, in turn, highlights why the focus of the Fiscal Review objective on economic rents is robust.

As a separate but important point, it is necessary to note that in addition to Ricardian rents petroleum exploitation can also give rise to Hotelling rents at the post-appraisal stage.[127] This concept is based on the Hotelling Model[128] which suggests that in order for an investor to maximise the returns from a

Box 2.1 Hotelling model[132]

The Model herein is considered within perfect competition where owners of the oil fields are price-takers, and as such their extraction rates cannot influence the price of oil in of themselves. The Model also assumes that the market is at equilibrium under free competition, and that the oil field owners are rational actors with correct expectations of future oil prices. It also assumes that at each time t the oil is supplied exactly at the level of the demand q_d at the equilibrium price of $p(t)$ at time t. The price for the discussions herein is additionally assumed to be net of costs of extraction and of getting the oil to the market.[133] It is further assumed that the quantity demanded is a function only of price, so that $q_d = f(p) = q_d p(t)$. Finally, the model assumes that as the price moves along the equilibrium price path all of the resource is extracted.[134]

After time t, then, the present value of a unit of profit is $e^{-\gamma t}$, where γ is the continuously compounded rate of interest, or as Hotelling himself called it, the 'force of interest'.[135] Since there are no uncertainties in this simplified Model the size of the resource is known and finite, and it is denoted as S. This also means that the exhaustion of the resource will happen at a finite time, T. Therefore, it can be inferred that with the extraction rate $q(t)$ at time t the net present value of such extraction would be $q(t)p(t)e^{-\gamma t}$ where $e^{-\gamma t}$ is the discount factor at time t. It can also be inferred that $q(t)$ will be 0 for all $t > T$. Based on the assumptions above, then, the equilibrium price at time 0 would be equal to $p(t)e^{-\gamma t}$ for all t until it is equal to T. Furthermore, extraction of all the resource until such time T implies that

$$S = \int_0^T q(t)\, dt = \int_0^T q_d p(t)\, dt$$

The behaviour of price along the equilibrium path then can be ascertained by the derivative of the net present value with respect to time equal to 0,

$$\frac{\partial p}{\partial t} = \frac{\partial p(t)e^{-\gamma t}}{\partial t} = \gamma p(t)$$

Alternatively, this can be written as

$$p(0) = \frac{p(1)}{(1+\delta)} = \frac{p\,(2)}{(1+\delta)^2} = \frac{p(3)}{(1+\delta)^3} = \frac{p(T)}{(1+\delta)^T}$$

This may be referred to as Hotelling's γ-percent rule as the net price, and therefore the net profit, from extracting a unit of oil rises at the rate of discount, δ, along the equilibrium price.[136]

Graphically this is can then be represented as follows:

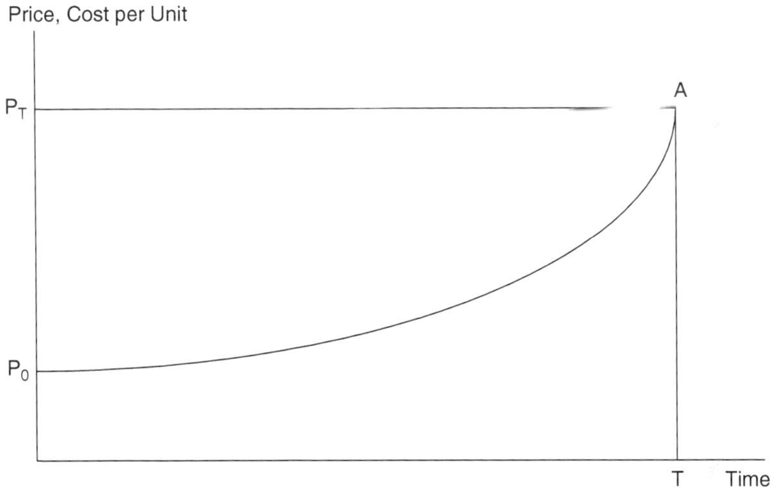

Graph 2a.1

It can be observed that the net price P_0A rises at a discount rate, δ, until the oil field is exhausted at time T. The price starts at P_0 and ends at P_T.

The price of oil has to grow at the rate of δ since, if they are not equal, then the rational resource owner would respond accordingly. By leaving the oil in the ground, the field owner would earn a capital gain of $\frac{\partial p}{\partial t}$. On the other hand if the owner extracts the resource the return would be p(t) which can then be reinvested to earn $\delta p(t)$. If for example, the discount rate, δ, is greater than the growth rate of oil price, then the return on the natural resource through capital gain will be less than the market rate of return. A value-maximising field owner will consequently choose the option that will create the greater return and thus, will sell more oil. Since the field size is fixed at S, this will reduce the amount of oil available for future, increasing the growth rate of oil price. The same is true for the reverse whereby the position of δ being less than the growth rate of oil would result in a reduction in the latter. This would continue until both are equal.

resource extraction, the values of extracting a unit of resource discounting to the present values[129] has to be equal at all times.[130] This is based on the understanding that by extracting a resource in the current period there is a cost imposed due to the foregone revenue as a result of not being able to extract the same resource in the future. This is referred to as the Hotelling rent.[131]

Although it is an important concept in the natural resource literature, 'the taxation of rents over a project's life does not require any measurement of Hotelling rent, or even any use or understanding of the concept'.[137] Instead, natural resource taxation regimes, at least ideally, focus on the Ricardian rent as it is the Ricardian economic rent and not the Hotelling rent the fiscal and quasi-fiscal instruments aim to capture. This is precisely why this work focusses on Ricardian economic rents in assessing the reforms introduced by the government and the new fiscal regime proposed in this work.

With this understanding of the Fiscal Review objective, it is now possible to develop an in-depth understanding of its guiding principles. The next section, therefore, discusses how this objective of 'fair return' in the form of economic 'rent' can take into account prices and costs, and how the tax take of the government can be flexible in tandem with maturity. The discussion exclusively considers the methodologies investors employ in assessing potential upstream opportunities in order to develop a robust understanding of the guiding principles.

2.3. Understanding Fiscal Review principles: investment evaluation methodologies

In order for investors to part with their money they require a return on their investment sufficient to compensate not only costs but also the risks of a given project.[138] The investors' goal can therefore be seen as maximising the long-run post-tax return from a project,[139] which is similar to the definition of 'satisfactory expected commercial return' in the first Strategy of the OGA.[140]

Towards this end, investors carry out detailed economic analyses to ascertain the viability of each investment opportunity. Although not all the methods are relied on equally, the investors commonly consider five main criteria and yardsticks used in the *field development* stage namely the payback period, the maximum cumulative cash exposure, the real Net Present Value (NPV), the real Internal Rate of Return (IRR) and the Profit/Investment ratio. At the *exploration* stage the investors also consider the Expected Monetary Value (EMV) technique which weighs the potential returns by the odds of discovering a commercially viable field in the first place. It must be emphasised though that none of these techniques, criteria or yardsticks can in themselves be sufficiently useful as a basis for judgment and 'usually two or three are used in combination. That is, a prospect must be acceptable by more than one standard'.[141]

Before discussing these techniques, however, it is important to highlight some of the issues taken into account when investors are deciding on an upstream hydrocarbon investment. For example, at the time of appraising potential investment decisions the stocks of reserves are not fully known. The same is true for the exploration and development costs which can differ significantly over time.

The latter issue has certainly been the case in the UKCS. In 2002, the average cost of operating in the UKCS was little under £4 per barrel of oil equivalent (boe).[142] By 2013, this figure was as high as £17 per boe which then reached the record high of £18.5 per boe in 2014.[143] These dramatic increases in per barrel costs were attributable not only to the underlying cost dynamics but also to equally rapidly declining production.[144]

The volatility of the average daily oil prices during this period were even stronger, ranging from little over $20 at the beginning of 2002 to about $110 a barrel by the end of 2013, which dropped down to approximately $45 by September 2016.[145] It is highly unlikely that investors would have expected such large scale variations in costs, or in prices, even at the beginning of the millennium.[146] Due to these issues, it is important to look in detail at the investment appraisal tools commonly used to identify the effects of such variabilities and uncertainties on investment decisions and the ways in which it can inform the tax policies. Only with this understanding can the guidance provided within the Fiscal Review be viewed in an informed light.

2.3.1. Investment appraisal techniques employed at the field development stage

This section discusses the five main tools employed in assessing a possible investment opportunity in an oil field at the development stage. These tools don't take probabilities and the corresponding errors into account. That is, the models are built with variables such as oil prices and costs pre-determined. Such determinations are not based on the likelihoods of those values occurring, nor do they change. The values are instead chosen for analytical purposes and in carrying out analyses these variables may manually be altered from their pre-determined levels to understand the impact of such changes, say for example, in oil prices. This is why they are frequently referred to as *deterministic models*.[147]

This deterministic approach subsequently forms the basis for further discussions that incorporate probabilities of success and error.[148] Although these tools are commonly used by investors in the upstream sector, they are not employed as the sole decision makers. The decision will also likely depend on the returns the same amount of investment would yield elsewhere, on competition, and on inflation dynamics, among others.[149] Nevertheless, these tools are sufficiently robust to be able to clarify what is meant by the Fiscal Review regarding the concept of flexibility and how prices and costs can be taken into account.

2.3.1.1. Payback period

Investors use the payback period method to measure how long it takes to get the investment back in a project. In technical terms this method is defined as 'the length of time required to receive accumulated net revenues equal to the investment'.[150] This relatively simple method can be expressed in terms of either before or after tax. All things being equal the investors, of course, would prefer those projects with the shortest payback period,[151], as the capital would be freed again sooner for reinvesting. A quick payback would also reduce the uncertainties of inflation, oil price and costs that tend to vary more as the timeline extends.[152]

Unfortunately, though, this method considers only the cash flows accruing from the moment of investment up to the payback period and, as such, not *all* the income and costs throughout the life of an upstream project. The consequence of this is that it does not measure the rate of earnings or profitability for the whole project.

A variant of this criterion called *the number of paybacks* somewhat addresses this issue. It looks at the number of times an investment would pay out from the entire life of the project.[153] In other words, it measures the extent of the operating profits covering the initial investment. If the operating profits are the equivalent of three paybacks, for example, an investor can effectively triple its investment. However, even then, this approach does not take the time value of money[154] or the cost of capital[155] into account. That is, it does not fully take into account the prices and costs. As such, it does not necessarily satisfy the Fiscal Review's third principle.

Nevertheless the payback technique is widely used by companies in various sectors, including the oil industry. In a survey carried out at the beginning of the millennium, 57% of the companies in different sectors confirmed that they rely on the payback period method, in their investment decisions in conjunction with other methods.[156] A possible reason for this may be that it takes account of risks[157] though this is rather an unconvincing point as there are other methods that are more robust in taking account of risks. Perhaps a better rationale for the use of this method may lie in the fact that an oil company will have a portfolio of projects. A company may employ this technique to quickly assess the extent of a project having a claim on its future funds.[158] It is also a relatively simple concept to communicate to a broader audience of decision-makers with backgrounds in disciplines other than economics or finance. It is an intuitive tool that discusses when the investments will be recouped.

2.3.1.2. Maximum cash exposure

Another tool that can be used in assessing a claim on the future funds of a project is the maximum cash exposure.[159] This tool is not necessarily employed in deciding definitively on an investment opportunity but rather used to highlight a feature of the project, namely the cash exposure, which can be taken into account in decision-making. This tool can be particularly handy when there is capital rationing within the company.

Looking at the cumulative cash flow the technique identifies the highest value, in absolute terms, of accumulated investment a company is expected to make for a given project. Chart 2.3 below illustrates the maximum cash exposure.

Like the payback method, it can be expressed in pre- or post-tax terms. It shows the total effect on an investor's budget. For limited budgets, the larger the claim the less is left for investing in other ventures. This method, however, suffers from the same issues as the payback method in that it does not measure profitability, nor does it take into account the time value of the money. Therefore, just as in the case of the payback method, it does not satisfy the third Fiscal Review principle.

However, it can nonetheless be considered a useful tool if a company is planning its investment budget for a number of years ahead since it shows the extent of which a given project will have a claim on that budget.

2.3.1.3. Net present value (NPV)

This third method employed by investors in assessing opportunities addresses the shortcomings of both payback and maximum cash exposure methods. Unlike these preceding two methods, this third tool, Net Present Value (NPV), takes into

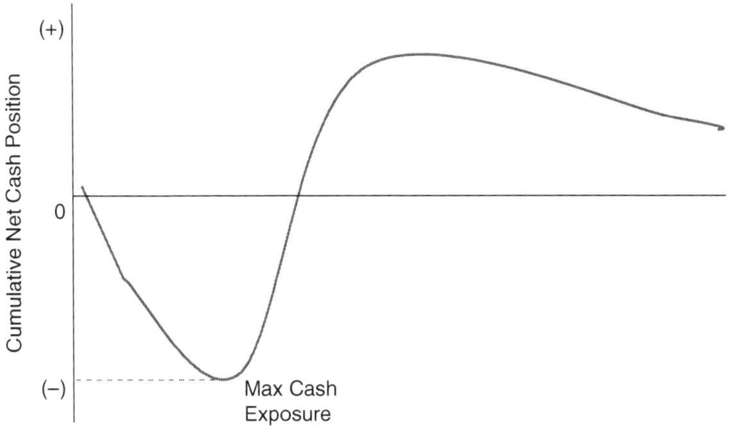

Chart 2.3 Maximum cash exposure

account the entire lives of projects and considers all the relevant costs and revenues associated with each of those projects. Thus, it satisfies the third principle of the Fiscal Review which requires that the concept of 'fair return' should 'take account of both prices and costs'.[160]

The NPV method also specifically highlights the wealth generated by each project and emphasises their scales. As an additional benefit, this method allows for meaningful comparisons between various projects because it is a monetary figure.

Investments in oil fields generate a number of cash flows in succession usually corresponding to each year of operation. Net Present Value (NPV) relates to those future cash flows in terms of their total value at the present time. The Present Value (PV) is obtained by calculating the current values of each of these future cash flows and then aggregating them together.[161] This value effectively represents the amount that needs to be invested today to generate those future cash flows. In other words, having this value in the bank today is the same as receiving those cash flows throughout the course of that project.[162] The 'Net' of Present Value is introduced with the investment. If the PV calculation subsequently takes the initial investment into account then it results in the NPV of that project.

In order to better understand the NPV approach Boxes 2.2 and 2.3 briefly discuss two important concepts: the cost of capital and the time value of money considerations. These considerations are important because they will provide the basis of obtaining present values for each of the future cash flows, and lead to the understanding of how prices and costs can be taken into account within a flexible framework as laid out by the Fiscal Review.

Box 2.2 Cost of capital

The terminology can be confusing as the cost of capital is not the same as capital costs. The latter is a term used more commonly in accounting and refers to those expenditures incurred 'not only once and for all, but with a view to bringing into existence an asset or an advantage for the enduring benefit of a trade'.[163] On the other hand, cost of capital is a term more commonly found in the disciplines of finance and economics and broadly refers to the cost of obtaining capital that is going to be invested in a project. This cost has a specific meaning whereby it is the *return expected* to be obtained from an alternative investment that has a similar risk profile and duration.[164] In other words, it is the foregone expected returns from an alternative investment as a result of investing in a particular project.[165] Naturally an investor would choose one project over another only if the expected returns from the foregone project are lower. In this sense, if the chosen project generates profits over and above the cost of capital, then taxing away those excess profits should not make that alternative investment more attractive. Of course, the cost of capital for each project would reflect the varying degrees of risks associated with each of these projects by including a corresponding risk premium over a risk-free interest rate.[166]

The level of how much it costs a given company to finance its operations, i.e. the cost of capital, depends on multiple factors including the cost of debt borrowed to finance the project, the cost of using the company's own equity, and the corporate capitalisation structure.[167] The cost of debt refers to the interest rate on that debt and can be viewed as the opportunity cost of capital for the lenders.[168] As lending itself is a risky investment for the lenders, it normally incorporates a risk premium.[169] It is important to note that the interest payments are usually deductible for corporation tax purposes.[170]

On the other hand, equity tends to be more expensive to employ than debt and usually without any benefits of tax deductibility. It is more expensive because debt holders have priority in receiving payments over the equity holders.[171] The following typical example illustrates the point.

Suppose a company requires £40m financing in order to extend the life of a producing asset which can either be acquired via borrowing from a bank at 5% per annum interest rate, or by selling 25% equity in the asset. Also suppose this asset generates an income of £20m the following year. If the company acquires the financing via debt then it retains £18m income after the interest payment of £2m.[172] If, on the other hand, it acquires financing via equity, it retains £15m, or 75% of the income. Therefore, it would be cheaper to acquire the £40m via debt than equity.[173]

Since it is cheaper to acquire, one may initially be tempted to finance the entire operation by borrowing. However, despite being cheaper, if the debt is very big then not only will the equity holder be worried that a bigger portion of income will go to servicing the debt but also the debt holders will get worried that the cost of debt will increase due to increased risks.

Continuing on from the above example, the risks become apparent when the project generates an income of £4m, instead of £20m, the following year. The company will still have to pay £2m interest on the loan, while retaining £2m for itself. In other words, a full half of the income is used in servicing the debt. Whereas, if the financing is acquired via equity the company then still retains 75%, or £3m, of the income.

Similarly, if instead the asset does not generate any income in the following year, there is still the obligation of interest payment, assuming the financing is acquired via debt. There wouldn't be a comparable liability of sorts under equity financing for this scenario. On the other hand, if the company goes bankrupt then the lender has a priority to the company's assets over the equity holders. This, inherently, highlights the risks in very big debt financing – at least from the equity holders' perspective.

Of course the choice between debt and equity is not binary. That decision can certainly be a combination of both. However, establishing an *optimal* debt-to-equity ratio is not easy. A lot of 'analysts prefer to determine discount rates, reinvestment rates, and company cost of capital by using weighted average cost of capital (WACC)'.[174] Under WACC, each of the financing components is weighted based on the proportion of that component in the overall financing structure.

For example, if the project in the example above is financed by 3 quarters of equity and 1 quarter of debt, then the WACC would be 20%.[175] This example is useful for illustrating the concept but in reality the determination of the market rate of interest is a subjective estimation as the beta[176] 'changes from one period to the next'.[177] As such, it is different for every company in any given year. For example, in 2014, the WACC for Exxon Mobil's assets in Texas is calculated to be 14.25%,[178] while in 2007 it was 16%.[179] Comparing these WACC figures to those of Occidental's rates of 15.69% in 2014 and 17.31% in 2007,[180] respectively, and to Pioneer's rates of 18.65% in 2014 and 12.48% in 2007,[181] respectively, makes it clear that there is not an agreed-upon WACC rate as the values vary in time and between the companies. Despite such variability, WACC is commonly relied upon in determining the discount rates, which in turn are used in investment appraisals.[182]

Box 2.3 Time value of money

In addition to the cost of capital, the second important concept in understanding the NPV approach is the concept of time value of money. This concept is important because an oil project requires quite substantial upfront costs for rewards in the future. Therefore, for an assessment of an investment opportunity to be healthy it needs to take into account the time value of money.

The basic principle of this concept is that the same amount of money, say £100, today and a year from now will not have the same worth – even in the absence of inflation – because that amount can be invested today to earn interest which will end up being larger than £100 in a year's time. Hence, the notion that the money today is more valuable than the same amount in the future.[183]

Given that the money can be invested today, this future value concept can be thought of effectively as a function of three things: the initial investment amount, the interest rate and time. This relationship, referred to as compounding, is the basis of all of the time value of money considerations[184] and is expressed as:

$$FV = C(1 + r)^n \tag{2.1}$$

where C is the value of the principal sum today,[185] r is the interest rate, n is the number of years between FV and C, and FV is the future value of C in n years. This equation is referred to as *compounding*.

The present value concept is the exact opposite of the future value in that it calculates how much investment is required today in order to receive a return of a certain specified value in a year's time, or in another future period. Effectively this relationship, referred to as discounting, is the reverse of compounding and can be expressed as,

$$PV = C = \frac{FV}{(1 + r)^n} \tag{2.2}$$

whereby, present value, PV, is equal to the principal sum, C, today.[186] It can be deduced, therefore, that the further the future value is from today, i. e. the larger n is, the bigger the denominator will be, reducing the PV.[187] Therefore, based on the definition of the PV, the further in time a future value is the smaller its present value will be. That is, the present value of a £100 in 2049 will be considerably smaller than the present value of a £100 in 2019.

These two important concepts, the cost of capital and the time value of money, provides the basis for the NPV method. This method can be defined as the sum of all the present values of the profits after the initial investment costs, which can be expressed as:

$$NPV = -I_0 + \sum_{i=0}^{i=n} \frac{R_i - O_i}{(1+r)^i} \tag{2.3}$$

where I_0 is the initial investment costs and thus negative, $R_i - O_i$ is revenue minus operating costs, thus profits, and r is the discount rate, or the 'average opportunity rate'[188] and can be thought of as the cost of capital to the investor.[189] The upper-case sigma symbol $\sum$ is essentially an instruction to sum each present value of the cash flow stream up to and including the year n.

Expressed as either before- or after-tax, NPV effectively shows the wealth generated by the project over its lifetime. If NPV is positive, the investor is not only earning a rate of return equal to r, but also a sum equal to NPV at time zero. This means that wealth is being created for the investor over and above the cost of capital, and as such, the investor can invest in the project.

The corollary to this is that the positive NPV value can be invested in the project in its entirety and still the investor would receive a return equal to the cost of capital. When the NPV is negative, on the other hand, the return on the project would be less than the cost of capital and the investor would reject the investment opportunity since this investment option would be less attractive than its opportunity cost.

At this point, one assumption of the time value of money needs to be underlined. The future value calculation, and thus the present value calculation, assumes that the returns at each period and the original capital are re-invested at the interest rate, r. This assumption has a particular impact on the NPV and Internal Rate of Return calculations discussed below.[190]

It is also important to highlight that the NPV is not without its limitations. The limitations exist because the NPV method does not take into account the absolute values of cash flows. For example 2 projects may have the same NPV, say +£100,000. This means both projects would create a wealth of £100,000 over and above the cost of capital. However, what the NPV measure does not tell the investor, at least directly, is the required level of investment. If one project requires \$300m initial investment, while another only \$50m, then the investor would presumably choose the latter project as it would yield the same return for a lower level of investment. This limitation, then, is resolved using the fourth assessment method, the Profit/Investment Ratio.

2.3.1.4. Profit/investment (P/I) ratio

Also referred to as a Return-On-Investment (ROI),[191] this is a useful tool to rank projects particularly in the presence of budget restrictions. Whether internally or externally imposed, a budget generally has to be rationed among projects as all the investors have, to a greater or lesser extent, budget constraints. In these circumstances it is important to obtain the greatest return from a limited budget. By displaying the profit-per-pound of investment, this ratio allows for a meaningful comparison between different projects competing for the same budget.

This is also a useful tool when viewed against the payback period method since the latter does not consider total profitability. Since P/I is a ratio of discounted (NPV) net profit[192] to investment it certainly does consider the total profitability. The P/I ratio can too be expressed either in before- or after-tax terms as long as all the ratios being compared are expressed in the same terms.

2.3.1.5. Internal rate of return (IRR)[193]

The fifth and final tool employed by investors is called the Internal Rate of Return (IRR). In the simplest terms, IRR is the average return an investment opportunity earns[194] and refers to the level of discount rate that makes the NPV zero.[195] It is defined as the

> interest rate which equates the value of all cash inflows to the cash outlays when these cash flows are discounted or compounded to a common point in time. Stated differently, it is the interest rate which makes the present value of net receipts equal to the present value of the investments.[196]

Thus, deriving from Equation 2.3 above IRR can be thought of as the r in the following equation where an investment is equal to the total present values of the cash flows:

$$I_0 = \sum_{i=1}^{i=n} \frac{R_i - O_i}{(1+r)^i} \tag{2.4}$$

Therefore IRR is the rate of return on the investment taking into account the time value of money. The IRR rate can be interpreted as the return on the project sufficient enough to cover the investment and a return of r on the outstanding balance of that investment. It should be noted that a negative rate of IRR would not have any meaning. IRR would also be meaningless, or cannot be calculated at all, when attempting to calculate a rate of return on a dry hole,[197] on circumstances where the investment is paid out of future revenues,[198] or on those productions that deplete prior to reaching payback.[199]

Determination of the IRR is a process of trial and error.[200] As a first step, all the future net cash flows generated from the initial investment in a project are discounted at an arbitrary interest rate[201] to determine their present values. If the sum of these net present values of future cash flows is higher than the initial investment, then the discount rate applied is deemed too low.[202] The process, then, would be repeated with higher discount rates until that sum is equal to the initial investment. That discount rate would, by definition, be the IRR. This process is now instantaneous with modern computers.

Once IRR is computed, an investor would invest in a particular project if its IRR is larger than the returns that investor would get from different projects with similar duration and risks.[203] Alternatively, if the investor is considering a single project only, then that project would be investment-worthy if the IRR is larger than the cost of capital.[204]

IRR is presumably popular as an investment appraisal tool because it takes into account the time value of money. It is also comparable to interest and loan rates as well as to certain benchmarks established by the management including the cost of capital and the growth rate objectives.

Similar to the problems present in the NPV calculations, however, it is a profit indicator that does not consider the magnitude of the cash flows. As such, it allows for a comparison of the rate of return on different projects independent of how expensive each project is. Problems would also arise when the time values of money are not the same for each project in comparison.

Also, if a company is not able to reinvest the net cash flows each year at the IRR rate[205] for the entire duration of the project then the IRR would not be a realistic measure of profitability. This is because the underlying assumption of a discount rate is that when received, all cash flows would be reinvested at the rate of IRR.

In addition, magnitudes of investment capital are also important in ascertaining a desirability of a project. This point is further developed in Box 2.4 discussing the interaction of IRR with NPV.

It can be concluded that for the investors assessing an investment opportunity at the development stage IRR is comparatively a more optimal tool than payback and maximum cash exposure measures, particularly because, like NPV, it takes into account the time value of money. If projects are for similar durations and have similar cash-flow patterns, IRR is also a useful tool in comparing the relative profitability.

2.3.2. Inflation

A separate but important comment is required for the concept of inflation in addition to the investment appraisal tools. An investor would necessarily take inflation into account as it may have a serious impact on the investment decisions, particularly if the rate is significant.[206] It is therefore important to adjust the investment assessments for inflation and especially express the NPV, IRR and NPV/I Ratio in inflation-adjusted, or in *real*, terms. This is because compared to the *nominal*, or Money-of-the-Day (MOD), terms a project may be uneconomical when viewed in real terms.[207]

2.3.3. Investment appraisal techniques employed at the exploration stage

The five investment appraisal tools discussed above do not incorporate the concept of risk into their assessments. Yet in the upstream petroleum sector a number of different and specific risks are present. These include exploration risks, reservoir risks, uncertainty of flow rates, oil price uncertainty and certain other political risks including fiscal and regulatory risks.[208] In addition, cost overruns and completion delays also present high uncertainties.[209] A delay of a

Box 2.4 Relationship between NPV & IRR

Given that both the NPV and the IRR take into account time value of money and profitability, it is important to briefly discuss the relationship between the two methods in evaluating investment potentials.

When evaluating two projects the comparison may not be as straightforward as the foregoing discussions suggests. To illustrate we can look at the NPV profiles of two projects in Chart 2.4 below.

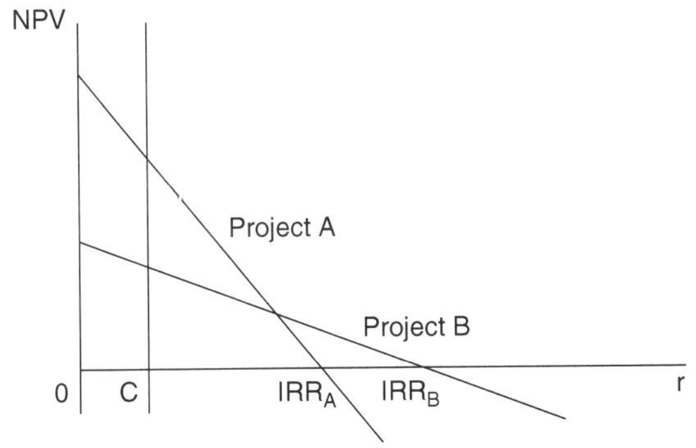

Chart 2.4 Relationship between NPV & IRR

The NPV profiles of projects A and B are graphed with the NPV on the vertical axis and the discount rate, r, on the horizontal. The intercepts on the horizontal axis are the IRR rates of each of the projects since the NPV is zero at those points. Therefore the IRR rate for project B is higher than A. However, if the cost of capital is the same for both projects (depicted as the vertical line C) then the project A would be preferable as it would generate more wealth then project B for the same cost of capital, as illustrated by the higher NPV.

The reason for differing slopes lies in the varying lives of the fields. The discounting process and a combination of different fields produce this phenomenon. For longer duration projects with large fields the NPV curve would be steeper and *vice versa*. Therefore, from an investment appraisal standpoint relying on a single indicator can be hazardous. This is why the investors tend to compare the projects using some or all of the tools discussed above concurrently.

single year in completion, for example, would have a knock-on effect on the cash flow of every subsequent year. This would result in a large reduction in the NPV calculation due to time value of money considerations. Therefore, all of these risks ought to be taken into account in investment decisions.

The technique that is employed in incorporating risks at the exploration stage is called Expected Monetary Value (EMV) where the NPV[210] and appraisal costs are weighted by the chance of discovery. This means that the assessment allows for the possibility of not finding a commercial discovery, and such possibility, accordingly reduces the value of NPV. The relationship is defined as

$$EMV = P(NPV) - E - P(A) \tag{2.5}$$

where, the EMV is arrived at by first weighing the NPV by the chance of discovery, *P*. Since the NPV is calculated at the post-appraisal stage the exploration costs, *E*, and appraisal costs, *A*, are both deducted from the probability-adjusted NPV, *P(NPV)*. However, since there would not be an appraisal if there is not a commercial discovery, the latter is also adjusted for the chance of discovery, *P(A)*. The exploration costs would nonetheless be incurred, and therefore, there would not be any adjustments to it.

Given that the EMV calculation is based on the NPV, all the positive attributes and limitations of NPV equally apply to the concept of EMV. Accordingly, EMV is a very useful tool as it considers the entire life of a project and all the relevant costs and revenues associated with that project. The method not only highlights the wealth generated by a project and emphasises the scale of that project but also adjusts them for the possibility of not finding a commercial discovery. Since it is a monetary figure, various projects can also meaningfully be compared.

Similarly, as in the case of NPV method, the EMV measure too does not tell the investor, at least directly, what the required level of investment is. However, a ratio of EMV per each pound invested, i.e. EMV/I ratio similar to the P/I ratio discussed in Section 2.4.1.4 can likewise alleviate this issue.

Thus, the foregoing discussion offers an understanding as to how the investors take into account prices and costs in investment decision-making. Particularly the NPV method, and to a large degree the IRR method, considers prices and costs for the entire duration of the project. These discussions, in turn, clarify the Fiscal Review's guiding principles for tax reform and provide the tools to rely on in conforming to these principles.

However, in order to be able to evaluate the tax reforms' levels of robustness in attaining the Fiscal Review objective a set of criteria are required. Based on the understanding developed in the preceding sections of the Fiscal Review's objective, and its guiding principles, the next section lays out the necessary criteria to set the assessments against.

2.4. The Fiscal Review principles and the assessment criteria

The most straightforward way of assessing a fiscal or a quasi-fiscal instrument would be to judge the degree of its ability to capture the economic rents. Unfortunately, doing so would not be easy because of the difficulties in measuring these rents.

One of the central problems with measuring economic rents, and why the capturing of it is an elusive quest, is that for the same upstream project its economic rent can vary for each investor. This is because the decision-making criteria, particularly the supply prices of investments[211] and the costs of exploitation,[212] will differ for each investor. Even if there was not a variation in the supply prices of investments, and more broadly in the investment appraisal tools employed by the investors,[213] it still would not be possible to observe the actual economic rents until after a project ceases and is completed. Of course, waiting for decades until the upstream operations are completed so that only the true economic rents can be taxed is simply unacceptable to governments. This is why the fiscal instruments *try* to get as close to capturing the economic rents as possible while taxing periodically throughout the lives of the projects.

This limitation does not make it impossible however to develop a set of criteria for assessing the degree of robustness of fiscal instruments in their ability to capture economic rents, or the degree of attaining the Fiscal Review objective. In fact, there are already a number of criteria to guide the fiscal system designs in general and assess the tax instruments against. These general criteria, in turn, can assist in developing a set of criteria specific to petroliferous trade. The discussion therefore ought to first focus on the original criteria put forward by Adam Smith that dates back to the 18th century.[214]

According to Adam Smith, an optimal tax should incorporate the maxims of equality, certainty, convenience and efficiency.[215] These maxims are applicable to taxation in general but they also lend themselves to petroleum taxation specifically. Particularly the maxim of efficiency has a specific application within the context of natural resource fiscal design.[216]

The first maxim, equality, concerns the distribution of tax liability. According to this criterion, the contribution of the taxpayers should be 'in proportion to their respective abilities';[217] that is, the tax liability ought to be similar for those earning at similar levels and different for those in different levels. The former is commonly referred to as the 'horizontal equity'[218] whereby the oil fields with similar cost structures and physical characteristics ought to be taxed in the same manner. The latter, on the other hand, is called 'vertical equity'.[219] To satisfy this maxim, a tax regime can be designed in a way that is either proportional, progressive or regressive. If proportional, the rate of tax would be the same for all taxpayers regardless of the income levels. Under this approach, a higher earner would still pay more in absolute terms since, say, 10% of 500,000 is higher than 10% of 10,000. If progressive, the rate itself would increase incrementally with the increase in income. If, on the other hand, it is regressive, a larger fraction of the earnings would be paid in tax as the earnings decrease. Although regressivity may intuitively seem to be counter to the equality maxim, it still satisfies this maxim as those at similar levels of income would also pay tax at similar levels.

At this point, it is important to distinguish the *design* from the *effect* since a proportional tax mechanism by design can nonetheless have a regressive effect. VAT, for example, is a proportional tax as it is levied at the same rate for everyone. However, its effect is regressive as it claims a larger portion of income from those who earn less. This distinction is fundamental as it informs the criteria employed in the assessments of fiscal instruments applicable to petroliferous trade.

Accordingly, petroleum tax design ought to concern itself with the *effects* and avoid regressivity within that context. This is because such an effect will artificially and adversely alter the investment decisions. The artificial and adverse nature would inevitably arise because a given project a tax with a regressive effect would claim a larger portion of the profits as the profitability decreases which would leave increasingly smaller amounts for investing. This can, for example, happen when the production from a field is in decline. As a result, an investor would be forced to stop producing from that field at an earlier time than that investor would otherwise have in the absence of a regressive tax. Investors would similarly be discouraged for the same reasons from investing in marginal projects because of the regressive effects of a tax.

Adam Smith's second maxim, certainty, highlights the importance of stability, consistency and clarity in tax design. This importance arises because a presence of arbitrariness in taxation can create incentives for corruption.[220] In fact, Adam Smith presents certainty as the most important maxim so much so that 'a very considerable degree of inequality' he argues, 'is not near so great an evil as a very small degree of uncertainty'.[221] Of course, in the upstream petroleum sector, where each project can last for a number of decades, this issue of certainty is frequently emphasised but seldom observed. This, in turn, highlights one of the tensions between the theory and the practice. Although theoretically certainty is a strong requirement, in practice politics, short-termism and less than full understanding of the petroleum sector tend to translate into frequent modification of applicable tax regimes. This will be particularly evident when discussing the UK's upstream taxation regime in the next Chapter.

Convenience, Adam Smith's third maxim, is concerned with the administrative side of fiscal measures in that taxes ought to be paid in a way that is the most convenient for the taxpayer.[222] Although this maxim is not a direct reference to simplicity in design, it can nonetheless be deduced that as the complexity of a tax system increases more time and human capital are required by a company for its internal assessment and, consequently, the less convenient it becomes. This, again, becomes evident when discussing the UK's regime with its specific allowances and charges in the next Chapter. Adam Smith extends the convenience concept into the discussion of the next, and his last, maxim, efficiency.

Efficiency, for the most part, concerns both the design and administration of taxation. This criterion highlights the need for achieving a balance between public and private welfares by keeping 'out of the pockets of the people as little as possible over and above what it brings into the public treasury of the state'.[223] Whatever the causes of it may be, an inefficient tax system would create disincentives and discourage investment. This is because, according to Adam Smith, an inefficient regime

> may obstruct the industry of the people, and discourage them from applying to certain branches of business which might give maintenance and unemployment to great multitudes. While it obliges the people to pay, it may thus diminish, or perhaps destroy, some of the funds which might enable them more easily to do so.[224]

It is this latter part – referred to as *economic efficiency* – that lends itself directly to the application of the criterion to the petroleum sector. Insofar as the upstream petroleum sector[225] is concerned, an efficient tax system would avoid creating disincentives to explore for and develop petroleum, or to incrementally invest to extend field life. Such a system would equally avoid encouraging early abandonment, overinvestment or gold-plating,[226] and would refrain from artificially altering the decisions on production rates.[227] In short, such a system would avoid distorting investment decisions.[228] This is why, after almost 250 years, it is this maxim of Adam Smith that is still being relied on in natural resource tax design,[229] since it is still the case that an optimal tax design ought to 'leave the investment decision undistorted' in order to 'enable the host government to maximize the capture of resource rent from any particular deposit without deterring investment'.[230]

Accordingly, the fiscal systems that are not targeting economic rents can be considered inefficient since taxing more than the economic rents can distort investments as discussed in Section 2.3 above.[231] Even a system that captures quasi-rents[232] would 'discourage' companies from 'applying to certain branches of business' and carry out exploration in the long-term. Thus, efficiency in this sense would be the first criteria for assessing the extent of tax reforms in attaining the Fiscal Review objective.

This maxim, in turn, can lend itself in developing the second criteria, flexibility, in assessing the degree of robustness of a natural resource taxation mechanism. It can be asserted that for a system to be efficient, and therefore target economic rents, it ought to be flexible. In the absence of flexibility, high variability in profits can necessitate artificial, discretionary, and, at times, arbitrary interference and adjustments to the tax regime which would increase the 'evil' uncertainty. Although the inherent uncertainties over a number of variables, particularly the oil prices and the various costs, would still be present, a responsive tax regime would allow the parties to predict the potential changes in the tax liability in response to changes in these uncertain variables. This flexibility, together with its potential for predictability, of the system would increase the 'revenue-raising potential of the tax'.[233] Therefore, a flexible system that can adjust to variations in field sizes, oil prices and costs would target economic rents efficiently.[234] The variations in these variables are particularly important as almost all the risks in the sector, from political to technical, would inevitably impact at least one of them. An evaluation of a fiscal mechanism, therefore, ought to employ an analysis of the *response* of that regime in the event of any given risks materialising.

In addition to the first criteria, efficiency, an interrelated concept referred to as neutrality is equally important. Given the microeconomic theory suggesting that companies maximise revenue when marginal revenues are equal to the marginal costs[235] a neutral tax regime that avoids creating a bias for a particular investment over another would be economically efficient.[236] In other words, aside from a reduction in income, a neutral tax would not artificially change a decision on investment. Such an artificial change may happen, for example, when the internal rankings of the attractiveness of various investment options gets reordered due to the impact of a non-neutral tax.

The IMF also employs this approach in its work regarding natural resource taxation which considers a tax to be neutral 'if it leaves the pre-tax ranking of possible investment outcomes equal to the post-tax ranking'.[237] As Garnaut and Ross highlight, the 'quest for complete neutrality in taxation very often reduces itself to a quest for finding ways of extracting no more and no less than...economic rent'.[238] This, therefore, is an 'important criterion' in determining the relative efficiency of different instruments employed in capturing economic rent.[239]

These criteria of neutrality, efficiency and flexibility are precisely why this work welcomes the first and the third principles stated in the Fiscal Review.[240] Both principles are underpinned by tax theory. The first principle directly underlines the importance of flexibility stating that the tax regime applicable to the UKCS ought to respond to the varying degrees of maturation by corresponding decreases in the tax imposition.[241] Complementing this position, the third principle then provides a clear direction of taking into account of both prices and costs[242] which again highlights the clear underpinnings of flexibility and the associated efficiency and neutrality criteria.

2.5. Conclusion

The purpose of this Chapter was to understand the government's rationale for reform and ascertain the specifics of the Treasury's objective for that reform and its associated guiding principles. This, in turn, yielded a set of objective criteria to be used in evaluating both the reforms introduced by the Treasury and the one advocated in this book.

Unfortunately, the reforms that ensued, both immediately and subsequently, fell considerably short of what was required. Even the industry, despite its initial positive response, expressed the need for further measures and pleaded with the Chancellor to introduce more significant changes in the 2015 Budget.[243] The need for further measures were also echoed in the Oil and Gas Authority's first report which committed to consult with the industry in considering reforms to the fiscal regime.[244] These were then followed up by the most recent changes[245] in 2016.[246]

In order to understand these changes, the reasons why the then current regime required reforming, and the reasons why this work still advocates yet another fiscal reform, the existing fiscal regime prior to the Fiscal Review ought to be discussed first. This discussion is necessary in order to understand the government's reforms post-Fiscal Review and why they are still short of the Treasury's own criteria. The next Chapter, therefore, discusses the fiscal regime in place prior to the Fiscal Review first before looking at the ensuing reforms in subsequent Chapters.

Notes

1 HM Treasury, '*Driving Investment: a plan to reform the oil and gas fiscal regime*' (Report, HM Treasury December 2014).
2 George Osborne, '*Chancellor George Osborne's Budget 2014 Speech*' (Speech, HM Treasury 2014).
3 Sir Ian Wood, '*UKCS Maximising Recovery Review: Final Report*' (Report, 25 February 2014).
4 Edward Davey, '*Written Ministerial Statement by Edward Davey: Review of UK Offshore Oil & Gas Recovery*' (Written Statement, DECC 10 June 2013).
5 Davey (n 4)
6 Wood (n 3) 2.1
7 Oil and Gas Authority, '*Summary of UK Estimated Remaining Recoverable Hydrocarbon Resources 2015*' (Report, OGA 2016).
8 Oil and Gas Authority (n 7)
9 Oil and Gas Authority (n 7)
10 Oil and Gas Authority (n 7)
11 Davey (n 4)
12 Formerly, the Wood Group. Wood plc was created following the 2017 acquisition of Amec Foster Wheeler by Wood Group. See Wood, *Investors* (2017) <https://www.woodplc.com/investors> accessed 15 October 2017
13 Davey (n 4)
14 Wood (n 3)
15 Sir Ian Wood, 'UKCS Maximising Recovery Review: Interim Report' (Report, 11 November 2013).
16 Wood (n 3) 2.3.i
17 Wood (n 3) 2.3.i
18 Wood (n 3) 2.3.i
19 Wood (n 3) 2.3.ii
20 Wood (n 3) 2.3.ii
21 Wood (n 3) 2.3.iii
22 Wood (n 3) 2.3.iii
23 Wood (n 3) 2.3.iv

24 Wood (n 3) 2.3.iv
25 Wood (n 3) 2.3.v
26 PILOT is a joint Government-industry initiative chaired by the Secretary of State for Energy. See PILOT, *'About PILOT: What is PILOT?'* (2010) <http://www.pilottaskforce.co.uk/data/aboutpilot.cfm> accessed 16 January 2015
27 Wood (n3) 2.3.vi
28 PILOT (n 26)
29 PILOT, *'Priority Areas'* (2010) <http://pilottaskforce.co.uk> accessed 08 April 2015
30 PILOT Progressive Partnership Work Group, *'The Work of the Progressive Partnership Group'* (PILOT 2002) para 3.2. Also see Greg Gordon, 'Petroleum Licensing' in G Gordon, J Paterson and E Usenmez (eds), Oil and Gas Law: Current Practice and Emerging Trends (2nd Ed, DUP 2011).
31 PILOT (n 30). PILOT, *'Maximising Economic Recovery of the UK's Oil and Gas Reserves: Context for the Brownfields Challenge'* (Report, PILOT March 2005). Also see Greg Gordon and John Paterson, *'Mature Province Initiatives'* in G Gordon, J Paterson and E Usenmez (eds), Oil and Gas Law: Current Practice and Emerging Trends (2nd Ed, DUP 2011).
32 Detailed discussions of these recommendations are beyond the scope of this work. This work solely focuses on the fiscal aspects.
33 Sir Ian refers to this as the 'MER UK strategy'.
34 Wood (n 3) 3.1
35 Wood (n 3) 3.1
36 Wood (n 3) 3.1 and 3.3
37 Wood (n 3) 4.1
38 Wood (n 3) 4.2
39 Wood (n 3) 4.3
40 Wood (n 3) 4.4
41 Wood (n 3) 4.5
42 Wood (n 3) 4.6
43 Wood (n 3) 3.3
44 Wood (n 3) Annex A
45 Wood (n 3) 3.3. In other words, it will focus only on the MER objectives. Wood (n 3) Annex A
46 Wood (n 3) 3.3.v
47 Wood (n 3) Annex A
48 Wood (n 3) 2.3.iii
49 A discussion on the historical repetition of the claims of under-funded and under-resourced Regulators in the oil industry in the UK and the very similar remedies recommended is beyond the scope of this work. For a concise discussion of this please see Emre Usenmez, *'Optimising Offshore Health and Safety Inspections: How the Markets Could Help'* in M Baram, P Lindoe and O Renn (eds), *Risk Governance of Offshore Oil and Gas Operations* (Cambridge University Press 2014).
50 Note that history has demonstrated that this is a very big if.
51 See Usenmez (n 49)
52 For an example of how solutions for health and safety inspections in the UKCS can be developed within a similar set of constraints see Usenmez (n 49)
53 See Chapter 5
54 See Chapter 5 for a detailed discussion on the theoretical Brown Tax.
55 See Chapter 5 for a discussion on the Australian and the Norwegian proposals and the reasons behind reeling back on their adoptions.
56 Wood (n 3) 3.3
57 Wood (n 3) 3.3 Recommendation 3.i.

58 Wood (n 3) 3.3 Recommendation 3.ii.
59 Wood (n 3) 3.3 Recommendation 3.v and iii
60 Wood (n 3) 3.3 Recommendation 3.iv. Operating and Technical Management Committees are the consortium meetings that determine the course of action to take in regards to the licenced asset. A detailed discussion of these Committees is beyond the scope of this work. For a discussion see Scott Styles, *'Joint Operating Agreements*' in G Gordon, J Paterson and E Usenmez (eds), *Oil and Gas Law: Current Practice and Emerging Trends* (2nd Ed, DUP 2011)
61 See Chapter 5
62 Wood (n 3) 4.2
63 In July 2016 the Departments of Energy and Climate Change (DECC) and Business, Innovation and Skills (BIS) merged to form a new Department for Business, Energy & Industrial Strategy (BEIS). See Department for Business, Energy & Industrial Strategy, 'About us' (DBEIS) <https://www.gov.uk/government/organisations/department-for-business-energy-and-industrial-strategy/about> accessed 05 March 2017
64 Oil & Gas UK, '*Wood Review Final Recommendations Can Be Game Changers for UK Continental Shelf*' (Press Release, Oil & Gas UK 24 February 2014)
65 Department of Energy & Climate Change, '*Wood Sets Out £200 billion Roadmap for Future of Offshore Oil and Gas Industry & World's First Gas CCS Plant Planned*' (Press Release, DECC 24 February 2014)
66 Department of Energy & Climate Change, '*Government Response to Sir Ian Wood's UKCS: Maximising Economic Recovery Review*' (Report, DECC July 2014)
67 HC Deb 6 November 2014 vol 587, cols 52-53WS (Davey)
68 Department of Energy & Climate Change (n 66)
69 Though it is now exempted from the obligation under the Companies Act 2006 of using 'limited' in its name and is officially changed from Oil and Gas Authority Limited to Oil and Gas Authority under the Energy Act 2016 s 1
70 Oil and Gas Authority Limited, Registered in England and Wales Company Number: 09666504. 100% of the shares are owned by the Secretary of State for Energy and Climate Change. The sole director of the Company is Stephen John Charles Speed, an employee of DECC, and the Company Secretary is Quayseco Limited, a law firm.
71 This intention of establishing a State Owned Enterprise was provided in Department of Energy & Climate Change (n 66) 2.10
72 Enacted on 12 May 2016
73 Energy Act 2016 s 39
74 Petroleum Act 1998 s 9A(1) as inserted by the Infrastructure Act 2015 s 41
75 Petroleum Act 1998 Part 1A as inserted by the Infrastructure Act 2015 s 41
76 Petroleum Act 1998 s 9A(3) as inserted by the Infrastructure Act 2015 s 41
77 Petroleum Act 1998 s 9F as inserted by the Infrastructure Act 2015 s 41. These strategies are subject to revision every four years. Though, the Secretary can review the strategy or strategies sooner than four years if he/she deems it appropriate.
78 Department of Energy & Climate Change and Oil and Gas Authority, '*Maximising Economic Recovery of UK Petroleum: the MER UK strategy*' (Strategy, DECC and OGA 18 March 2016), also see Department of Energy & Climate Change, 'Maximising Economic Recovery of Offshore UK Petroleum: Draft Strategy For Consultation' (Consultation, DECC November 2015)
79 Department of Energy & Climate Change (n 78) para c
80 Department of Energy & Climate Change and Oil and Gas Authority (n 78) para 3.
81 Department of Energy & Climate Change and Oil and Gas Authority (n 78) Annex – Definitions, emphasis added. Note that the theoretical underpinnings of this definition will be discussed in Sections 2.3 and 2.4
82 Department of Energy & Climate Change and Oil and Gas Authority (n 78) para 4

83 This safeguard is provided under Department of Energy & Climate Change and Oil and Gas Authority (n 78) para 6
84 Department of Energy & Climate Change and Oil and Gas Authority (n 78) para 7
85 Department of Energy & Climate Change and Oil and Gas Authority (n 78) para 7
86 Department of Energy & Climate Change and Oil and Gas Authority (n 78) paras 1, 9–22
87 Department of Energy & Climate Change and Oil and Gas Authority (n 78) paras 26–34
88 Department of Energy & Climate Change and Oil and Gas Authority (n 78) paras 30–34
89 Petroleum Act 1998 s 9C as inserted by the Infrastructure Act 2015 s 41; the second strategy has been published on 30 June 2016 which focusses on decommissioning. See Department of Energy & Climate Change and Oil and Gas Authority, '*OGA Decommissioning Strategy*' (Strategy, DECC and OGA 30 June 2016)
90 Though, initially two-year period before moving to annual schedule. Petroleum Act 1998 s 9D as inserted by the Infrastructure Act 2015 s 41
91 Petroleum Act 1998 s 9D as inserted by the Infrastructure Act 2015 s 41
92 Petroleum Act 1998 s 9D as inserted by the Infrastructure Act 2015 s 41
93 Infrastructure Act 2015 s 42
94 Department of Energy and Climate Change (n 66) 2.15
95 Department of Energy and Climate Change (n 66) 2.17
96 Osborne (n 2)
97 HM Treasury (n 1)
98 Wood (n 3) Action 20 and Annex E
99 Wood (n 3)
100 See HM Treasury (n 1) Appendix B for the list of entities that provided evidence for this consultation.
101 HM Treasury (n 1) 3.12
102 HM Treasury (n 1) 3.12
103 HM Treasury (n 1) 3.17. Also see Oil & Gas UK, 'Economic Report 2014' (Report, Oil & Gas UK 2014).
104 HM Treasury (n 1) 3.22
105 See the discussions in the subsequent Sections of this work.
106 HM Treasury (n 1) Box 4a The concept of economic rent will be discussed in Section 2.3
107 HM Treasury (n 1) Box 4a. This first principle of tax burden moving in tandem with maturity can be interpreted as flexibility. This position is also supported by the requirement of the Chancellor of a tax regime that can adapt to the changing economics of the UKCS when he requested the Fiscal Review.
108 HM Treasury (n 1) Box 4a
109 HM Treasury (n 1) Box 4a
110 HM Treasury (n 1) 4.2
111 HM Treasury (n 1) Box 4a
112 David Ricardo, *Principles of Political Economy and Taxation* (1817).
113 Ross Garnaut, and Anthony Clunies Ross, '*Uncertainty, Risk Aversion and the Taxing of Natural Resource Projects*' (1975) 85 The Economic Journal 338, 272–287
114 Alexander G Kemp, *Petroleum Rent Collection around the World* (The Institute for Research on Public Policy 1987).
115 Most common factors of production are capital, labour and land.
116 Joseph E Stiglitz and Carl E Walsh, *Principles of Microeconomics*, (WW Norton 4th Ed 2006) 298
117 John Cordes, '*An Introduction to the Taxation of Mineral Rents*' in James Otto (ed), *The Taxation of Mineral Enterprises* (Graham & Trotman 1995) 26

118 In fact even the World Bank publications still refer to David Ricardo's analysis directly. See for example, Robin Boadway and Michael Keen '*Theoretical perspectives on resource tax design*' in P Daniel, M Keen, and C McPherson (eds) *The Taxation of Petroleum and Minerals: Principles, Problems and Practice* (Routledge 2010) and James Otto, Craig Andrews, Fred Cawood, Michael Doggett, Pietro Guj, Frank Stermole, John Stermole, and John Tilton, *Mining Royalties*, (World Bank 2006).
119 See Kemp (n 114) Ch 2
120 Kemp (n 114) Ch 1
121 Christopher Snyder and Walter Nicholson, *Microeconomic Theory: Basic Principles and Extensions* (11th International Ed, South-Western, Cengage Learning 2012) Ch 10. This is calculated by finding the change in total costs per change in output and includes an element for normal profits.
122 Although it is drawn as a straight line for the purposes of illustrating the concepts, in economics they are referred to as curves since the marginal costs are theoretically somewhat U-shaped curves.
123 Snyder and Nicholson (n 121) Ch 10
124 Revenue is calculated by multiplying price with quantity produced which is depicted as the 0-P-MC_{LR}-Q square in Chart 2.2
125 Kemp (n 114) Ch 1
126 Kemp (n 114) Ch 1
127 Harold Hotelling, '*The Economics of Exhaustible Resources*' (April 1931) 39 The Journal of Political Economy 2, 137–175
128 See Box 2.1 for a detailed explanation of Hotelling Model.
129 See Section 2.4.1.3
130 Hotelling (n 127). If it was not the case, the producers would adjust their activities so that the present values would be the same. See Hotelling (n 127) and Garnaut R and Ross A C, *Taxation of Mineral Rents* (Clarendon Press 1983) Ch 3
131 Boadway and Keen (n 118)
132 The discussion in this Box looks at the Hotelling model in a highly simplified form and omits the technical details found in the original 1931 work as inclusion of those details will not have significantly alter the arguments here.
133 This is also the case in Hotelling's original work, Hotelling (n 127). For a discussion where price is not net of extraction costs see Joseph Swierzbinski, '*Chapter 162: The Economics of Exploration for and Production of Exhaustible Resources*' in Jason Shogren (ed), *Encyclopedia of Energy and Natural Resource and Environmental Economics* (Vol 3, Elsevier Press 2013).
134 All of these assumptions can be found in Swierzbinski (n 132)
135 Hotelling (n 127) p 140.
136 Swierzbinski (n 132)
137 Boadway and Keen (n 118) 16
138 Sylvana Tordo, '*Fiscal Systems for Hydrocarbons: Design Issues*' (World Bank Working Paper No 123, 2007)
139 United Nations Centre on Transnational Corporations (UNCTC), *Financial and Fiscal Aspects of Petroleum Exploitation* (UNCTC Advisory Studies, Series B No 3, ST/CTC/SER.B/3, 1987)
140 See Section 2.1 above
141 Arthur W McCray, *Petroleum Evaluations and Economic Decisions* (Prentice-Hall Inc. 1975) 2; there are, however, certain characteristics of a 'realistic measure': 1) It must be suitable for comparing and ranking the profitability of investment opportunities; 2) The parameter should reflect the firm's 'time-value' of capital. That is, it should realistically represent the policies of the firm, including future reinvestment opportunities; 3) The parameter should provide a means of telling whether profitability exceeds some minimum, such as the cost of capital and/or the firm's average

earnings rate; 4) It should include quantitative statements of risk (probability numbers); 5) It would be desirable to have the parameter reflect other factors, such as corporate goals, decision-maker's risk preferences, and the firm's asset position, if possible. Paul Newendrop, *Decision Analysis for Petroleum Exploration* (Planning Press 1975) 12. It should be noted that it is not the purpose of this work to rank the techniques discussed herein on their desirability but instead to consider the circumstances in which they may be useful and their limitations.

142 Oil & Gas UK, '*Activity Survey 2014*' (Oil & Gas UK 2014) 28. Also see James Edens, '*Extracting Maximum Value from a Maturing Basin: Case for Fiscal Incentives*' (CNR International presentation, 28 Feb 2012)

143 Oil & Gas UK, '*Activity Survey 2015*' (Oil & Gas UK 2015) 2.7. By 2015 the unit operating costs fell to £13.70 per boe due to decline in oil prices which are often tracked by cost trends, reduction in operating expenditures 'in an attempt to maintain positive cash flow position amidst falling revenues', 'high volume of "one-off" maintenance work that was carried out from 2011 to 2014', and to efficiency improvements. Oil & Gas UK, '*Activity Survey 2016*' (Oil & Gas UK 2016) 5.4

144 Oil & Gas UK (n 137) 2.7

145 These are in money of the day terms for the Brent Crude spot FOB prices. Note that on 10 December 1998, the price was as low as $9.1. US Energy Information Agency, '*Petroleum & Other Liquids: Europe Brent Spot Price FOB*' (US EIA 15 September 2016). Also see Appendix I for the historical Brent Oil Prices from 20 May 1987

146 In fact the OPEC was of the opinion in early 2000s that the price band of $22–28 per barrel was 'fair and reasonable'. Dr Maizar Rahman, *Forecast of the World Oil and Gas Market Development*, (Speech at the 4th Russian Oil and Gas Week, OPEC, Moscow, Russia, 26–28 October 2004)

147 McCray (n 140) Ch 2

148 See Chapter 4 for the detailed technical discussion.

149 McCray (n 140) Ch 2

150 Newendrop (n 140) 14. Note that Newendrop refers to this as 'payout' and not 'payback'.

151 In fact, in earlier periods of the industry, a payback of 3 to 5 years from a well would be considered acceptable. See McCray (n 140) Ch 2

152 McCray (n 140) Ch 2. Note that McCray also includes 'equipment failures and increased pressure from competitors'.

153 McCray (n 140) Ch 2

154 This is the 'most basic principle of finance: *a dollar today is worth more than a dollar tomorrow'*. Richard A Brealey, Stewart C Myers, and Franklin Allen, *Principles of Corporate Finance: Global Edition* (10th Ed, McGraw-Hill 2011) Ch 2. This is because a dollar today can be invested at an interest rate that yields a return by tomorrow. See Jonathan Berk and Peter DeMarzo *Corporate Finance: Global Edition* (3rd Ed, Pearson 2014) Ch 3. Also See the discussion in Section 2.4.1.3.2 below.

155 See the discussion in Section 2.4.1.3.1 below.

156 John Graham and Campbell Harvey, '*The Theory and Practice of Corporate Finance: Evidence from the Field*' (2001) 60 Journal of Financial Economics 187

157 Particularly the exploration risk.

158 Berk and DeMarzo (n 153) Ch 7 also highlights the simplicity as another reason for employing this technique, particularly if the investment consideration is very small.

159 UNCTC (n 138). This publication plagiarises from Kemp (n 114) verbatim without acknowledging Kemp's work.

160 HM Treasury (n 1) Box 4a

161 Berk and DeMarzo (n 153) Ch 4

162 Berk and DeMarzo (n 153) Ch 4
163 *Atherton (HM Inspector of Taxes) v British Insulated and Helsby Cables, Limited* [1925] KB 421, 10 TC 155 (CA) 192–193. However, please note that it is not defined in any statute. The determination of capital is a question of law. In those systems where the rights to exploitation of hydrocarbons are granted via contractual mechanisms, the capital costs would be defined in the contract which may be different than the traditional separations between the operating and capital costs. See Charlotte J Wright and Rebecca Gallun, *International Petroleum Accounting* (PenWell 2005) Ch 3
164 Berk and DeMarzo (n 153) Ch 10
165 Braeley, Myers, and Allen (n 153) Ch 2. This is why it is also referred to as the 'opportunity cost of capital'.
166 Berk and DeMarzo (n 153) 10. Note that the risk-free interest rate generally refers to the government bonds. The terminology can be misleading as the government bonds themselves have inherent risks.
167 Capitalisation structure is 'essentially the corporate balance of equity (common stock) and debt financing'. Daniel Johnston and David Johnston, *Introduction to Oil Company Financial Analysis* (PenWell, 2006) 46
168 Braeley, Myers, and Allen (n 153) Ch 9
169 These tend to be '1.5%–2.5% above long-term government bond rates'. Johnston and Johnston (n 166) 46
170 Berk and DeMarzo (n 153) Ch 15
171 Berk and DeMarzo (n 153) Ch 14
172 5% interest on £40m equals to £2m
173 At first it may seem that if in this hypothetical example only the 10% of the equity was sold the investor would have been indifferent to using debt or equity as in either case the investor would have retained £18m the following year. However, if the expected future incomes are constant at £20m every year, the investor would have paid back the debt in less than 3 years. Whereas, with equity financing it would have continued to retain £18m even after year 3.
174 Johnston and Johnston (n 166) 49
175 (One quarter of cost of debt) + (Three quarters of 25% equity) = (0.25*5%) + (0.75*25%) = 1.25% + 18.75% = 20%
176 Based on Capital Asset Pricing Model, beta is the 'trading price volatility relative to either a stock market index or an industry-related index of stocks'. Johnston and Johnston (n 166) 48
177 Johnston and Johnston (n 166) 50
178 With only 1.55% of capital is acquired via debt. Susan Combs, '*2014 Property Value Study: Discount Range for Oil and Gas Properties*' (Texas Comptroller of Public Account, August 2014) 2. The Texas Comptroller of Public Accounts calculates the WACC for 18 oil and gas companies operating in Texas.
179 With only 1.4% of capital acquired via debt. C P Schumann, P C, 'Oil & Gas Royalty Interest Valuations' (2015) <http://www.cpschumannco.com/business.asp?subject=11> accessed 24 February 2015, citing Texas Comptroller of Public Accounts. Unfortunately, the Texas Comptroller of Public Accounts only provides the latest available WACC assessments. Accordingly, the dissertation had to rely on a secondary source.
180 With debt financings of 8.4% and 2.72% in 2014 and 2007, respectively.
181 With debt financings of 9.18% and 32.4% in 2014 and 2007, respectively.
182 Clarence Harden, '*Discount Rate Development in Oil and Gas* Valuation', (Society of Petroleum Engineers Hydrocarbon Economics and Evaluation Symposium SPE-169,862-MS 19–20 May 2014)
183 Braeley, Myers, and Allen (n 153) Ch 2

184 Newendrop (n 140) 17
185 I.e. in time zero.
186 Of course if the interest rate is compounding/discounting more frequently than a year, then the expression becomes $PV = C = \frac{FV}{(1+r/m)^{n*m}}$ where m is the period the interest rate is applicable in a year. So if it is quarterly *m* is 4, if it is monthly *m* is 12 etc.
187 This is why completion delays have large impact on project NPVs as discussed further below in NPV and IRR interaction.
188 Newendrop (n 140) 32
189 The concept of cost of capital will be further discussed below in Further Issues. It is also occasionally called 'hurdle rate'. See Braeley, Myers, and Allen (n 140) Ch 2
190 See Section 2.4.1.6 below.
191 Newendrop (n 140) 15
192 Though, alternatively, it can also be undiscounted net profit. However, if this variant is used then it raises a problem of lacking time-rate patterns as it does not reflect time-value of money.
193 This is also known as discounted rate of return, internal yield, internal rate of return, profitability index (PI), discounted cash flow (DCF) rate of return, and marginal efficiency of capital. For the sake of consistency it will be referred to as IRR in this dissertation.
194 Berk and DeMarzo (n 153) Ch 7.2
195 In other words the investment would be equal to present value of cash flow. Johnston and Johnston (n 166) 44
196 Newendrop (n 140) 21
197 Since all the cash flows would be negative.
198 Since all the cash flows would be positive.
199 Since the money-of-the-day revenues would be lower than the investment.
200 According to the Descartes' Law of Signs, a change in the sign (− / +) of the cash flow is required to determine a solution for IRR. In fact, because of this law, there can be more than one IRR if the signs (− / +) of the cash flow changes more than once.
201 'In making the trial-and-error computations the rule to follow in selecting the rate for the next trial is as follows: if the sum [less initial investment] is positive use a higher discount rate for the next trial. If it is negative, use a lower discount rate for the next trial…A useful rule of thumb for estimating the first discounting rate to try is to divide *100%* by the number of years of payout'. Newendrop (n 140) 22
202 This can be seen in the IRR equation. If $I_0 < \sum_{i=1}^{i=n} \frac{R_i - O_i}{(1+r)^i}$ then a higher rate of r would increase the denominator, reducing the sum of present values closer to I_0
203 Berk and DeMarzo (n 153) Ch 7.2
204 Braeley, Myers, and Allen (n 153) Ch 5
205 This is one of the fundamental assumptions of compounding and discounting. See the discussions in Section 2.4.1.3.2
206 See McCray (n 140) 11–16 for further discussion.
207 This is why the modelling in Chapters 4 and 5 will be carried out in real terms.
208 For a discussion on these risks, see Frank Jahn, Mark Cook and Mark Graham, *Hydrocarbon Exploration and Production* (2nd Ed, Elsevier 2008)
209 Note that the terms risk and uncertainty are used interchangeably.
210 Note that the EMV calculation cannot use IRR as the result would not be interpretable.
211 Which is a behavioural concept in of itself. See Garnaut and Ross (n 130) Ch 4.
212 Kemp (n 114) Ch 1

213 Discussed in Section 2.4
214 Adam Smith, *An Inquiry Into the Nature and Causes of the Wealth of Nations* (1776) Book 5, Ch 2
215 Smith (n 213) Book 5, Ch 2
216 In addition to Adam Smith's maxims a further set of concepts in the form of simplicity, neutrality and international competitiveness can also be included in the list of criteria for assessing a tax regime. However, the former two can be viewed within the Adam Smith's maxims of convenience and efficiency, respectively. The latter highlights the fact that for investment purposes a tax regime tends not to be viewed in isolation but in contrast to other jurisdictions. Although this latter criterion is a very important element, the international competitiveness will not be developed in this dissertation as this is not a comparative work. For a treatment of the fiscal regimes in various jurisdictions see, for example, Alexander Kemp and David Reading, '*The Impact of Petroleum Fiscal Systems in Mature Field Life: A Comparative Study of the UK, Norway, Indonesia, China, Egypt, Nigeria, and United States Federal Offshore*' (1991) North Sea Study Occasional Paper No. 32
217 Smith (n 213) Book 5, Ch 2
218 Louis Kaplow, '*Horizontal Equity: Measures in Search of Principle*' (1985) Harvard Law School Program of Law and Economics Discussion Paper No. 8, 5/85
219 Kaplow (n 217)
220 Smith (n 213) Book 5, Ch 2
221 Smith (n 213) Book 5, Ch 2
222 Smith (n 213) Book 5, Ch 2
223 Smith (n 213) Book 5, Ch 2
224 Smith (n 213) Book 5, Ch 2
225 Also to a large extent the mining sector.
226 Gold plating refers to the concept of after tax returns becoming more attractive as the costs of the project increase. This would be largely due to large reduction in tax base and tax payments. A detailed discussion on gold plating is beyond the scope of this dissertation. For a discussion on this topic please see Alexander Kemp and Peter D A Jones, '*Progressive Petroleum Taxes and the "Gold Plating" Problem*' (1996) North Sea Study Occasional Paper No. 59 and Rob Fraser, '*On the Neutrality of the Resource Rent Tax*' (1993) 69 The Economic Record 56–60
227 Kemp (n 114) Ch 4
228 Garnaut and Ross (n 130) Ch 7
229 See for example, Land B C, 'Resource Rent Taxes: A Re-Appraisal', in P Daniel, M Keen, and C McPherson (eds) The Taxation of Petroleum and Minerals: Principles, Problems and Practice (Routledge, 2010), Baunsgaard T, A Primer on Mineral Taxation (IMF Working Paper No. 01/139, IMF, 2001) and Otto et al (n 118). Also see the discussion on neutrality below.
230 Land (n 228) 248 Please note that in that text, 'resource rent' refers to economic rent.
231 Similarly, from the governments' perspective, taxing less than the economic rents would leave money on the table.
232 See the discussion in Section 2.3, above.
233 Garnaut and Ross (n 130) Ch 7
234 Kemp (n 114) Ch 4
235 Taxation in this respect can be considered as cost. Snyder and Nicholson (n 121) Ch 11
236 Ken Henry, Jeff Harmer, John Piggott, Heather Ridout, and Greg Smith, '*Australia's Future Tax System: Report to the Treasurer*' (Commonwealth of Australia The Treasury, December 2009)
237 Baunsgaard (n 228) 17

238 Garnaut and Ross (n 130) Ch 7
239 Kemp (n 114) Ch 4
240 The second principle concerns with the 'wider economic benefits' though it is unclear as to the meaning of this in fiscal policy terms.
241 HM Treasury (n 1) Box 4a
242 HM Treasury (n 1) Box 4a
243 Oil & Gas UK, '*Oil & Gas UK meeting with Chancellor George Osborne*' (Press Release, Oil & Gas UK 25 February 2015)
244 Oil & Gas Authority, '*Call to Action: The Oil and Gas Authority Commission 2015*' (Report, the OGA Commission 25 February 2015)
245 At the time of writing.
246 See Chapter 4

3 The UKCS fiscal regime prior to the fiscal review and the case for its reform

3.1. Introduction

The Fiscal Review highlighted the fact that the UKCS could not continue to receive investments at its current levels unless the applicable tax regime was reformed.[1] Although the tax burden imposed by the existing system was reported to be 'roughly average' compared to other tax regimes around the world, it was recognised, in line with its first guiding principle,[2] that the maturity of the basin, and the higher costs and the smaller reserves these entail, necessitated a reduction in the tax burden to 'compensate.'[3]

Yet the ensuing changes fell short of both the Fiscal Review objective and the criteria contained in its guiding principles. In order to understand these changes, the reasons why the then current regime needed to be reformed in the first place, and the reasons why these changes did not satisfy the Treasury's own guidance and objective, the fiscal regime in place at the time of the Fiscal Review must be studied first. This is because, only through studying the then existing tax regime would it be possible to understand in what way the regime was changing and what the Treasury's reforms were intending to achieve.

Therefore, while giving a detailed descriptive account of the then existing regime the focus will be on establishing the instability highlighted in the Wood Review[4] and the extent of a fair share the government used to receive from petroleum revenues at the time. It is envisaged that this approach will yield an understanding as to how far the then existing regime was from achieving the Fiscal Review objective. Developing this understanding is the main purpose of this Chapter. To develop this understanding, the discussions of the fiscal regime in place prior to the Fiscal Review changes will be complemented by their analysis and evaluations. These evaluations will be based on the criteria of efficiency, neutrality and flexibility established in the preceding Chapter. It is envisaged that these evaluations will not only understand the drivers but also the nature and characteristics of the most current tax regime applicable to the UKCS. Only with this understanding will it be possible to develop subsequent discussions on the extent to which the ensuing changes introduced by the Treasury attains the Fiscal Review objective and what is required to further improve the regime.

Accordingly, this Chapter first discusses the existing regime prior to the recent modifications to understand how the current system has changed and to which technical aspects these modifications apply. The discussions focus on illustrating how far it further strayed away from the criteria established in Chapter 2. This in turn provides both the understanding as to why the fiscal system needed to be reformed and the basis for developing a discussion on the robustness of the subsequent changes introduced.

One of the fundamental issues of the then existing tax regime, as highlighted by the Wood Review,[5] has been its instability. Especially since 2002, the fiscal *certainty* in the UKCS has all but disappeared. Since that time the system has been through a series of significant changes that not only made the tax burden heavier but also the entire system considerably more complex.[6] In fact during this period the business of exploitation of the hydrocarbon reserves in the UK has been the 'most highly taxed' activity in the UK.[7] Until the recent changes were announced following the Fiscal Review,[8] the applicable marginal tax rates were either 81% or 62% depending on the relevant tax treatment.[9] In comparison, the standard corporation tax rate for the non-upstream businesses was set at 20% at the time of the Fiscal Review.[10] If this separate, and quite heavy, tax treatment of the upstream sector was not sufficient enough to make the investors think twice, instability of the system has not been of help in alleviating the investor worries either. This situation was made worse by the additional layers and complexities in the form of allowances introduced during this period of fiscal tinkering. These additional layers moved the regime further away from the simplicity of tax design.

The tax regime at the time was not only uncertain and inconvenient either. It was also *economically inefficient,* or not *neutral,*[11] since the specific details of each of the fiscal regime's components were likely to distort investment decisions.[12] This chapter, therefore, looks individually at the components that make up the upstream fiscal regime and assesses them against these criteria – particularly against *neutrality* – to highlight the inefficiencies and underline the reasons for reform. Thus, the chapter studies the extent to which the then existing regime was allocating a fair share from the petroleum revenues to the government.

Accordingly, the makeup of the fiscal regime applicable at the time, and also to an extent now,[13] to the hydrocarbon Exploration and Production (E&P) activities in the UK consists of three pillars. The first fiscal pillar, referred to as the Ring Fence Corporation Tax (RFCT), is a modification of the usual corporation tax that all companies, including oil companies, are subject to. It has a separate headline tax rate that applies specifically to profits generating from upstream activities which are ring fenced. Section 3.2 discusses this fiscal pillar and looks at the components that make up the ring fence profits, namely the ring fence income and the treatments of relevant expenditures. Within the discussions of expenditures, it particularly looks at the specific allowances within this fiscal pillar including the plant and machinery allowances, mineral extraction allowance, research and development allowances, decommissioning expenditure allowances and ring fence expenditure supplement. These discussions are important because the modifications introduced with the Fiscal Review applies specifically to these components. Without a clear understanding of these components a discussion on the post-Fiscal Review changes would be incomplete.

The second fiscal pillar applicable to the UKCS is a relatively recently introduced additional imposition called the Supplementary Charge (SC). Section 3.3 discusses the rationale behind the introduction of the SC before looking at its components including the relevant allowances and reliefs that have been subject to changes with the Fiscal Review. Specifically, this Section discusses the allowances that relate to small fields, ultra-heavy oil fields, and ultra-high pressure and high temperature fields. This discussion also includes the latterly introduced additional allowances for large deep-water oil fields, large shallow-water gas fields, deep-water gas fields and brown fields. This Section then looks at the reliefs available for expenditures associated with decommissioning.

The final pillar, the Petroleum Revenue Tax (PRT), is a specific tax applicable not to corporate profits but to individual *field* profits arising from the pre-1993 fields instead. Section 3.4, therefore, first discusses the statutory components of the profit/loss arithmetic arising out of a field. These include among other items, tariff incomes and the various treatments of sales of production depending on whether the transactions are at an arm's length or not. This is then followed by a discussion on the treatment of the expenditures. Specifically, the Section looks at the differing treatments of expenditures on long-term and non-long-term assets. It also discusses the expenditure supplement called 'uplift' before looking at certain carve-outs from the PRT regime in the form of oil allowances and safeguard. A detailed discussion of these components are necessary as they form the basis for the new fiscal regime proposed in Chapter 5.

Although the discussions initially look at these three pillars separately, they do not exist in isolation. Section 3.5 therefore looks at the interaction between them and discusses the pillars holistically as the upstream fiscal regime applicable to the UKCS.[14] While doing so it focuses on setting the regime against the theoretical framework discussed in the preceding Chapter. It is envisaged that analysing the fiscal pillars based on the theoretical underpinnings can assist in understanding the fiscal regime better and aid in the assessment of the existing regime before discussing the potential ways forward based on the same theoretical foundations.

Finally, before looking at these fiscal pillars in detail, it is important to note that between 1975 and 1982, and then partially between 1982 and 2003, a royalty system was in place in the UKCS. A 12½% royalty was retrospectively introduced in 1975 based on semi-annual production volumes,[15] whereby the monetary equivalent of 1/8th of semi-annual production was paid by the investors to the UK as the owner of the petroleum *in situ* before any of the tax calculations took place. A royalty mechanism can have quite a regressive effect as they are insensitive to variations in costs of production and field sizes throughout the life of a field, which can deter investments, particularly in marginal fields. In fact, the decline in development activity in the early 1980s, particularly of those marginal fields, were given as the reason for the abolition of the royalty regime.[16] However, the abolition of the royalty mechanism was gradual. Initially only those fields that received a development consent from 1st of April 1982 onwards were royalty-free.[17] It was then abolished entirely from 1 January 2003.[18] As it was no longer applicable at the time of the Fiscal Review, it will not feature in the detailed discussions below. Instead, the following sections discuss the three fiscal pillars as they were applicable prior to the recent fiscal reforms before looking at the changes brought about in the subsequent Chapter.

3.2. The first UKCS fiscal pillar: ring fence corporation tax

Originally introduced in 1975,[19] the RFCT can be considered as a modified application of the standard corporate income tax[20] specifically to the UK's petroleum sector. In its standard form the corporate income tax is a levy usually charged as a flat rate on annual net corporate incomes after a certain set of deductions and allowables. This is the same for RFCT, though it applies these standard UK corporation tax rules with a number of important modifications.

One of the modifications concerns the separation of upstream petroleum activities from all the other activities the company may also be engaging in.[21] Referred to as *ring fencing*, this separation means, for tax purposes, isolation of the petroleum exploitation activities[22] from other activities, such as refining. This arrangement is in place in order to avoid losses that may arise from time to time in these other activities reducing the taxable profits arising from the upstream activities.[23] However, it is important to note that reliefs in the opposite direction are possible. That is, it behaves like 'a valve…in that it acts one way only; thus, if the ring fence shows a loss, it can be set off against profits earned outside the ring fence subject to the usual rules and restrictions,' though not *vice versa*.[24] The reasoning behind this is that by allowing the losses in one direction the potential investments into the upstream activities in the UKCS are not discouraged as the investors would have an avenue to relieve these losses.[25]

The RFCT rate has been one of the more stable components of the entire fiscal regime. The current rate[26] is 30% which has been the case since the first of April 2008,[27] while the standard corporation tax has gradually declined from 28%[28] for the 2008–2009 fiscal year to 20% for the fiscal year beginning on 1 April 2015,[29] and will be 17% by 2020.[30]

What the rate applies to, on the other hand, has been less stable than the rate itself. The RFCT rate applies to upstream profits, which are the ring fence incomes[31] left after all losses, expenditures and interest payments are considered, and after taking into account all the associated allowances and reliefs.[32] Table 3.1 shows the relevant components of the RFCT calculation. A brief

Table 3.1 RFCT calculation

Add	*Subtract*	*£*	*Chapter Subsection*
Ring Fence Income		I	3.2.1
	Ring Fence Losses	L	3.2.2
	Expenditures	E	3.2.3
	Financing Costs	F	BOX 3-2
Chargeable profit		P = I-L-E-F	
RFCT at 30%		T = P*30%	

discussion of each these components is pertinent to understanding the extent to which this pillar, and the fiscal regime as a whole, falls short of the Fiscal Review objective.

3.2.1. Ring Fence Income

The majority of the ring fence income is determined based on the disposal of petroleum obtained from the ring fence activities.[33] Since it can be disposed of via transactions that are either at arm's length or non-arm's length, the methods for valuation of petroleum is distinguished between the two.[34] For the former, the value is determined based on the realised prices after adjusting for the transportation costs.[35] For the non-arm's length transactions the values are instead ascertained from the market values of the petroleum disposed.[36] For this latter determination, the HMRC publishes a list of statutory market values for various types of crude oils.[37]

Another component of the ring fence income consists of tariff receipts.[38] These are payments received as a compensation for the use of a company's ring fence assets or services by a third party.[39] For example, a company may receive a tariff payment for allowing access to its offshore facilities to separate and process petroleum from a nearby field owned and operated by a third party. That company may also receive payments for allowing access to its pipeline infrastructure to convey the petroleum to its own facilities from the third-party field, and, after separation and processing, for conveying it to a nearby terminal. Such payments are considered as part of ring fence income for the RFCT purposes.[40] The treatment of tariff receipts is particularly important not only in this pillar but in the other pillars as well.[41] The importance arises because their tax treatment may contribute to the problem of third-party access, which has been highlighted in the Wood Review as one of the issues.[42] This is partially attributable to the possibility of the tax treatment removing the financial incentives for allowing access.[43]

It is also important to note that incomes derived from derivative contracts on crude oil are not within the RFCT, but considered as income for the general corporation tax purposes.[44] Derivative contracts are financial instruments where the payoffs are solely based on the price performance of underlying crude oil, and include such tradable instruments as futures and options contracts and Contracts For Differences (CFDs).[45] Any incomes generated through these means are outside of the RFCT but are captured by the general corporation tax rules instead.

3.2.2. Ring fence losses

Under the standard corporation tax rules, which is the non-RFCT regime that applies to all the businesses in the UK, a loss can be deducted from all other profits of the company in the same period and in the immediately preceding year.[46] If this is not possible, or only a portion of the losses can be relieved this way, then this 'unrelieved loss' can be carried forward to be set against the profits in the subsequent periods,[47] starting with the accounting period that immediately follows.[48] Such loss reliefs are not available for losses arising from commodity futures trading.[49]

Within the RFCT regime the treatment of a loss is almost the same but with some important variations. A loss can only be deductible from the RFCT income if the loss has arisen from oil extraction activities or oil rights.[50] If it is allowable under the RFCT system, then the loss is first relieved against other ring fence profits in the same period and in the immediately preceding 3 years.[51] If this is not sufficient to relieve the entire loss then this period can be extended back further to 17 April 2002.[52] Following the extended period if there is still some unrelieved losses left, they can then be carried forward indefinitely so long as the ring fence trade carries on.[53] Should the trading cease, the carry back provisions of loss relief for the first 3 preceding years and then subsequently all the preceding periods until 17 April 2002 continue to apply.[54]

It should be noted that the losses from non-ring fence activities cannot be set against ring fence income,[55] though a similar restriction does not exist for the reverse.[56] That is, losses from ring fence activities are allowable against both the ring fence and non-ring fence profits.

3.2.3. Ring fence expenditures

The treatment of expenditures is the least stable component of the RFCT pillar. It is also one of the most important. It is important because the tax treatment of expenditures differs depending not only on the type of expenditures, but also on the type of investors that incur those expenditures. Having an insight into this multilayered treatment is germane to both understanding the ensuing changes and what those changes were trying to address, and to the analysis of this fiscal pillar with respect to its ability to achieve the Fiscal Review objective.

As Table 3.1 above shows the expenditures are deducted from the ring fence income before the RFCT can apply. However, as in the case of a loss, the timing of the deductibility of those expenditures is quite important. This is because, due to time value of money, the longer it takes to recover an expenditure incurred the lower its value will be, even if numerically the recovered expenditure is the same as the expenditure incurred.[57]

Particularly for a newly established commercial entity, or a new non-UK entrant undertaking exploration and production activities,[58] the date on which the trading commences can be especially important as the expenditures and losses cannot be set against income until such date.[59] In so far as the petroliferous trades are concerned, neither the exploration activities, nor the sale of petroleum 'produced as a by-product of exploration' constitute a commencement of such trades.[60] According to the HM Revenue & Customs (HMRC), this type of trade instead commences when an entity *decides to proceed*[61] to develop its first commercial field 'that will lead to production.'[62] Therefore, until that time, all the relevant exploration costs do not qualify for a relief, thus creating a delay in recovering those expenditures. The longer the delay the lower the actual value of the recovered costs will be – despite the numerical value being the same – due to time value of money.[63]

Regardless of the duration of the recovery, the way in which the expenditures are treated depends on whether they are categorised as revenue or capital. This is important because while the former is deductible as it is accrued, the latter type of expenditure is not allowed as a deduction.[64] This approach is consistent with the standard international practice as certain costs including salaries and purchases that cause 'decreases in equity, other than those relating to distributions to equity participants,'[65] are usually deducted in full immediately.[66] On the other hand, those that can be distributed to equity participants are considered to be assets given that 'future economic benefits' from those resources 'are expected to flow' to them.[67] Therefore, the distinction between the two types of expenditures is quite significant as investors would prefer not only to be able to deduct the expenditures but also to be able to deduct them in full as they are incurred. Yet this would not be possible if the expenditures are capital in nature.

Unfortunately, there are no clear-cut rules separating capital expenditures from those of revenue.[68] The legislation only states the types of expenditures that are excluded from the definition of capital expenditures, but it does not clearly define what it is.[69] It simply states that the capital expenditure designation excludes those expenditures that are deductible in taxable profit calculations and those that are treated as income receipt by the recipient of the expenditures.[70]

In distinguishing expenditures that are capital in nature from those of revenue the principles of accounting are of no help either. In *ECC Quarries Ltd v Watkins*[71] Brightman J stated that an

> unchallenged evidence, or a finding, that a sum falls to be treated as capital or income on principles of correct accountancy practice is not decisive of the question whether in law the expenditure is of a capital or an income nature.[72]

Thus, the treatment of capital expenditures in commercial accounts has no bearing in tax computation insofar as the law is concerned. For example, a capital expenditure can be depreciated for commercial accounts.[73] Yet, they will not be allowed as a deduction for tax purposes.[74]

In fact, to have a clearer understanding of the distinction between the two categories of expenditures one instead has to turn to the courts. In the 1926 decision by the House of Lords in *British Insulated and Helsby Cables Ltd v Atherton*[75] Viscount Cave LC stated that the determination of whether expenditure is that of a capital or a revenue in nature is

> a question of fact which is proper to be decided by the commissioners upon the evidence brought before them in each case; but where...there is no express finding by the commissioners upon the point, it must be determined by the courts upon the materials which are available and with due regard to the principles which have been laid down in the authorities.[76]

As it was affirmed that the courts were the appropriate forum for the determination of the nature of the expenditure, they naturally were also the forum for establishing the test for identifying expenditures capital in nature. This legal test for capital expenditure was also provided in the same case while it was at the King's Bench in 1925, before it was appealed to the House of Lords. In *Atherton v British Insulated and Helsby Cables, Limited*[77] Viscount Cave LC stated that when an expenditure is incurred

> not only once and for all, but with a view to bringing into existence an asset or advantage for the enduring benefit of a trade...there is very good reason (in the absence of special circumstances leading to an opposite conclusion) for treating such an expenditure as properly attributable not to revenue but to capital.[78]

In other words, capital expenditures are those expenditures that add an 'asset or advantage to the business of a permanent character.'[79]

Conversely, in a 1979 decision it was affirmed that those expenditures that reduce or alleviate a disadvantage were also capital in nature.[80] This test, however, did not necessarily clarify the distinction of the nature of expenditures incurred in the upstream petroleum sector, where, more complex arrangements including the hiring of rigs are common. Such clarification of the nature of expenditures, as emphasised by Lord Upjohn in *Strick (Inspector of Taxes) v Regent Oil Co Ltd*,[81] was a question of 'fact and degree and above all judicial common sense in all the circumstances of the case.'

A specific clarification regarding the expenditures incurred in the upstream sector only came in 1987 from the Chancery Division of the High Court. In *RTZ Oil and Gas v Elliss*[82] – merits of which are provided in Box 3.1 – Vinelott J affirmed that a considerably large segment of expenditures incurred throughout

Box 3.1 Merits of *RTZ Oil and Gas v Elliss (inspector of taxes)* [1987] 1 WLR 1442, [1987] STC 512 (Ch D)

RTZ Oil and Gas (RTZ) was a licensee on the Argyll field in the central North Sea that began producing on 11 June 1975.[83] At the time, the licensee was not expecting production to last longer than three years so it resorted to hiring drilling rigs and tankers and modified them to satisfy the technical requirements of the Argyll field with the obligation to reconvert them back to their original state before returning them to their owners at the end of their use.[84] Immediately following the commencement of production, RTZ made provisions in its accounting periods ending on 31 December 1976 and 1977 for the plugging and abandonment costs that included the costs of removal and reconversion of the rigs and tankers. RTZ treated these expenditures as revenue, thus deducting them in full immediately and reducing its taxable profits arising from the Argyll field.[85]

Following the HMRC's tax assessment of the same accounting periods which ended up being substantially different from the RTZ's accounts, the oil company appealed for a determination to the Commissioners for the Special Purposes of the Income Tax Acts.[86] The decisions of the Commissioners on three separate issues, however, were unsatisfactory to both RTZ and the inspector of taxes.[87] Both parties therefore required the Commissioners to 'state a case for the opinion of the High Court' on a number of questions of law, the most important of which, for the purposes of this work, on the determination of the nature of the expenditures.

Accordingly, Vinelott J affirmed that regardless of whether RTZ purchased or hired a drilling rig, it was to be treated as a capital cost.[88] If it was purchased, clearly an asset was added to the business 'of a permanent character,' thus satisfying the *Atherton v British Insulated and Helsby Cables*[89] test. If it instead was hired, Vinelott J affirmed that it was still a capital expenditure because if the benefit of the hiring contract was to be sold then the proceeds would have been considered as capital too.[90] To illustrate the point further, Vinelott J drew the analogy of a leased land on which a business was being conducted was an asset.[91] Since lease payments were treated as capital under the capital gains tax legislation applicable at the time[92] the lease payments for the drilling rig were therefore costs incurred on an asset, and, as such, were also capital in nature.

The case also affirmed that the capital expenditure categorisation was also appropriate for the costs incurred in converting or modifying the rig to 'adapt it for the purposes of the trade' and reconverting it back to its initial condition,[93] for drilling boreholes and wells, and for putting in place the associated manifolds and flow and control lines.[94] This was because, if the costs of hiring a rig was treated as capital expenditure, the costs of modifications for the purposes of the trade and the subsequent remodifications were also naturally capital expenditures.[95] Similarly, given that boreholes, well heads, flow lines, manifolds, loading lines and buoys were all parts of a 'comprehensive installation designed to obtain access to and to win and transport oil from the oilfield to onshore facilities' it was impossible to distinguish them individually, and therefore their costs were all capital in nature.[96] This is despite the fact that the boreholes were not drilled simultaneously but over time. Vinelott J affirmed that they were still to be treated as capital expenditures as the boreholes and the associated well heads and flow lines were all parts of a 'continuing programme of capital expenditure.'[97]

Similarly, the majority of the expenditures incurred during the production phase, especially at the earlier stages, were deemed as capital in nature. Particularly, the costs incurred in laying a pipeline, acquiring a tanker and modifying it to transport the production, reconverting it back,[98] and putting a buoy in place for a tanker to anchor for loading[99] were affirmed by Vinelott J as capital in nature. This was because such expenditures were incurred in order to make the assets 'more advantageous as income winning assets,'[100] satisfying the criterion laid out by Lord Scrutton in *Atherton v British Insulated and Helsby Cables.*[101]

In so far as the decommissioning costs are concerned, *RTZ v Elliss* case also confirmed that they are largely capital in nature. This is because the capping of wells and removing all the relevant assets were considered as a 'continuing programme of capital expenditure' that started with exploration and as such treated as capital in nature.[102]

the life cycle of petroliferous trade from exploration to decommissioning are deemed as capital in nature.

Consequently, this means that a very large majority of upstream expenditures are not deductible in calculating the RFCT liability.[103] Such a position, however, would make the system extremely regressive[104] as the RFCT would effectively apply not to ring fence *profits* but rather almost exclusively to ring fence *income*. As such, the tax regime would be insensitive to the variations in costs, claiming a larger portion of the same income as the costs increase. As asserted in Chapter 2, a regressive effect would artificially alter the investment decisions and therefore the petroleum tax design ought to avoid it.[105]

In order to avoid such regressivity there is therefore a system of capital allowances in place. The intention of such a system is for it to somewhat mimic, or behave similar to those of depreciation and amortisation schedules found not in legal but in commercial accountancy principles,[106] which allow for the deduction of certain capital costs over a period from ring fence profits.[107]

This allowance system, however, may itself give rise to distorting or regressive effects, and thus violate the neutrality criteria developed in the preceding chapter, largely due to the issues concerning the timing and the pace of the deductions. This possibility arises because of the impact on tax savings such timing and pace may have. From an investor's perspective the faster the speed of cost recovery the more preferable it is since the tax savings decline as the time stretches due to time value of money considerations.[108] This is why the timing of cost write-offs is as equally important as the statutory tax rate.

Traditionally the duration of depreciation has been aligned with the 'useful service life' of the asset.[109] However, for oil projects that last for a few decades such an approach means certain assets would have to be depreciated over their physical life as opposed to their economic life. The latter recognises the fact that while an asset is creating an income stream its own value is diminishing faster than its physical life due to 'obsolescence.'[110] A smartphone can be used as an illustration for the difference between the physical and economic life. The physical life of a smartphone can last for perhaps a decade. Yet it is obsolete after a couple of years with its value in rapid decline each year following its first introduction to the market. The same argument goes for the assets in use for upstream activities.

Accordingly, setting the annual depreciation to the asset's *decline in value* is theoretically ideal as it avoids creating distortions,[111] and maintains neutrality. This can be seen by looking at the effects of different speeds of depreciation. If the depreciation is spread out over longer durations, say to the life of an asset, then investors have an incentive to invest in assets with shorter lives. On the other hand if the depreciation is more rapid than its economic life, then those assets with longer life will have a disproportionate benefit for the investor as the effective tax rate will be lower.

The effective tax rate shows the reduction in income due to tax in percentage terms and is calculated by dividing the difference between the pre- and post-tax income by the pre-tax income.[112] As such, it is a function of both the statutory rate and the speed of the depreciation. If, and only if, the tax depreciation is set at an asset's economic life then an investment decision is not artificially altered by the length of the asset's life.[113] At this level, the statutory tax rate will be the effective tax rate.

However, accurately determining economic depreciation is very difficult. The obsolescence rates will vary for each asset.[114] Furthermore, in the petroleum industry, uncertainties regarding the oil prices and recoverable reserves in a project make it difficult to accurately estimate, each year, the reduction in the present values of the cash flow.[115] This is further exacerbated by the issues surrounding the choice of appropriate discount rate to arrive at present values.[116] 'In practice, depreciation has to be calculated on some arbitrary rule, and in those circumstances the tax may discriminate between different time patterns of receipts and hence between different techniques, products, and industries.'[117] These discriminatory outcomes due to arbitrary depreciation rules are certainly present in the UK's upstream petroleum fiscal regime prior to the Fiscal Review.

Before looking at the then existing depreciation system, however, it is important to emphasise a distinguishing feature of the petroliferous trades in relation to the capital expenditures. The petroleum industry is different from manufacturing and other industries in the sense that the obsolete equipment can be replaced by new capital investment in the latter sectors. This is not the case with the highly risky exploration investment, especially if a commercial discovery is absent at the end of exploration efforts.[118] Therefore a rapid depreciation of exploration costs is desirable and 'likely to be consistent with economic depreciation.'[119] This understanding and the difficulty in determining the precise depreciation for each asset informs the ways in which the capital expenditures are treated in the UK's petroleum fiscal regime, both pre- and post-Fiscal Review.

3.2.3.1. Capital allowances

The system of capital allowances permits annual write downs of certain portions of capital expenditures.[120] These allowances within the RFCT are broadly split into five sub-categories of plant and machinery,[121] mineral extraction,[122] research and development,[123] decommissioning expenditures[124] and ring fence expenditure supplement.[125] Since these particulars of the capital allowance regime within the RFCT was subject to the changes introduced by the Fiscal Review these sub-categories are briefly discussed in turn.

3.2.3.1.1. PLANT[126] AND MACHINERY ALLOWANCES

Under the accounting rules, fixed assets such as plants and equipment are depreciated.[127] Yet in tax calculations they are not deductible.[128] The plant and machinery allowances fill that gap by giving tax relief at certain prescribed rates in lieu of depreciation of these assets.[129] In order for the expenditures to qualify for this allowance within the RFCT regime the assets must be employed within the ring fence.[130]

The plant and machinery expenditures[131] within the ring fence, incurred on or after 17 April 2002,[132] are allowed for 100% deduction in the first year[133] as long as such assets are used solely in the ring fence trade within the first five years.[134] In other words, these capital expenditures are treated as an expense instead and as such written off in full immediately.[135] Certainly there are a number of exceptions to this allowance though not all of them are directly relevant to the oil exploitation sector.[136]

3.2.3.1.2. MINERAL EXTRACTION ALLOWANCES (MEA)

There are three sub-categories of MEA that are subject to three different deduction rates. The first of these concerns the post 17 April 2002 ring fence expenditures on *mineral exploration and access* which are allowable on a 100% first-year basis.[137] Mineral exploration and access effectively refers to Exploration and Appraisal (E&A),[138] and therefore, most of the capital expenditure in the E&A phase will be within the 100% first-year allowance. However, the costs of obtaining a licence itself, or, more broadly, of acquiring a mineral asset,[139] are explicitly excluded from the 100% first-year allowance.[140] These costs, nonetheless still qualify for the MEA. They are instead written-down annually at 10% on the reducing balance of that expenditure.[141] Other qualifying expenditures,[142] those that fall outside of these two sub-categories and yet still within the MEA, are written down at 25% on the reducing balance of those costs.[143]

Of course, if a 100% allowance is being claimed for an MEA-qualifying expenditure, a subsequent write-down on reducing balance cannot also be claimed for the same expenditure.[144] This possibility arises if a claim for the 100% first-year allowance is not for all of the expenditure that could have qualified for it.[145] What this means is that if the 100% first-year allowance is not claimed in part or in its entirety when the qualifying expenditures are incurred,[146] they will instead be subject to the write-down on reducing balance methods.

3.2.3.1.3. RESEARCH AND DEVELOPMENT (R&D) ALLOWANCES

For qualifying capital expenditures the R&D allowance is 100% which means capital expenditures on 'research' are deductible in their entirety.[147] Naturally, a company cannot claim reliefs for the R&D allowances and the MEA for the expenditures that qualify for both but instead has to choose between the two.[148] In practical terms it wouldn't matter which one is chosen as long as a relief is not claimed twice for the same capital expenditure under the two capital allowance schemes.

In order to qualify for the R&D allowances the capital expenditures need to be considered as R&D under the 'normal accounting practice'[149] and in conformity with the guidelines issued by the Secretary of State.[150] Interestingly, for the purposes of these allowances, capital expenditures on E&A activities are also considered as research.[151] Therefore, the costs of exploring for petroleum, and the costs of discovery and testing to ascertain its commerciality do qualify for the R&D allowance.[152]

At first glance it may appear perplexing that the E&A activities are deemed as 'research.' Yet, this has been affirmed both in a 1967 memorandum agreed between the then Board of Inland Revenue and the oil industry[153] and in the case law.[154] Following a decision by the Commissioners for the Special Purposes of the Income Tax Acts in 1984,[155] Gaspet Ltd appealed for a decision to the High Court.[156] The decision sought was on whether it could be deemed as Gaspet Ltd itself incurred the capital costs that qualify for the R&D allowance even though the relevant exploration work was carried out by two other consortium partners.[157] Although the facts of the case and the decision were not directly concerned with whether the E&A activities were considered as 'research,'[158] the Special Commissioners and Justice Gibson both commented on this point and affirmed in the positive. They both stated that it was 'common ground' between the taxpayer company and the Crown that 'scientific research' included E&A for the purposes of R&D allowance.[159]

Despite this, an 'appropriate body of Commissioners,'[160] and as of 2009, instead a 'Tribunal body,'[161] has the right to a final determination whether given expenditures come within the R&D allowance.[162] This, though, did not necessarily mean a greater fiscal uncertainty given that those capital expenditures that did not qualify, or were deemed unallowable by a Tribunal body, could qualify for the MEA instead, and thus could still be deductible in full, the same year they are incurred. Therefore, inevitably, through one capital allowance mechanism or another, most of the E&A expenditures were deductible in full.

Additionally, from 1 April 2013[163] there was a new credit in place available at 49%[164] for the ring fence companies incurring certain R&D expenditures.[165] Called 'Above the Line'[166] (ATL), this credit has been operating in a similar way to a grant, in that if a company could not reduce its corporation tax liability due to an overall loss position it could receive the credit amount as a direct payment from the HMRC.[167] This feature of the ATL credit is particularly important for the new regime proposed in Chapter 5 as the proposed regime also involves payments from the Treasury.

For the ATL credit, the expenditures ought to be incurred generally on those items that are *revenue* in nature including staffing costs, software or consumable items, and externally provided workers.[168] Interestingly, the gross credit itself is treated as income and taxable, although the ATL is designed to reduce the overall corporation tax liability. The effect of this is that for every pound spent on an ATL-qualifying ring fence R&D expenditure a company receives £0.8062 tax relief. This is illustrated in Table 3.2:

Table 3.2 Hypothetical application of the ATL credit

	Without ATL	*With ATL*
Income (£m)	500	500
R&D Expenditure (£m)	No deduction	-100
ATL Income (49% of R&D)	-	49
Taxable Profit (£m)	500	449
Tax Liability @ 62%* (£m)	310	278.4
ATL Credit reducing tax liability	-	-49
Net Tax Paid (£m)	*310*	*229.4*
Profit After Tax (£m)	190	219.6

* Tax is levied at 62% because RFCT at 30% + SC (discussed below in Section 3.3) at 32% = 62%

Thus, in the above example based on the regime prior to the changes introduced by the Fiscal Review the effective tax relief as a result of the ATL credit is £80.6m.[169]

3.2.3.1.4. DECOMMISSIONING[170] EXPENDITURE ALLOWANCES

The fourth sub-category of capital allowances within the RFCT regime concerns those expenditures incurred for decommissioning which has been subject to frequent changes with the resultant fiscal instability and uncertainty.[171] The tax treatment of this sub-category has frequently changed largely because, as some of the older assets began approaching the point of being decommissioned, the tax treatments of the expenditures on decommissioning these assets have gained prominence.[172]

Most of the decommissioning expenditures are deemed as capital[173] and the capital allowance mechanism provides for 100% deduction.[174] In order for the expenditures to qualify, they have to be incurred in compliance with an approved decommissioning plan,[175] and on decommissioning of offshore installations, pipelines or those plant and machinery that are part of such assets used in the ring fence trade.[176] Furthermore, from mid-2013, the applicable net has been widened to include certain onshore installations that are incidental to the offshore assets.[177] The types of qualifying decommissioning expenditures also include those incurred in preservation of the qualifying assets in anticipation of their demolition or reuse, and in preparing or arranging to reuse them.[178] The relevant legislation distinguishes between the decommissioning expenditures incurred before and after the cessation of the ring fence trade[179] in its tax treatment.

There is a special 100% allowance[180] available pre-cessation of ring fence trade for general decommissioning expenditure[181] incurred after mid-March 2008.[182] As part of anti-avoidance measures,[183] the conditions for this special relief have been further restricted for the decommissioning expenditures incurred from April 2009 in a way that a relief cannot be claimed prior to the accounting period in which the general decommissioning work has been carried out.[184] An election for this special relief, which is irrevocable,[185] can be made within two years after the end of the relevant chargeable period.[186]

There is also a 100% allowance[187] available for those decommissioning expenditures that is instead incurred after the cessation of ring fence trade.[188] Such relief would be added to the final accounting period in which the ring fence trade was ongoing.[189] As in the case of pre-cessation of trade, and for the same reasons, from April 2009 this relief is not available prior to the work being carried out.[190]

As the decommissioning issue has been gaining prominence the frequent modifications of its tax treatment, and the uncertainty ensuing therefrom, have been identified as potential deterrents to new investments into the mature UKCS.[191] In recognition of this, the government promised in 2011 to work on bringing a 'long-term certainty' to the treatment of decommissioning expenditures.[192] In the subsequent budget the government announced a consultation on the implementation of a contractual arrangement 'to provide assurance' to the investors on the reliefs they will receive when decommissioning.[193] By July 2012, the consultation was announced on the implementation of Decommissioning Relief Deeds (DRDs), standardised contracts between the government and the investors providing assurance as to the tax treatments of the decommissioning expenditures. Under the DRD contracts, if in the future the tax treatment of decommissioning expenditures changes from the applicable legislation as at July 2013 to the detriment of a taxpayer,[194] the government is to pay the difference so as to neutralise the effects of such changes.[195] This feature of the DRD system, like the ATL credit for certain R&D expenditures, is also particularly important for the new regime proposed in Chapter 5 since the proposal also involves payments from the Treasury.[196]

In 2013, the government also introduced the legislation that gives the authorisation to enter into such contracts.[197] Accordingly, the government is statutorily obliged to pay the investor should such a liability under a DRD arises.[198] Moreover, such payments are not to be treated as income and as such not subject to a tax.[199] The legislation, though, is silent as to the timing of the payment if a claim under a DRD is triggered. That information is instead provided in the DRD itself.[200] Accordingly, from the date a DRD becomes effective, for each Tax Period,[201] if the applicable tax regime at that time with respect to decommissioning expenditure is to the detriment of the investor, compared to the position as on 17 July 2013,[202] then the government is obligated to pay[203] the difference to the investor within either 60 or 120 days depending on whether the relevant field is a PRT-liable one or not.[204]

3.2.3.1.5. RING FENCE EXPENDITURE SUPPLEMENT (RFES)

A final component of the capital allowance mechanisms is the Ring Fence Expenditure Supplement (RFES). This system is a fundamental component in tailoring the tax treatment depending on the investor type and is in place for those capital expenditures, particularly the E&A expenditures, that cannot be relieved immediately, or losses incurred that cannot be offset against any taxable profits.[205] These measures were introduced in 2010,[206] broadening and replacing similar measures previously found under the Exploration Expenditure Supplement (EES).[207] While the latter has applied only to E&A expenditures incurred between 2003 and 2005,[208] the RFES applies to *any* expenditure incurred in oil extraction activities from 1 January 2006 onwards.[209] This expansion of its applicability has been deemed necessary to incentivise the 'exploration and development of the most difficult fields' and to counter the increase in the headline supplementary charge[210] rate.[211]

With the RFES it is intended to avoid putting those E&A companies that don't have a corporation tax liability[212] at a disadvantage. A disadvantage would arise because even though the E&A expenditures would qualify for the allowances discussed above, it would not be possible to offset them until an income is generated[213] – which may not happen for several years. Due to the concept of time value of money[214] companies in this circumstance would not enjoy the same *value* of benefit as those who can claim the relief immediately against its ring fence profits. Therefore, in order to maintain the value of the relief, all the oil extraction expenditures are uplifted under the RFES.[215] This uplift has initially been set at 6% until 2012.[216] From then onwards, however, the uplift further increased to 10% to align it with 'the discount rate typically used by the sector.'[217] This way it is envisaged that the fixed 10% uplift can alleviate the value erosion of capital expenditures that cannot be claimed immediately under various allowances. The RFES, however, is not available indefinitely but, at the time of Fiscal Review, could only be claimed for up to 6 years, though not necessarily consecutively.[218]

The revenue costs and depreciation and the treatment of capital expenditures are not the only components of costs in defining the tax base for the RFCT mechanism. Another component concerns the financing costs of the projects which are treated as an expense and deducted in full in the year they are incurred. Box 3.2 discusses this.

Box 3.2 Treatment of financing fosts under RFCT

Treatment of interests

Interest can be seen as the price, or even as the salary, of a borrowed fund. Although, certainly, a portion of an interest payment to the lender can also be seen as a compensation 'for the fall in real value of the debt' due to inflation.[219] Yet generally these inflation-induced changes in the real value are not necessarily a part of considerations. Usually the interest payments are deducted at nominal values and, particularly in the high inflationary environments, the gains obtained from the reduction in the real value of debt are not taken into account.[220]

Interest payments as a cost of financing obtained for the purposes of a company's trade are treated as an expense under the standard corporation tax rules in the UK.[221] No distinction is made between different types of interest and as such various types including short and annual interests as well as bank interests are allowable as long as the financing is for the purposes of a company's trade.[222]

For the RFCT system the 'purposes of a company's trade' is restricted to ring fence activities.[223] This means, the money borrowed must be used in financing oil exploitation activities including acquiring rights from an unconnected party.[224] If the financing is obtained from a related entity on a non-arm's length basis there is a possibility for assuming, with certain exceptions, the arrangement was established on an arm's length basis.[225]

If, however, the financing is done by using own equity then a similar relief is not available for the associated financing costs, which inevitably creates a bias in favour of debt over equity in financing projects.[226] Worse, if unchecked, this bias can also incentivise tax avoidance schemes whereby financing an operation almost exclusively by loans from the parent company can be used as a mechanism to repatriate profits with minimal tax liability.[227] The parent company may also lend at interest rates differing from those that can be obtained from the market. Such artificially high interest costs can then be used in further minimising tax liability.[228]

In order to prevent these, there are certain thin capitalisation rules. These rules are found within the transfer pricing legislation and are aimed at preventing gains of tax advantage by exploiting the differing rules in multiple jurisdictions.[229]

Thin capitalisation rules

According to the HMRC, thin capitalisation effectively means that a company has more debt than it 'either could or would borrow'[230] which can only happen if the financing was not at an arm's length or if it was borrowed from third parties 'on the strength of group support, usually in the form of guarantees.'[231] There is not a specific ratio prescribed as to how much of the financing can at most be obtained via debentures without being considered as 'thinly capitalised,'[232] but in the event of such a determination by the HMRC, the relief is readjusted on the basis of financing costs that would have been charged at an arm's length.[233] The adjustment is such that the excess part of financing costs, over and above what could have been obtained at an arm's length, is not deductible for tax purposes.[234] However, not all of the financing from connected parties are synthetic measures to minimise tax liability. If a non-arm's-length financing is arranged for genuinely commercial reasons the European Court of Justice (ECJ) affirmed that no adjustments are necessary.[235]

Comprehensive business income tax (CBIT)

Another possible solution may be to disallow the interest payments in defining the tax base,[236] which is commonly referred to as the Comprehensive Business Income Tax (CBIT).[237] This may be an unsound proposition, however.[238] This is not only because such payments are certainly a part of the costs of doing business,[239] but also because the foreign investors, particularly those based in the countries where the tax is applied to their worldwide income, ought to be able to get a tax credit at home as opposed to a deduction in order to avoid double taxation issues. The difference may be subtle but very important. A tax deduction reduces the worldwide *income* that is subject to tax at home, while the tax credit reduces the tax *liability* on the worldwide income.[240] An example may aid in highlighting the difference.

Assume that an oil company has generated a \$100m gross income in a foreign country \$40m of which have been paid in taxes. For simplicity, assume that the company has no other income from or costs in anywhere else. If the home country's statutory income tax rate is 30%, the company would have an $18m tax liability at home under the deductibility rules. This is because the taxable worldwide income of $100m would be reduced by the $40m tax paid abroad before being subject to the home tax rate.[241] On the other hand, if the creditability rules apply, not only would the company not have any tax liability but also it would have $10m tax credit to carry forward into the next period. This is because the tax credit of $40m would be deducted from the $30m tax liability on the worldwide income.[242]

It is clear that obtaining a tax credit is highly advantageous for the investor. In highly simplified terms,[243] in order to qualify for the tax credits the tax paid abroad has to be an income tax.[244] This means, the income tax paid abroad should include all the things deductible including the interest payments on financing.[245] This is why disallowing the interest payments in corporate income tax payments would not be a sound policy as it can discourage investment. This is also why many governments have instead adopted policies restricting debt financing, requiring some sort of a debt-to-equity ratio.[246]

A third possibility may be to allow the costs of equity financing to be deductible. Referred to as Allowance for Corporate Equity, this mechanism may alleviate the bias towards debt though possibly less so of the avoidance mechanisms.

Allowance for corporate equity (ACE)

Like the CBIT system, the ACE system[247] is designed to address the imbalance created by the corporate income tax regime in favour of using debt in financing projects, albeit in a diametrically opposing structure. While the former does not allow any deduction for financing costs at all, the ACE system allows for the deduction of costs of both debt and equity.[248] This means, the opportunity cost of tying up equity in a venture needs to be accurately calculated to reflect the cost of equity. However, the difficulty and the administrative cumbrance of this have put off policy-makers from giving much consideration to accounting for equity cost.[249] Instead, cash-flow taxation[250] has been advocated.[251]

However, for regimes that employ corporate income tax, the ACE system can be relied on to avoid the distorting effects and approximate neutrality in terms of the investors' decision-making. Instead of attempting to calculate the opportunity cost of the shareholder equity individually, the ACE system proposes, along with the deduction for the cost of debt, an allowance for equity finance calculated by multiplying the previous year's total equity[252] with an 'appropriate nominal interest rate.'[253]

The appropriate interest rate would usually be set at the risk-free nominal interest rate given that the system is symmetric[254] and the 'tax advantages are certain.'[255] This is justified regardless of how the shareholders are disposed towards risk. The equity owners, particularly the risk-averse ones, would demand a higher interest rate as a compensation for risk. Receiving compensation at the risk-free rate would therefore reduce the equity holders' expected return. However, due to the symmetry of the ACE system, the variations in the possible returns also decline, 'thereby reducing the risk premium that shareholders require. Intuitively, the government becomes a sleeping partner in the risky project, sharing in the return, but also sharing some of the risk.'[256]

The ACE system removes the artificial bias towards debt financing under the corporate income tax regime. It also does not discourage investment into marginal projects.[257] Interestingly, the depreciation methods employed become less relevant under the ACE system. If the system allows for accelerated depreciation, the base the corporate tax is applicable to is naturally reduced. However, such a depreciation schedule also reduces the capital stock[258] and subsequently the total equity to be multiplied by the risk-free interest rate in calculating the ACE for the next period.[259] Finally, the ACE system does away with inflation indexation as it is 'unaffected by inflation.'[260]

On the other hand, as the allowance for the cost of using corporate equity reduces the tax base, some critics point out that a higher corporation tax rate needs to be applied to maintain the tax revenue levels.[261] A higher tax rate, in turn, can play a discouraging role to the investors as it signals a higher tax environment.[262] The strength of these arguments, however, is questionable. ACE effectively allows the tax regime to target economic rents,[263] and as such, those investors earning 'just or less than the minimum required rate of return pay little or even no tax.'[264]

Administratively, the ACE system does not require any specialist expertise[265] and since it does not require any calculations for cost of equity capital it is relatively simple, at least simpler than the Resource Rent Tax.[266] Since it does not create distortions in investment decisions and in decisions of financing those investments, it is neutral and efficient, thus targeting the economic rents.

With the multilayered treatments of financing costs, capital costs, revenue costs and losses the determination of the RFCT base has never been a simple task since its inception. Yet, as complex a fiscal regime as the foregoing discussions may suggest the RFCT is only one of the three fiscal pillars employed in the taxation of upstream petroleum activities in the UK, which collectively formed the subject of the Fiscal Review. Another of these pillars, a relatively recent imposition called Supplementary Charge, is discussed in the next Section.

3.3. The second UKCS fiscal pillar: supplementary charge

The second fiscal pillar that has been subject to the Fiscal Review reforms[267] is the Supplementary Charge (SC). Since its inception it has been subject to frequent changes and has contributed considerably more than the RFCT to the fiscal instability issue highlighted by the Wood Review.[268] It was introduced initially in 2002[269] as a 10% extra levy on the ring fence profits in addition to the RFCT.[270] The rationale for this additional imposition was to counterbalance the generosity of the government in allowing a 100% first year deduction within the RFCT mechanism.[271] The then Economic Secretary, Ruth Kelly, summarised the Government's reasoning as thus:

> It is clear that oil companies are generating excess profits, and ours is the only major oil-exporting economy that does not have a special regime to reflect that…It is [also] abundantly clear that the regime is not securing a fair deal for the nation from this national resource, and the changes introduced in the Bill will remedy that for the future. We have listened to industry, and the package that we are introducing…focuses on investment. Companies that invest in the North Sea will receive full and immediate [100 per cent] relief against any tax liability, while those which do not do so will rightly pay a higher share of corporation tax, together with a supplementary charge. In future, therefore, the Government will take a much greater share of the risk of investing in the future of the North Sea. It is right that, as a consequence, the nation should take a higher share of the profits of that investment.[272]

This was at a time when the average daily spot FOB[273] price of Brent was fluctuating around $25.[274] When the average price for the same crude rose to over $54 in 2005,[275] the applicable rate for the SC also increased to 20% at the beginning of 2006, responding to the then 'recent significant rises in oil prices.'[276] To compensate, the government at the time simultaneously extended the EES[277] within the RFCT regime by introducing the RFES to include all the ring-fenced oil extraction activity.[278] As an additional sweetener, the government also promised that there would be 'no further increases in North Sea oil taxation during the life of this Parliament.'[279]

Yet, when the life of that Parliament came to an end the subsequent government again increased the rate of the SC in March 2011, this time to 32%,[280] which remained as the rate at the time of the Fiscal Review. The reason for this increase was again the rise in the Brent spot FOB price[281] which was averaging around $80 in 2010 and had passed the $100 barrier by February 2011.[282] At the same time of this increase in the SC rate, the government also promised that if the oil price dropped below $75 in the future they would 'reduce the new oil tax in proportion.'[283] However it was never made clear what that proportion would look like.

Although the SC has quite a lot of similarities to the RFCT, it should be emphasised for the avoidance of doubt that the SC is not a corporation tax.[284] Rather, it is an annual charge levied 'as if it were an amount of corporation tax chargeable on the company.'[285] What this means is that the administration of the SC is the same as that of the RFCT, and also that of the corporation tax. This is also true for the provisions on returns, assessment, collection and receipt of corporation tax, appeals, and, 'administration, penalties, interest on unpaid tax and priority of tax in cases of insolvency.'[286]

However it is not a corporation tax because while the corporation tax is charged on a company's overall profits,[287] and the RFCT on its ring fence profits,[288] the SC is levied on a company's 'adjusted ring fence profits' instead.[289] What the 'adjusted' refers to is the exclusion of the interest costs of debt financing[290] when calculating the deductible expenditures. Thus the tax base is wider than that of the RFCT, increasing the potential tax take over what it would have been had the tax base been the same as the RFCT, holding everything else constant.

Since it differs from the RFCT, the SC also has, or at least had at the time of the Fiscal Review, its own set of allowances and reliefs in calculating the adjusted ring fence profits. These are briefly discussed next not only to highlight the complexity of the allowances and reliefs found within the SC pillar and the instability arising from that complexity but also to identify the specific changes introduced to this pillar with the Fiscal Review.

3.3.1. Allowances and reliefs

From the time it was introduced the allowances within the SC regime concerned only certain, specific types of oil fields. The first three of these specific types related to those new fields that received development consents after 21 April 2009.[291] These qualifying fields were eligible for certain field allowances that were deductible from their *adjusted* ring fence profits.[292] These allowances ranged from £75,000,000 to £800,000,000 depending on the field type.[293]

In order to qualify for the allowances a new field had to either be a small field,[294] an ultra-Heavy (uH) oil field,[295] or an ultra-High Pressure/High Temperature[296] (uHP/HT) field.[297] While both the new uH and uHP/HT fields were eligible for allowances of £800m, the small oil fields received allowances of up to £75m.[298] Although, the latter figure was raised to £150m for the small oil fields that received authorisation after 21 March 2012.[299]

The fiscal instability was further exacerbated in 2012 with the introduction of an additional set of allowances.[300] This new set was brought within the umbrella of what was termed as an 'additionally-developed field' which itself was defined as a *project* 'described in an addendum' to the development consent that has also been authorised[301] by the Secretary of State.[302] The definition also required that such a project also needed to meet the conditions set out in the subsequent orders by the HMRC.[303]

Such orders were duly published in 2012[304] and 2013,[305] respectively. The earlier one introduced three additional specific types of fields that now also qualified for field allowances. These three additional types were categorised based on their water depth, the hydrocarbon state and size. Accordingly, large deep-water oil fields,[306] large shallow-water gas fields[307] and deep-water gas fields[308] were all eligible for field allowances for the SC purposes up to £3 billion, £500 million and £800 million, respectively.

The latter order, commonly referred to as the 'Brown Field Allowances,'[309] introduced an allowance for those projects that aimed at incrementally increasing the existing production levels. Accordingly, those post-6 September 2012, DECC-approved projects[310] which were aiming to increase the production levels from existing fields were to receive field allowances of up to £50 per tonne of additional oil reserves that materialise as a consequence of the project, though with an upper ceiling of £250,000,000.[311] For such projects to qualify, however, their expected capital costs per tonne of anticipated additional reserves had to exceed £60.[312]

A final relief within the SC pillar was applicable to the decommissioning expenditures. At the time when the SC headline rate was raised to 32% the government simultaneously announced a restriction of 20% on the reliefs that could be claimed for decommissioning expenditures in order to 'avoid incentivising accelerated decommissioning' as a consequence of the increased tax rate.[313] Consequently, from 21 March 2012,[314] a fraction[315] of the decommissioning costs relieved were to be added back to the adjusted ring fence profits before applying the SC,[316] effectively widening the base for which the tax applied.

As the foregoing suggests, the SC was not only subject to very frequent changes but also increased complexities due to increase in the layers of capital allowances. However, despite this multilayered allowance and relief mechanisms within the SC, the complexity of the fiscal system applicable to the petroleum exploitation was not limited to mechanisms applied at the corporate income level. In contrast to the RFCT and the SC pillars, the third component of the overall system was quite distinct in that it applied at a project level. This project-specific application, as discussed in the next section, meant that although this third pillar was also contributing to the fiscal instability highlighted by the Wood Review,[317] the magnitude of that contribution was lower than that of the SC.

3.4. The third UKCS fiscal pillar: petroleum revenue tax

This project specific third fiscal pillar applicable to the petroleum exploitation in the UK, the petroleum revenue tax, can be considered as a modified application of the theoretical Resource Rent Tax (RRT) developed by Garnaut and Ross in the 1970s.[318] Box 3.3 below briefly elaborates on this theoretical RRT.

The PRT regime, as an application of RRT, does not share all its theoretical benefits. There are certain peculiarities in the design of PRT that move it away from the Fiscal Review objective leaving only very specific circumstances in which the objective might be achievable. Accordingly, the mechanics and the components of the PRT are discussed below to illustrate this position.

Box 3.3 Resource rent tax (RRT)

RRT is a tax on annual net cash flows with 100% allowance on all expenditures except for interest payments and other financing costs.[319] If a cash flow is negative it is carried forward at a specific *threshold rate*. That is, this year's loss is artificially inflated at the threshold rate and included in the next year's calculation. Once an annual net cash flow turns positive in subsequent years, it is then taxed at the legislated tax rate every year until the annual net cash flow turns negative again. At that stage, it is again carried forward at the threshold rate.[320] This system effectively allows an investor to achieve a rate of return equal to the threshold rate before the project becomes taxable.[321]

Theoretically the system may capture economic rents efficiently, and thus satisfy both the purpose of petroleum taxation in general and the specific objective set out in the Fiscal Review.[322] The RRT can achieve this because it is a tax on a project's cash flow and as such it would satisfy the criteria developed in Section 2.5. That is, as a tax on cash flows it would be highly sensitive to the changes in oil prices, various costs and the sizes of the fields. As the cash flows fluctuate the system would automatically react, capturing larger share when positive cash flows increase and vice versa. 'The sensitivity would be strong enough to ensure that government would always obtain an "adequate" share of the economic rents while field developments would never be deterred when they were viable on a pre-tax basis.'[323]

3.4.1. The mechanics of PRT

PRT was introduced at the same time as RFCT with a similar ring fence concept albeit with a narrower ring. While the determination of the RFCT's tax base required aggregation of the profits from all upstream activities, the PRT was levied on an individual field basis,[324] charged at 50% at the time of the Fiscal Review. The application of this fiscal pillar, though, has been limited in that it has been only applicable to relatively older fields that received development consents prior to 16 March 1993.[325]

Upon its introduction, the PRT was regarded as a 'completely new concept in UK taxation – a self-contained piece of legislation separate and distinct from the main corpus of the law of Income Tax (IT), Corporation Tax (CT) and Capital Gains Tax (CGT).'[326] This self-contained nature of the PRT meant that the procedures for calculating the PRT liability were not one of accounting employed to ascertain company accounts, but instead laid out in a statute.[327] This could possibly be attributable to the differing objectives between financial and tax accounting.[328] While the former would intend to inform the 'capital providers'[329] the goal of the latter would be to generate income for the government.[330] Therefore the legislated methodology for calculating field profits would inevitably 'differ dramatically from financial accounting standards and procedures.'[331]

Accordingly, the relevant legislation[332] stated that the PRT rate was to be applied to 'assessable profit'[333] after being adjusted for specific oil allowances and reduced by certain allowable losses.[334] Once the PRT liability is calculated it may also be further limited by a protective mechanism called 'safeguard.'[335] Table 3.3 below illustrates the PRT calculation:

Table 3.3 PRT calculation

Add	*Subtract*	£	*Chapter Section*
Assessable profit		π	3.4.2
	Allowable loss	λ	3.4.2
Chargeable profit		$\Pi = \pi - \lambda - \alpha^*$	
PRT at 50%		$\iota - \Pi * 50\%$	
PRT liability, τ, may further be limited due to Safeguard.			3.4.3
**α denotes oil allowance*			

Each of these components contain specific methodologies that feed into the proposed fiscal regime in Chapter 5 and therefore merit a brief discussion.

3.4.2. Assessable profits and allowable losses

Assessable profits and allowable losses are two sides of the same coin. For any given period, a participant's share of the income generated from a *field* after allowing for certain expenditures gives a company's *field profits*. It is considered as negative field profits, or an 'allowable loss' if the field income is lower than the relevant expenditures; or positive, if the converse is true, which is deemed as an 'assessable profit.'[336] If it is an allowable loss, then these losses can be set against any previous or subsequent chargeable periods, further reducing the assessable profits for those periods.[337]

The procedures for calculating the assessable profits, or the allowable losses, are considered to be 'the greatest contrast with corporation tax'[338] because the '[a]ccounts are completely ignored and instead the profit or loss for each field in which a participator is interested is arrived at by aggregating positive amounts and negative amounts.'[339] For example, under standard corporate accounting, assets may be depreciated. This is not the case under PRT. Similarly, under general corporation tax, and under RFCT, the expenditures are treated separately depending on whether they are revenue or capital in nature.[340] The PRT regime does not apply that distinction[341] and instead the treatment of expenditures are legislated as positive and negative amounts.[342]

Table 3.4 Assessable profits calculation

Positive Amounts	*£*	*Negative Amounts*	*£*	*Chapter Section*
Gross Profit	X	Gross Loss	Y	3.4.2.1
Tariff Receipts	X	Tariff Receipt Allowance	Y	3.4.2.2
Expenditure Credit	X	Expenditure Debit	Y	3.4.2.3
Licence Credit	X	Licence Debit	Y	Box 3.4
Licence Payments bar Royalty	X	Licence Payments bar Royalty	Y	Box 3.4
Disposal Receipts	X			Box 3.4
Assessable Profit	$\pi = \sum X - \sum Y$			

The positive amounts include gross profits, asset disposal receipts,[343] tariff receipts,[344] licence credits and payments,[345] and expenditure credits. The negative amounts include gross losses, tariff receipt allowance, licence debits and payments bar royalty,[346] and expenditure debits. Table 3.4 below summarises the calculation for the assessable profits.

Some of these components of the positive and negative amounts are pertinent to the fiscal regime proposed in Chapter 5 because their existing design within the PRT regime are aligned with the Fiscal Review guiding principles. This is why, specifically, the gross profits and losses, the tariff receipts and allowances, and the treatment of expenditures will be discussed – not only examine the conditions within which the PRT can be aligned with achieving the Fiscal Review objective – but also to identify the key details of the Assessable Profits components that can be utilised for the fiscal regime advocated in this work.

3.4.2.1. Gross profits and losses

For the purposes of the calculations in Table 3.4, the gross profits are more or less the same as the value of the production in the relevant period.[347] However, the determination of the value is only for a portion of a given volume of production because the legislation allows for a certain level of PRT-free production[348] in recognition of, and in order to prevent, the economic burden the PRT regime may impose on 'smaller, more marginally economic fields.'[349]

Such protection is afforded for each chargeable period whereby a portion of a participant's share of the production in that period from the PRT-liable field is subject to a mechanism called 'oil allowance' as a tax wrapper.[350] That is, a portion of the production – ranging from a maximum of 125 to 250 tonnes per period with a 5 to 10 million limit depending on when, and for which location, a development consent has been granted[351] – is protected from the PRT regime and the participant would be liable for the PRT only if the field profits exceed the oil allowance.[352]

The determination of the quantity of production that comes within the PRT calculation is only one aspect of arriving at the gross profits. Assessing the value of that production can also be complex as it depends on whether the production is sold or appropriated, and if the former, whether they are sold at an arm's length or not.[353] If the production is appropriated then it is deemed as a sale at a non-arm's length.[354] When the sale is deemed as not at an arm's length the HMRC divides the crude oil sales into two categories.[355] One category is for those crude oils which are traded in sufficient volumes to yield a price discovery. These include the Brent, Ekofisk, Flotta, Forties blends and the Statfjord oil.[356] The second category is for those crude oils that are outside of the first category.[357] The valuations of these two vary in certain specific details. Although that variation is not pertinent to the arguments presented in this work,[358] Box 3.4 below provides a brief explanation of valuations of petroleum and other positive amounts under PRT.

Box 3.4 Valuation of petroleum and other positive amounts under PRT

Value of production: arm's length sale

The tax point for the sale of a production, insofar as the PRT is concerned, is the time when it is delivered to a buyer as long as the sale is at an arm's length.[359] However, the types of sales that are deemed as at an arm's length are quite limited. This is because for a sale to be at an arm's length the seller must demonstrate that the sale has not been affected by other commercial relationships or transactions.[360] Specifically, a sale needs to possess the following characteristics:

(a) The only consideration for the transaction is the price,
(b) Any existing commercial relationships between the parties or their connected entities do not influence the Terms and Conditions (Ts&Cs) of the sale, and
(c) The seller, or any one of its directly or indirectly connected entities, does not have 'any interest in the subsequent resale or disposal of oil or any product derived therefrom.'[361]

These characteristics seriously restrict what qualifies as an arm's length sale. For example, if an upstream company sells its equity crude to an unconnected refinery which then sells a portion of the refined products to a petrochemical company affiliated with the upstream company, then the sale of the crude is not considered as at an arm's length.[362]

On the other hand, for companies with both an upstream and a marketing subsidiaries a sale may be considered at an arm's length depending on the circumstances of the sale.[363] For example, the upstream subsidiary may sell its equity oil to the marketing subsidiary at a price $0.40 above[364] a price reporting agency's Brent assessment[365] around the Bill of Lading.[366] The marketing subsidiary then sells this and other third-party crudes to an unconnected refinery at a price differential of $0.45 to the same assessment. The HMRC would then deem the difference of $0.05 as a 'reasonable marketing fee,' and, consequently, the sale between the upstream and marketing subsidiaries would be considered as at an arm's length.[367]

Nevertheless, it is very difficult for a company to demonstrate that an existing commercial relationship does not have an impact on the Ts&Cs of a sale as the 'HMRC is inclined to argue that the mere existence of another commercial relationship will affect the terms of the sale.'[368] Therefore, it has been suggested that the parties may be better off negotiating within the rules for non-arm's length sales as to avoid 'adverse adjustment' by the HMRC.[369]

Value of production: non-arm's length sale

For the purposes of the PRT, the valuations of non-arm's length transactions are conducted separately for oil and for gas.[370] Calculations for oil vary depending on which of the 2 categories it belongs to.[371] Specifically, Category 2 oils are all of the oils that are outside of the Category 1 oils.[372] The categorisation depends on whether the types of oil have a 'widely commercially available published price assessment or not.'[373] Accordingly, the Category 1 oil include those crude oils:

(a) that arrive at Sullom Voe Terminal in Shetland Islands through either the Brent or Ninian pipeline systems (these oils are referred to as 'Brent blend'),
(b) that arrive at Teeside Oil Terminal in Seal Sands through the Norpipe pipeline (these oils are referred to as 'Ekofisk blend'),
(c) that arrive at Flotta Oil Terminal in Orkney Islands and that originate from the Flotta catchment area (these oils are referred to as 'Flotta blend'),
(d) that arrive at Cruden Bay, Aberdeenshire through the Forties pipeline system (these oils are referred to as the 'Forties blend'), and
(e) 'Statfjord oil' to which 'article 23 of the Agreement between Her Majesty's Government of the United Kingdom and Northern Ireland and the Government of the Kingdom of Norway relating to the exploitation of the Statfjord Field Reservoirs signed at Oslo on 16th October 1979 applies'.[374]

The market value of a Category 1 oil,[375] therefore, is determined by discovering the market price of that particular quantity and quality of crude oil which has been sold at a non-arm's length.[376] For this, the benchmark market contract must be for an arm's length sale of one standard cargo of the oil with a loading duration of 3 days – after allowing for initial treatments prior to delivery.[377] The oil should also be delivered 'at the place of extraction' if it is onshore, or at the nearest location 'at which the seller could reasonably be expected to deliver' it, if it is offshore.[378] To qualify within this Category the terms regarding the payment should also be those customarily used in the arm's length oil sales.[379]

The valuation of the Category 2 oils is almost identical to the valuation of the Category 1 oils except for two differences. First, rather than the benchmark market contract being of one standard cargo, it instead 'provides for delivery of the oil on the notional delivery day[380] for the actual oil or within such period that includes that day as is normal under a contract at arm's length for the sale of oil of that kind.'[381] Second, rather than the market contract specifying the 3-day loading period, it instead has to be made on a date prior to the notional delivery date that is a 'normal' duration for the arm's length sale of oil of that kind.[382]

Finally, the valuation of the light gases,[383] is also determined by discovering the market price of that particular quantity and quality of light gas which have been sold at a non-arm's length.[384] For this, a market contract must be for an arm's length sale of the light gas after allowing for the initial treatment prior to the delivery.[385] Like in the case of the benchmark market contracts for oil, the delivery point for the market gas contracts should also be the 'place of extraction' if onshore, or the nearest location 'at which the seller could reasonably be expected to deliver the gases' if it is offshore.[386]

Value of production: appropriation

As opposed to selling it, when the oil is instead secured for refining, or any other use with the exception of production purposes, then it is deemed as 'relevantly appropriated.'[387] For the PRT calculations, 'production purposes' not only includes the drilling and other production operations but also initial treatment and pumping of the oil to the delivery point.[388]

In so far as the valuation of the appropriation is concerned, it is treated as a non-arm's length transaction and the procedures are virtually the same as those laid out for the non-arm's length sales.

Disposal receipts

From 1 July 1982, proceeds from the disposals of qualifying assets are brought within the PRT calculation as part of the 'positive amounts' in arriving at assessable profits.[389] In addition to the income obtained from disposing of an asset, such receipts also include insurance receipts arising from loss or destruction of an asset.[390] However, it does not constitute a disposal receipt if the payment received is either 'for the purpose of obtaining a direct or indirect interest in oil won or to be won from an oil field,' or for the financing charges on amounts a company has lent.[391] In other words, if the transaction is a transfer of field interest, or if it is an interest receipt, then the proceeds do not constitute a disposal receipt.[392]

Licence credit/debit and licence payments bar royalty
In calculating the assessable profits there is also a relief available for the annual licence fees.[393] The PRT mechanism additionally provides for the apportionment of payments in relation to multiple fields,[394] and for catching all the payments to and from the Secretary of State that falls outside the items specified in the PRT legislation.[395]

3.4.2.2. Tariff receipts and tariff allowances

One of the important components of the PRT's Assessable Profits calculation concerns the treatment of tariffs. As will be discussed below, the design of the tariff allowances and the interpretation by the courts of that design may have contributed, in the early stages, to the third-party access to infrastructure issues highlighted by the Wood Report.[396]

The tariff payments have been included in the 'positive amounts' computation since 1 July 1982,[397] unless a tariff contract was entered after 8 April 2003, and the payments for which were received within a chargeable period ending on, or after, 30 June 2004.[398] These latter *new* tariff payments have been excluded from the PRT calculations in their entirety.[399]

For PRT purposes, the definition of 'tariff receipts' include all types of payments regardless of whether they are capital or income in nature, in so far as it is paid in exchange for the use of a 'qualifying asset'[400] of the company, or for the 'provision of services' of any kind 'in connection with the use.'[401]

Despite the old tariff payments being considered as 'positive amount' in assessable profit calculations there nonetheless exists a tax protection in the form of Tariff Receipt Allowances (TRA). The TRAs act as a tax wrapper for a portion of tariff income by reducing certain qualifying tariff receipts liable to the PRT[402] by the monetary equivalence of 250,000 metric tonnes.[403] The monetary equivalent is calculated by multiplying the tariff payments received[404] for each tonne of oil with the TRA.[405] This allowance is available for every chargeable period as there are not any cumulative or time limits. If the total oil throughput[406] from the user field[407] in a chargeable period is less than the TRA, then there would be no PRT liability arising from the 'tariff receipts' in that period as the monetary equivalent would simply be the entire tariff payments received.[408]

Although the legislation is quite clear as to the TRA being 250,000 metric tonnes,[409] it is less so when it comes to the multiple tariff payments for separate uses of assets in the same field. This is because the amount of throughput oil is defined as the

> 'oil won from that user field which, in that chargeable period, is extracted, transported, initially treated or initially stored (or subject to two or more of those operations) by means of the asset to which the qualifying tariff receipts are referable.'[410]

The issue with this definition is the use of the word 'asset' in its singular form as opposed to 'assets' together with the 'tariff receipts' because treating the use of each asset separately with corresponding tariff receipts can mean multiple TRAs, which in turn would mean a significant reduction in the PRT liability. Naturally, the clarification on this issue had to come from the courts which did not arrive until December 1991.[411] The House of Lords decision was that the separate uses would be taken in aggregate, generating a single TRA.[412] Box 3.5 provides a discussion on the simplified facts of this case.

This outcome, however, may have contributed to the longer-term issues surrounding the difficulties for smaller third-party assets in gaining access to existing infrastructures[422] given that separate TRAs for each tariff generating activity may have incentivised the asset owners to be less draconian in granting access. This issue has also been highlighted in the Wood Review,[423] with a strong recommendation for a regulatory intervention as a solution.[424] Perhaps a

Box 3.5 BP oil development Ltd v commissioners of inland revenue [1992] STC 28, 64 TC 498 (Ch D)

In 1980, Marathon Oil UK Ltd (Marathon) entered into an agreement with BP Oil Development Ltd (BP) to process and throughput its petroleum from the Brae field via BP's assets in the Forties field. This naturally required separate accesses to BP facilities with differing tariff schedules. The first access was in relation to transporting the petroleum from the Brae field to BP's Forties field, separating the Brae crude and raw gas, temporarily storing the crude and then delivering it to a shipping terminal.[413] This was charged at £0.5 per barrel.[414] The second access concerned the processing of the Brae raw gas to obtain dry gas, propane, butane and C5+ condensate, temporarily storing all the gases bar the dry gas, and delivering them to Grangemouth Dock among other locations.[415] This was charged at £14.50 per tonne of raw gas.[416] The final access was in relation to further processing, or sweetening, of the dry gas and the propane.[417] This was charged at £0.1 per barrel of the original petroleum throughput.[418]

Given that the legislation referred to 'asset' in the singular and not 'assets', BP argued that each of these tariff receipts required a separate TRA.[419] The Inland Revenue, not surprisingly, asserted that because the legislation referred to 'tariff receipts' in the plural the concept had to be viewed as an aggregate.[420] In their decision the House of Lords sided with the Inland Revenue clarifying the point that the interpretation of 'asset' can also include its plural form.[421] Although the poor drafting of the definition of throughput oil led to a quite plausible interpretation of BP that a separate TRA applies to each distinct tariff activity, the House of Lords judgment of limiting the applicability of TRAs ensured that the government could receive a tax income from tariff payments.

more liberal interpretation by the House of Lords would have made such an interventionist approach redundant. Unfortunately, given the House of Lords decision the position of the HMRC has been to allow for only one TRA for tariff receipts from each user fields regardless of any multiplicity of access.[425]

3.4.2.3. Treatment of Expenditures

The final item that features in the assessable profits calculation concerns the treatment of expenditures which is perhaps the most complex element of the PRT calculation. The simplest aspect involves those expenditures that are explicitly not allowable. These include interests on loans,[426] the costs of buying land and constructing structures onshore,[427] those expenditures based on the levels of production,[428] the costs of acquiring interest in the licence or the production therefrom,[429] and the tax payments of the non-resident contractors.[430] Additionally, payments in settling the abandonment liabilities which are matched by abandonment guarantees[431] are also excluded from the PRT calculations.[432] Outside of these costs other expenditures may be allowable depending on the types of those expenditures. This is where the complexity begins.

Unlike the treatment of expenditures under the RFCT,[433] the PRT system does not distinguish between capital and revenue expenditure.[434] Instead, the allowable expenditures are split into two based on whether they are incurred on long-term assets or not.[435]

In broad terms, expenditures incurred in obtaining, creating or increasing the value of a long-term asset[436] are fully allowable.[437] If such an asset is a non-dedicated mobile asset,[438] a fraction of the cost of that asset, based on how long it has been in use at the PRT-liable field in proportion to its expected life, can still be allowable.[439]

The expenditures that are incurred outside of the ones that are incurred on a long-term asset may also be allowable depending on the purpose for which they were incurred. Referred to as Section 3 expenditures, or the 'ordinary expenditure rules,' these expenditures are allowable as long as they are incurred for one of the 13 specific purposes.[440]

In addition to the foregoing, certain qualifying expenditures can also be subject to a supplement, or an 'uplift,' of 35%.[441] This means, if a particular expenditure qualifies, it will be inflated by 35% in calculating the negative amounts for the PRT calculation. Broadly, the qualifying expenditures include the exploration, appraisal, development and production costs,[442] together with the costs involved in transporting the production.[443] Though, such a supplement is not without limitation. Even if the expenditure incurred qualifies for an uplift, it is no longer available when the field payback period[444] is reached.

The HMRC gives the rationale for this uplift as a compensation for not allowing interest payments[445] as a deduction under the PRT regime.[446] Though, the case law is less clear on this point. In *IRC v. Mobil North Sea Limited*[447] the then High Court judge Harman J has rejected the argument that it is compensation for not allowing the financing costs and instead asserted that it is an incentive mechanism to attract investors to the North Sea.[448] When the case was appealed to the House of Lords, Lord Templeman however did connect the lack of financing cost deductibility and the uplift provisions:

> In calculating the profits or losses derived from an oil field in each chargeable period for the purposes of petroleum revenue tax, allowances are made under the Act of 1975 for expenditure on the exploration, operation and development of the oil field. No allowance is permitted for interest or other costs of borrowing but certain types of expenditure qualified for an additional deductible allowance, described as supplement, originally equal to 75 per cent of the amount of the qualifying expenditure.[449]

Unfortunately, Lord Templeman's understanding of the purpose of uplift is less accurate than the then High Court judge Harman J's,[450] whose interpretation is not exactly right either. It is true that the uplift mechanism creates incentives. However, the purpose of the uplift is perhaps less to do with creating an incentive as it is to do with avoiding creating distortions and disincentivising the investors. This is because this uplift can be considered almost the same as the threshold rate within the theoretical RRT regime. As discussed in Section 3.5, the RRT regime can be neutral. Yet, this neutrality would hold if and only if the threshold rate set by the government is the same as the investor's discount rate. If the threshold rate is higher than the investor's discount rate then the government would not capture the economic rent efficiently[451] and if it is lower than the investor's discount rate then it would discourage investment.[452] Therefore, theoretically, the threshold rate ought to be set at the investor's discount rate in order to avoid disincentivising investment.[453] Thus, the uplift mechanism is in place to avoid distortions and disincentivisation, and not necessarily to incentivise.

One final point regarding the treatment of expenditures under the PRT mechanism concerns the non-field expenditures. Although the PRT is a field-based regime, there are nonetheless certain expenditures incurred, and negative amounts acquired, outside a field that can be brought within the PRT calculations.[454] These include certain research expenditures,[455] 'unrelievable field losses'[456] from another PRT-liable field and 'cross-field allowances.'[457]

Once the expenditures and other negative amounts are set against the positive amounts in arriving at the gross profits and once the PRT liability is calculated, that tax liability may further be reduced through a mechanism called the 'safeguard.'

3.4.3. Safeguard

The safeguard mechanism may be elected after the PRT liability is calculated. It limits the total amount of PRT liability payable which effectively guarantees a certain return to a participant.[458] Like the oil allowance mechanism[459] it too is in place in recognition of the possible burden PRT may impose on the marginal fields.[460] Unlike the oil allowance, however, it is not a device to reduce the assessable profit to which the PRT rate applies, but instead calculated separately. Once calculated, a participant's total PRT liability is determined by the lowest figure of either the amount reached via the safeguard calculation or via the standard PRT calculation in the absence of the safeguard.[461]

To calculate the safeguard 'adjusted profits'[462] are set against a particular threshold. If it is lower than the threshold, then no PRT liability arises. If it exceeds the threshold, then the PRT liability is limited to the 80% of that excess above the threshold.[463] This threshold is set at 15% of the 'accumulated capital expenditure.'[464] The Table 3.5 below illustrates the steps involved in calculating the PRT liability with a safeguard.

The number of times the safeguard can be utilised is not unlimited, however. The safeguard is only available until the payback period is reached[465] plus half the time it takes to reach it.[466] As such, this mechanism seems to be more aligned with the purpose identified by the High Court judge Harman J than the uplift.[467] In other words, the safeguard is in place as an incentive mechanism for the investors.

Unfortunately, with these incentive mechanisms the complexity of the PRT pillar is further exacerbated. In addition to this, since neither the PRT, nor the SC, nor the RFCT apply in isolation, the fiscal system as a whole becomes even more complex. The next Section discusses this complexity through the interactions between these fiscal pillars.

3.5. Interaction between the fiscal pillars

When calculating the RFCT liability the PRT payments can be deducted from the ring fence income in the same accounting period, further reducing the chargeable profits to which the RFCT rate applies.[468] This also means if a participant receives a repayment due to a carry back of a PRT loss, then that repayment is treated as income for RFCT purposes.[469]

Since the adjusted ring fence profits calculation under the SC closely follow that of ring fence profits calculated under the RFCT, the PRT payments are also allowable under the SC calculation. Similarly, the repayments of the PRT loss carry backs are also treated as income.

Another interaction between the SC and the PRT pillars concerns the Brown Field Allowances introduced in 2013.[470] Those projects, approved by the

Table 3.5 Safeguard calculation

	(£)
Adjusted Profit	*AP*
Threshold: 15% of Accumulated Capex to end of Period	TH = 15% * Acc. Capex
Excess	Ex = AP – TH
Safeguard PRT	S.PRT = 80% * Ex

Secretary of State after 6 September 2012, that aim to increase the production from existing fields[471] receive an allowance of £50 for each tonne of additional oil reserves that materialise as a consequence of the project.[472] Usually there is an upper limit of £250,000,000 to this allowance.[473] However, if it is a PRT-liable field, then the upper limit is doubled to £500,000,000.[474]

When these interactions are taken into account it becomes evident the three fiscal pillars have jointly imposed very high marginal tax rates. At the time of the Fiscal Review the marginal tax rate was as high as 81% for the PRT-liable fields.[475] For all other fields this rate was 62%.[476] In addition to these very high marginal rates the system as a whole has not been granting a fair share of the revenues from petroleum exploitation to the government, and thus was not efficient.

In order to understand this inefficiency position, it is important to briefly revisit the concepts of *fair share* and *efficiency* developed in Chapter 2. These essentially refer to the ability of capturing economic rents. As emphasised in the Fiscal Review and underlined in Section 2.3, capturing economic rents is the ultimate goal of natural resource taxation. This is because, doing so, by definition, will grant the maximum tax receipts to the government without altering the decisions of the investors on continuing to invest in producing assets, or in developing discoveries or in exploring for new assets in the same jurisdiction. The investment decisions would not be altered since what is left for the investors after taxing away the economic rents are the amounts required to keep investing in this jurisdiction.

Yet neither in the RFCT, nor in the SC pillars, are the tax bases profits arising from individual *projects*. Instead they are the overall corporate ring fence profits arising from petroleum extraction. It is true that they focus on profits, which means they certainly take costs and prices into account, satisfying one of the Fiscal Review's guiding principles. However, despite this profit focus neither of them are very efficient as they are not directly targeting the economic rents of each project separately. This inefficiency may arise because each individual project will generate varying degrees of economic rents, and some will not generate at all. Yet the tax bases are either the ring fence profits in the case of RFCT or the adjusted ring fence profits in the case of SC, which are, in broad terms, the aggregate of all ring fence incomes left after all the relevant costs of different ring fence projects are taken into account. Thus, the effect of these fiscal mechanisms on individual projects will vary. For some of the projects, particularly those of higher costs and/or marginal fields, the RFCT may capture more than the economic rents generated from those projects; and for some others it may capture only a small share of the economic rent, leaving money on the table from the government's perspective. The same argument can readily be extended to the SC as well. It is, however, very difficult to pinpoint the effects as all the incomes and associated costs from petroliferous trades are aggregated before these mechanisms are applied.

On the other hand, they are taxes on profits. This means they respond, to some degree, to variations in oil prices, costs and production levels associated with a given field, which in turn would impact the ultimate recovered reserves from that field. As highlighted in Chapter 2, it is important to identify the extent to which a fiscal mechanism can respond to the changes in these variables in determining its efficiency. These variables receive particular attention because the materialisation of any risk, whether it is political, economic or technical, will inadvertently impact either the prices, costs or production levels, and in turn, the recoverable field sizes. An efficient fiscal tool, therefore, ought to be highly responsive to the changes to the field's costs and production levels along with what it receives for the produced oil.

Both RFCT and SC are responsive to the changes in these variables though not strongly. This is because, the effects of any variations at the field level will inevitably get diluted when aggregating with other ring fence projects to calculate the tax bases for either mechanisms.

For example, assume that rig rental costs for an upstream company operating in the UKCS declined. At the same time, operating costs of two other producing fields in the UKCS of the same company increased significantly, perhaps due to increased maintenance or access tariff costs. The responses of the RFCT and the SC regimes in this scenario would not directly be predictable as they would depend on the magnitudes of the reduction in rig rentals and of the increases in operating costs. They could possibly even cancel each other out. Yet individually each of these projects would have a different economic rent profile. The first project may not even generate any as there may not be a commercial find. This aggregation under both mechanisms means they would not be able to completely respond to the variations in each of these projects. The magnitude of their responses would be small in proportion to the aggregate outcome of the changes.

In addition to their aggregate position, within each of these fiscal pillars there are also specific elements that cause further distortion in investment decision-making. In all the fiscal pillars the timing and the pace of the cost write-offs are as important as their headline tax rates. For the RFCT and the SC mechanisms there are capital allowance regimes in place that are designed to behave like the depreciation found in corporate accounting. These effectively make certain capital expenditures deductible, despite the current tax law not allowing for the deductibility of capital costs.

Accordingly, for the RFCT pillar, those qualifying capital expenditures on plant and machinery,[477] on mineral extraction,[478] on research and development-[479] and on decommissioning[480] are deductible in full as they are incurred. Given that an investor would prefer immediate deductibility of capital costs due to the time value of money considerations this seems to be in line with expectations. However, for the sake of efficiency, or to avoid creating distortions, the capital assets ought to be written off on their decline in values based on their economic life. This is because extending the deductibility to longer periods incentivises the investors to invest in assets that have shorter lives. Similarly, reducing the deductibility to shorter periods, say to 100% first year, creates disproportional benefits for assets with longer lives as the effective tax rate will be lower for those. Thus, it can be argued that such capital allowances actually may artificially induce investors to invest in longer-life assets than they otherwise would.

It is, however, extremely difficult to set the right deductibility schedule for each capital asset, given that their individual rates of obsolescence will differ.[481] In addition, due to the price and reserve risks highlighted above, it is equally difficult to estimate the reduction in the present values of cash flows even without considering the problem of setting the right discount rate.[482] Thus the allowances for the capital costs have to be set at an arbitrary rate. The 100% first-year deductibility can, therefore, be justifiable as it may be in tandem with the government's wider objective of extending asset lives as expressed in the Wood Review.[483] Yet it nonetheless creates distortions and as such is not as efficient as it can be for the analytical purposes set out in this and the previous chapter.

Comparatively, all costs that are revenue in nature are expensed in full as they are incurred including certain financing costs.[484] This latter position, however, can create a bias towards debt over equity financing. Thus it can be seen that it may not be neutral as it may create distortions in the financing decisions.

One other interesting element within the RFCT pillar concerns the RFES mechanism that is in place to avoid disadvantaging those E&P companies that are not yet in a tax paying position.[485] By providing an uplift, it is envisaged that the RFES mechanism would alleviate the value erosion of capital expenditures that cannot be claimed immediately. However, as a consequence, the RFCT regime segregates an existing taxpayer from a new entrant. Even though the relevant legislation[486] is broad enough to cover all types of investors,[487] in practice the uplift provided within the RFES is significantly more likely to be utilised by a new entrant than an existing taxpayer as the latter will likely have other taxable ring fence income from other upstream assets. This segregation, along with a fixed uplift irrespective of the specificities of a given asset may create further distortions.[488]

Similar distortions on investment decisions are also found in the SC pillar. In fact, such distortive effects are precisely the reason behind limiting the decommissioning reliefs to 20% for the SC system.[489] It is presumed that by disallowing the four-fifths of decommissioning expenditures, in other words, by spreading the costs associated with decommissioning into a number of periods, the distortions of premature abandonment created by the SC regime may be countered.[490] Yet, as highlighted previously if the paces of capital cost write-offs are not aligned with their own economic lives then distortions may result. Setting an umbrella rate of 20% may therefore create a different set of distortions for various different capital costs.

Interestingly though, there are allowances within the SC regime that are project based. These, however, do not mimic a depreciation schedule. They instead provide a ring-fenced income that is protected from the SC. Consequently, any variations in oil prices or costs impact only the duration of these specific allowances. Since they reduce an individual project's adjusted ring fence profits they, in effect, incentivise investments into those specific assets, intending to counter the impact of the SC regime. Yet, they nonetheless distort investment decisions as investors with limited budgets are artificially induced by fiscal mechanisms to invest in these particular fields defined in the allowances, away from potentially more efficient investment alternatives.

On the other hand, unlike the RFCT and the SC regimes the PRT is a project-based fiscal mechanism. That is, it applies periodically[491] on the cash flows generated from an individual field. In calculating the cash flows financing costs among others are not relievable, though a large portion of relevant expenditures are relievable in full.[492] As such, it can be viewed as the implementation of the theoretical RRT system.[493]

Since it is a tax on a project's cash flow, the PRT system is highly sensitive to the changes in oil prices, costs and the sizes of fields which is also the case under the theoretical RRT regime. This means any change to these variables would immediately alter the cash flow, providing a larger share for the government when positive cash flows increase and vice versa. Thus, the system can be considered neutral and efficient.

However, the PRT system would be neutral only to the extent that the 35% uplift is the same as the investor's discount rate.[494] If the 35% rate is higher than the investor's discount rate then the government would effectively leave money on the table as it would capture a smaller portion of economic rent than it could have had the two rates been aligned. Conversely, if the rate is lower than the investor's discount rate then it would discourage investment, thus still less than efficient. In fact, in order to prevent such discouragement, the PRT pillar additionally provides Oil Allowance and Safeguard mechanisms.

Given that it is only in very limited circumstances neutrality and efficiency can hold true for the PRT regime, it is more likely to be less than efficient, or neutral, in most of the cases. The situation is further exacerbated by the fact that not only the discount rates[495] employed by the investors vary per project and among the investors, but also are confidential and unknown to the governments.[496] The government, and particularly the decision-makers within the government, may have less than aligned interests that could result in varying discount rates. The only jointly observable item for the parties is the profits which are by definition a combination of the returns required on capital and economic rents. So there is a real possibility that the point at which the resource rent is applicable may be below or above the investor's required rate of return.[497]

The fact that neutrality can be achieved only in limited circumstances gets further undermined when the inefficiencies of the RFCT and the SC system are taken into account and when the fiscal regime is viewed holistically. Even if, hypothetically, in those limited circumstances fiscal neutrality can be achieved under the PRT pillar for a given project, the combined effects of the RFCT and the SC pillars would subsequently not only dilute that neutrality through the aggregation of incomes but also introduce a number of distortions.

In fact, the distortions and inefficiencies would be particularly pronounced for the new UKCS investors since they would not be subject to the PRT pillar. This position, though, would certainly not be conducive to attracting investment into the UKCS which therefore would mean that it would also not achieve the purpose of the Wood Report.

As the foregoing suggests, the tax system at the time of the Fiscal Review was inefficient and in desperate need of reform. It also explains why the diagnosis of the Fiscal Review was correct when it argued that the UKCS could not continue to receive investments at its current levels unless the applicable tax regime was reformed.[498] The distorting effects of the inefficiencies of the system would certainly have continued to disincentivise investors. The Fiscal Review was also equally correct in establishing what the reform objectives had to be and the types of principles that were required to guide the reform process.What followed, however, has not only been surprising but also disappointing. The reforms presented in the Fiscal Review and the subsequent modifications have been significantly short of the goals and the principles highlighted in that very document. The next Chapter analyses these modifications and discusses the reasons behind why the reforms that have been introduced are unaligned with the Fiscal Review's own objectives and principles. Subsequent to those analysis and discussions, Chapter 5 will then present what the fiscal regime ought to look like when the Fiscal Review's arguments are taken to their natural conclusions.

Notes

1 HM Treasury, *'Driving Investment: a plan to reform the oil and gas fiscal regime'* (Report, HM Treasury December 2014) 3.20, 3.28 and 3.29
2 See Section 2.2
3 HM Treasury (n 1) 4.4
4 Sir Ian Wood, *'UKCS Maximising Recovery Review: Final Report'* (Report, 25 February 2014) 2.3.ii
5 Wood (n 4) 2.3.ii
6 Oil & Gas UK, '*Economic Report 2014'* (Report, Oil & Gas UK 2014) 48
7 Oil & Gas UK, Economic Report 2013 (Report, Oil & Gas UK 2013) 43
8 See Section 4.1 below for the details on the recent changes introduced.
9 See Section 3.5 below for the details on the marginal tax rates.
10 Finance Act 2014 Ch 1, which will reduce to 17% for the financial year 2020, Finance Act 2016 s 46
11 See Section 2.3 for a detailed discussion of these concepts.
12 See Section 2.3 above.
13 See Chapter 4
14 Note that this work limits itself to the tax regime applicable to the UKCS and therefore the fiscal treatment of onshore extraction is beyond the scope of this work.
15 Petroleum and Submarine Pipe-lines Act 1975 s 18
16 Emre Usenmez *'The UKCS Fiscal Regime*' in G Gordon, J Paterson and E Usenmez (eds), *Oil and Gas Law: Current Practice and Emerging Trends* (2nd Ed, DUP 2011)
17 Petroleum Royalties (Relief) Act 1983 s 1 read together with Finance Act 1983 s 36 (2). This assumes that those development consents were granted for those licences that incorporated the 1982 Model Clauses. Petroleum Royalties (Relief) Act 1983 s 1 (2)(a). The 1982 Model Clauses are set out in Petroleum (Production) Regulations 1982 SI 1982/1000 Sch 5

18 HM Treasury, '*Budget 2002 The Strength to make long-term decisions: Investing in an enterprising, fairer Britain*' (Report, HM Treasury 17 April 2002) 5.82
19 Oil Taxation Act 1975 s 13. This section has been repealed under Income and Corporation Taxes Act 1988 Sch 29 s 32, and re-enacted under Income and Corporation Taxes Act 1988 s 492 (1); which itself has recently (3 March 2010) been repealed under Corporation Tax Act 2010 Sch 1 s 62 and re-enacted under Corporation Tax Act 2010 s 279. Reliefs and allowances under ring fence corporation tax are further discussed in Section 3.1.3
20 See Section 2.4.4
21 Oil Taxation Act 1975 s 13; Income and Corporation Taxes Act 1988 s 492 (1); Corporation Tax Act 2010 s 279 read together with ss 274 and 277
22 These activities can range from acquisition of exploitation rights either onshore or offshore to abandonment.
23 HM Revenue & Customs, '*Oil Taxation Manual*' (Manual, HMRC 12 November 2014) OT00020
24 Hayllar R F and Pleasance R T, *UK Taxation of Offshore Oil and Gas* (Butterworths 1977) 20.01
25 See Section 3.5 for a detailed analyses of the RFCT.
26 As of Fiscal Year commencing on 01 April 2016
27 Finance Act 2008 s 6
28 Finance Act 2008 s 6
29 Finance Act 2014 Ch 1
30 Finance Act 2016, s 46
31 Ring fence income is defined as 'income arising from oil extraction activities or oil rights.' Corporation Tax Act 2010 s 275
32 Oil Taxation Act 1975 s 2
33 Corporation Tax Act 2010, s 280
34 Oil Taxation Act 1975 s2(5)
35 Oil Taxation Act 1975 s2(5), 2(5A) and Sch 3
36 Oil Taxation Act 1975 s2(5) and Sch 3
37 HM Revenue & Customs, *'LBS Oil and Gas Market Values for Category 1 crudes 2015'* (List, HMRC Large Business Service 2 June 2015)
38 Corporation Tax Act 2010 s 291
39 Oil Taxation Act 1983 s 6. Specifically, by a party other than a 'connected party' as defined in Corporation Tax Act 2010 s 1122
40 Corporation Tax Act 2010 s 291
41 Especially under the PRT pillar. See Section 3.4
42 See Section 2.1.1
43 See Section 3.5
44 Corporation Tax Act 2009 s 571
45 Corporation Tax Act 2009 s 577. Broadly, a future contract involves the sale of crude at an agreed future date for a price (or, a methodology for determining the price) agreed at the time of signing the contract. An option contract on the other hand, is almost identical to a futures contract with an important exception that the buyer of the contract has the right but not the obligation to exercise the contract. CFDs, by comparison, are financial swaps where the payoffs are dependent on the fluctuations of the crude oil price around an agreed and fixed price. Corporation Tax Act 2009 ss 580–582
46 Corporation Tax Act 2010 s 37. This period increases to immediately preceding 3 years if the trade ceases. Corporation Tax Act 2010 s 39. The cases in which a cessation of trade is deemed to have occurred are prescribed in Corporation Tax Act 2010 s 50
47 Corporation Tax Act 2010 s 45

48 Corporation Tax Act 2010 s 95

49 Corporation Tax Act 2010 s 52. Interestingly, this only covers those derivative contracts traded in a regulated exchange. It does not include the losses arising from bespoke swap contracts like contracts for differences (CFDs) as they are traded outside of an exchange. The tax treatment of both the futures and swaps are in capital gains tax legislation. See Taxation of Chargeable Gains Act 1992 Part IV

50 Corporation Tax Act 2010 s 304

51 Corporation Tax Act 2010 s 40

52 Corporation Tax Act 2010 s 42

53 Corporation Tax Act 2010 s 45

54 Corporation Tax Act 2010 ss 39 and 42

55 Corporation Tax Act 2010 s 304

56 Corporation Tax Act 2010 s 37

57 See Section 2.4.1.3.2 for the theoretical discussion on time value of money.

58 Under Corporation Tax Act 2009 s 1313 exploration and production (E&P) activities by non-residents are deemed to be carried out via a permanent establishment (i.e. via branch or agency) in order to bring them within the tax net.

59 Corporation Tax Act 2010 Chs 2 and 3

60 HM Revenue & Customs, *'Oil Taxation Manual'* (n 23) OT20252 and OT26035

61 The HMRC emphasises the decision to proceed in their manual. This is due to the fact that there may be substantial 'gap' between a decision that 'commercial development is considered worthwhile' and a decision 'to proceed with the commercial development of a discovery.' HM Revenue & Customs, *'Oil Taxation Manual'* (n 23) OT20250

62 HM Revenue & Customs, *'Oil Taxation Manual'* (n 23) OT20250

63 See Section 2.4.1.3.2 for a discussion on this concept.

64 Corporation Tax Act 2009 s 53. Please note that, despite the fact that capital expenditures are not allowable, there is nonetheless a capital allowance system in place. See the discussion in Section 3.2.3.1 below.

65 International Accounting Standards Board (IASB), *A Review of Conceptual Framework for Financial Reporting* (Discussion Paper DP/2013/1, IFRS Foundation 2013) Para 2.37

66 R A Musgrave and P B Musgrave, *Public Finance in Theory and Practice* (5th Ed, McGraw-Hill 1989) Ch 22

67 International Accounting Standards Board (IASB), *Conceptual Framework for Financial Reporting: The Objective of Financial Reporting and Qualitative Characteristics and Constraints of Decision-Useful Financial Reporting Information* (Exposure draft issued on 29 May 2008, IFRS Foundation 2008), para 49. For further discussion on the treatment of assets and the issues surrounding the concepts of assets, liabilities, expenses and income please see Peter Walton and Walter Aerts, *Global Financial Accounting and Reporting: Principles and Analysis* (2nd Ed, Cengage Learning 2009) Ch 3

68 Usenmez (n 16) para 6.12

69 Capital Allowances Act 2001 s 4

70 Corporation Tax Act 2009 s 931 and Capital Allowances Act 2001 s 4. The circularity of this provision together with the treatment of capital expenditures is noted. Effectively the legislation states that the capital expenditures are not deductible and those expenditures that are deductible are not capital expenditures.

71 *ECC Quarries Ltd v Watkins (Inspector of Taxes)* [1975] 3 All ER 843 (Ch D), (1977) 1 WLR 1386

72 *ECC Quarries v Watkins* (n 71) 862

73 Walton and Aerts (n 67) Ch 5

74 Andrew Farley and Martin Wilson, *'Capital Allowances'* in N Lee (ed) *Revenue Law: Principles and Practice* (21st Edition, Bloomsbury Professional Ltd 2013)
75 *British Insulated and Helsby Cables Ltd v Atherton* [1926] AC 205 (HL)
76 *British Insulated v Atherton* (n 75) 212
77 *Atherton (HM Inspector of Taxes) v British Insulated and Helsby Cables, Limited* [1925] KB 421, 10 TC 155 (CA)
78 *Atherton v British Insulated* (n 77) 192–193
79 *Atherton v British Insulated* (n 77) 441 (Lord Scrutton)
80 *Tucker (Inspector of Taxes) v. Granada Motorway Services Ltd* [1979] 2 All ER 801, [1979] STC 393 (HL) 396.
81 *Strick (Inspector of Taxes) v Regent Oil Co Ltd* [1966] AC 295 (CA)
82 *RTZ Oil and Gas v. Elliss (Inspector of Taxes)* [1987] 1 WLR 1442, [1987] STC 512 (Ch D)
83 *RTZ v. Elliss* (n 82) 512c
84 *RTZ v Ellis* (n 82) 512d
85 *RTZ v Ellis* (n 82) 512e
86 *RTZ v Ellis* (n 82) 514c
87 *RTZ v Ellis* (n 82) 514d-e
88 *RTZ v Ellis* (n 82) 542g-h (Vinelott J)
89 *Atherton (HM Inspector of Taxes) v British Insulated and Helsby Cables, Limited [1925] KB 421, 10 TC 155 (CA)*
90 *RTZ v Ellis* (n 82) 542h (Vinelott J)
91 *RTZ v Ellis* (n 82) 542g (Vinelott J). This analogy is present despite Justice Vinelott himself highlights the 'dangers in this context of reasoning by analogy' in rejecting the analogy of the RTZ Oil and Gas: 'trader who needs a fleet of vans and who hires suitable vans temporarily surplus to the requirements of another trader carrying on a similar trade and then adapts them by painting out the name of the trader from whom the vans are hired and substituting his own.' *RTZ v Ellis* (n 82) 543a-b (Vinelott J)
92 Capital Gains Tax Act 1979, s 106 together with Sch 3; this is still the case. See Taxation of Chargeable Gains Act 1992 s 240 with Sch 8
93 *RTZ v Ellis* (n 82) 542j (Vinelott J)
94 *RTZ v Ellis* (n 82) 544g-j (Vinelott J)
95 *RTZ v Ellis* (n 82) 542j (Vinelott J)
96 *RTZ v Ellis* (n 82) 544g-j and 545a (Vinelott J)
97 *RTZ v Ellis* (n 82) 544h-j (Vinelott J)
98 *RTZ v Ellis* (n 82) 542j (Vinelott J)
99 *RTZ v Ellis* (n 82) 543f (Vinelott J)
100 *RTZ v Ellis* (n 82) 543e (Vinelott J) citing *Pyrah (Inspector of Taxes) v Annis & Co Ltd* [1957] 1 All ER 196, [1957] 1 WLR 190, 37 TC 163, 195
101 *Atherton v British Insulated* (n 77) (Lord Scrutton)
102 *RTZ v Ellis* (n 82) 544j – 545a (Vinelott J)
103 Corporation Tax Act 2009 s 53
104 See Section 2.3 for the concept of regressivity.
105 See Chapter 2
106 Depreciation can be seen as a 'capital loss made on an asset.' Losses are approximated via depreciation allowances. 'However, it is difficult to assess the true costs of depreciation, and it becomes more difficult in the presence of inflation.' Malcolm Gammie, *Equity for Companies: A Corporation Tax for the 1990s: A Report of the IFS Capital Taxes Group Chaired by Malcolm Gammie* (The Institute for Fiscal Studies 1991) para 2.2.9
107 Hayllar and Pleasance (n 24) 19.10; and Farley and Wilson (n 74)
108 Discussed in Section 2.4.1.3.2
109 Musgrave and Musgrave (n 66) Ch 22

110 Musgrave and Musgrave (n 66) 383–384
111 Alexander G Kemp, *Petroleum Rent Collection around the World* (The Institute for Research on Public Policy 1987) 93–94
112 That is *Effective Tax Rate* $= \frac{\text{Pre-tax Income} - \text{Post-tax Income}}{\text{Pre-tax Income}}$
113 Musgrave and Musgrave (n 66) 384. Although it can create distortions in terms of encouraging current consumption over saving for future consumption. See R Garnaut and A C Ross, 'The Neutrality of the Resource Rent Tax' (September 1979) The Economic Record 193, 194
114 Musgrave and Musgrave (n 66) 384
115 Kemp (n 111) 94
116 Kemp (n 111) 94
117 Garnaut and Ross (n 113) 104
118 Kemp (n 111) 94
119 Kemp (n 111) 95
120 Capital expenditures are deemed to be incurred 'as soon as there is an unconditional obligation to pay it… [This] rule applies even if the whole or part of the expenditure is not required to be paid until a later date.' Capital Allowances Act 2001 s 5
121 Capital Allowances Act 2001 Part 2
122 Capital Allowances Act 2001 Part 5
123 Capital Allowances Act 2001 Part 6
124 Capital Allowances Act 2001 ss 162–165
125 Capital Allowances Act 2001 s 165 as amended by Finance Act 2009 Sch 38
126 Plant is not defined in statutes but instead framed out in case law. See *Yarmouth v France (1887)* 19 QBD 647, 57 LJQB 7 (QBD), *Hinton (Inspector of Taxes) v. Madden & Ireland Ltd* [1959] 3 ALL ER 356, [1959] 1 WLR 875, 38 TC 391 (HL), and *Benson (Inspector of Taxes) v Yard Arm Club Ltd* [1979] 1 WLR 347 (CA) for the relevant tests in determining a plant
127 IFRS, '*International Accounting Standards: IAS 16 – Property, Plant and Equipment*' (Standards, IFRS 2003)
128 Corporation Tax Act 2009 s 53
129 HM Revenue & Customs, '*Capital Allowances Manual*' (Manual, HMRC 11 February 2015) CA20006
130 Note that there is also an allowance scheme for plant and machinery expenditures under the standard corporation tax rules. However, the relevant treatment outside of the ring fence trade is beyond the scope of this work. For details please see HM Revenue & Customs, *'Capital Allowances Manual'* (n 129) CA20000
131 These expenses do not include those incurred before 2001 on seagoing ships and railway assets, plant and machinery bought for leasing purposes, and costs incurred for decommissioning. There is a separate relief for decommissioning discussed at Section 3.2.3.1.4
132 Finance Act 2002 ss 39 and 63 insert Sch 21 into Capital Allowances Act 2001 as s 45F and 45G
133 Capital Allowances Act 2001 Part 1, Ch 4
134 Capital Allowances Act 2001 s 45G
135 Capital Allowances Act 2001 Ch 19. Prior to 12 March 2008 there was a different treatment for those expenditures incurred on 'long-life assets' which were allowable only at 24% in the first year and 6% thereafter. Capital Allowances Act 2001 s 52(3) (original text) and s 102. Finance Act 2008 s 108 amended Capital Allowances Act 2001 s 52(3) disapplying the long-life asset regime so that a ring fence plant and machinery expenditure are allowable in full immediately regardless of whether it is incurred on long-life asset or not. An asset is considered to be a long-life asset if, when new, it has been anticipated to have a 'useful economic life of at least 25 years.' Capital Allowances Act 2001 s 91

136 Capital Allowances Act 2001 s 46(2). The most relevant of these to the ring fence activities are those exclusions for the expenditures incurred on ships and on the leasing of plant and machinery, including chartering or hiring of any ships. These expenditures are not allowed for deduction under the plant and machinery allowance within the RFCT regime. However, insofar as the expenditures on ships are concerned, the exclusion does not apply to offshore installations including 'most Floating, Production Storage and Offloading Vessels,' or FPSOs. In other words most FPSOs are likely to qualify for the plant and machinery allowance within the RFCT regime. Some of the exclusions that are not directly relevant include expenditures incurred on cars or on railway assets.

137 Capital Allowances Act 2001 s416A as amended by Finance Act 2002 Sch 21

138 Capital Allowances Act 2001 s 396 defines mineral exploration and access as 'searching for or discovering and testing the mineral deposits of a source, or… winning access to such deposits.' These deposits include oil Capital Allowances Act 2001 s 394

139 Capital Allowances Act 2001 s 397

140 Capital Allowances Act 2001 s 416B as amended by Finance Act 2002 Sch 21

141 Capital Allowances Act 2001 s 418

142 As defined at Capital Allowances Act 2001 ss 395 and 399, these for example include unsuccessful planning applications.

143 Capital Allowances Act 2001 s 418

144 Capital Allowances Act 2001 s 419

145 HM Revenue & Customs, *'Oil Taxation Manual'* (n 23) OT21250

146 Capital Allowances Act 2001 s 5 clarified as to when an expenditure is deemed to be incurred.

147 Capital Allowances Act 2001 s 441

148 Capital Allowances Act 2001 ss 7 and 8

149 Income and Corporation Taxes Act 1988 s 837A as amended by the Finance Act 2000 Schedule 19. This section defines 'normal accounting practice' as 'normal accounting practice in relation to the accounts of companies incorporated in a part of the United Kingdom.' Accordingly, the 'normal accounting practices' are set out in Accounting Standard SSAP 13, IFRS (n 108) 38 or Part 6 of FRSSE

150 Income and Corporation Taxes Act 1988 s 837A as amended by the Finance Act 2000 Schedule 19. The most recent guidelines on the meaning of R&D is Department for Business, Innovation & Skills, '*Guidelines on the Meaning of Research and Development for Tax Purposes'* (Guidelines, DBIS 2010)

151 Capital Allowances Act 2001 s 437(2)(b), and Income and Corporation Taxes Act 1988 s 82A(5) as inserted by the Finance Act 2000 Schedule 19

152 Income and Corporation Taxes Act 1988 s 837B as amended by the Finance Act 2000 Schedule 19. Note that the definition of E&A is also almost identical under Corporation Tax Act 2010 s 1134

153 HM Revenue & Customs, *'Oil Taxation Manual'* (n 23) OT26008

154 *Gaspet Ltd v Elliss (Inspector of Taxes)* [1985] 1 WLR 1214 (Ch D)

155 *Gaspet v Elliss* (n 154) 573

156 *Gaspet v Elliss* (n 154)

157 *Gaspet v Elliss* (n 154) 573–574. Previously, the Special Commissioners had determined that 'the taxpayer company had incurred the expenditure but that the expenditure was not directly undertaken on behalf of the taxpayer company' *Gaspet v Elliss* (n 154) 572

158 The case instead considers the meaning of 'on his behalf' in determining research allowance as the allowance is only available for the research directly carried out by the taxpayer or 'on his behalf'.

159 *Gaspet v Elliss* (n 154) 572 and 577. Note that this case refers to a previous legislation, Capital Allowances Act 1968 that allows for R&D capital expenditures under s 91
160 HM Revenue & Customs, *'Oil Taxation Manual'* (n 23) OT26008
161 From 01 April 2009, this responsibility is no longer with the Commissioner but instead moved to a Tribunal body. HM Revenue & Customs, *'Oil Taxation Manual'* (n 23) OT26013
162 However, the right to appeal to the Court is reserved. HM Revenue & Customs, *'Oil Taxation Manual'* (n 23) OT26008
163 Finance Act 2013 Sch 15 s 27
164 Corporation Tax Act 2009 s 104M as inserted by Finance Act 2013 Sch 15
165 Corporation Tax Act 2009 s 104A as inserted by Finance Act 2013 Sch 15
166 HM Revenue & Customs, *'"Above the Line" credit for Research and Development: response to consultation'* (Consultation, HMRC 27 March 2012)
167 Corporation Tax Act 2009 s 104N as inserted by Finance Act 2013 Sch 15
168 Corporation Tax Act 2009 ss 104C-104L
169 This is obtained by subtracting the tax paid under the ATL scenario, £229.4m from the non-ATL scenario, £310m
170 Relevant legislation used to refer to this as 'abandonment' until the terminology was changed to 'decommissioning' under the Finance Act 2008, s 109
171 HM Treasury, *'Decommissioning Relief Deeds: increasing tax certainty for oil and gas investment in the UK continental shelf'* (Consultation, HM Treasury 9 July 2012)
172 Oil & Gas UK, *'Decommissioning Insight 2014'* (Report, Oil & Gas UK 2014) and Oil & Gas UK (n 6)
173 *RTZ v Elliss* (n 82)
174 Capital Allowances Act 2001 ss 162–165
175 The requirement of compliance with a decommissioning plan approved by the Secretary of State, or with conditions attached to such approval are inserted into Capital Allowances Act 2001 s 163 by Finance Act 2009 Sch 38
176 Capital Allowances Act 2001 s 163 as amended by Finance Act 2008 s 109
177 Capital Allowances Act 2001 s 163 as amended by Finance Act 2013 s 90
178 Capital Allowances Act 2001 s 163 as amended by Finance Act 2001 Sch 20
179 'Effectively allowing for mid-life decommissioning.' KPMG, *A Guide to UK Oil and Gas Taxation: 2012 Edition* (Report, KPMG 2012)
180 After deducting the income that may be derived from resale of the scrap or from the remains of the asset. Capital Allowances Act 2001 s 164 as amended by Finance Act 2009 Sch 38
181 i.e. those expenditures that fit the definition in the preceding paragraph in this work.
182 Capital Allowances Act 2001 s 164 as amended by Finance Act 2008 s 91
183 KPMG (n 179) 13.3
184 Capital Allowances Act 2001 s 164 as amended by Finance Act 2009 Sch 38
185 Capital Allowances Act 2001 s 164 as amended by Finance Act 2009 Sch 38
186 Capital Allowances Act 2001 s 164 as amended by Finance Act 2009 Sch 38. The 'relevant chargeable period' can either be the period in which qualifying expenditure is incurred, or in which the decommissioning was carried out.
187 100% less any income that may arise from the sale of scrap or the remains.
188 Capital Allowances Act 2001 s 165 as amended by Finance Act 2008 s 110
189 Capital Allowances Act 2001 s 165 as amended by Finance Act 2008 s 110
190 Capital Allowances Act 2001 s 165 as amended by Finance Act 2009 Sch 38
191 HM Treasury, *'Decommissioning Relief Deeds: increasing tax certainty for oil and gas investment in the UK continental shelf'* (Consultation, HM Treasury 9 July 2012)

192 HM Treasury, Budget 2011 (Report, HM Treasury 23 March 2011) 1.149
193 HM Treasury, Budget 2012 (Report, HM Treasury 21 March 2012) 2.125
194 In other words, the applicable tax regime at the time of the enactment of Finance Act 2013
195 Finance Act 2013 s 80 read together with Cl 5 of DRD. A copy of a model DRD (hereinafter, Model Decommissioning Relief Deed) can be obtained from HM Treasury (n 191)
196 See Chapter 5
197 Finance Act 2013 Part 2
198 Finance Act 2013 s 80
199 Finance Act 2013 s 80(5)
200 Model Decommissioning Relief Deed Cl 6.1.5
201 Defined as accounting period for the purposes of the RFCT and the SC, and chargeable period for the PRT calculations. Model Decommissioning Relief Deed Cl 1.1
202 Model Decommissioning Relief Deed Cl 1.1, Cl 5 and Sch 1
203 Model Decommissioning Relief Deed Cl 5
204 Within 60 days if the relief is claimed under the RFCT or SC pillars, and 120 days if it is claimed under the PRT pillar. Model Decommissioning Relief Deed Cl 6.2.5. See Sections 3.2 and 3.3 for discussions on SC and PRT, respectively.
205 Corporation Tax Act 2010 ss 307–329
206 Corporation Tax Act 2010 Chapter 5
207 Income and Corporation Taxes Act 1988 Sch 19B
208 Income and Corporation Taxes Act 1988 Sch 19B
209 Corporation Tax Act 2010 s 312
210 Discussed below at Section 3.3
211 HC Deb 5 December 2005, vol 440, col 612
212 For example, the start-up upstream companies.
213 I.e. when the ring fence trade commences.
214 This concept is discussed in the previous chapter. See Section 2.4.1.3
215 HM Treasury, *Britain meeting the global challenge: Enterprise, fairness and responsibility* (Pre-Budget Report, HM Treasury 5 December 2005) 5.130
216 Corporation Tax Act 2010 s 310 as enacted.
217 HC Deb 5 July 2011, vol 530, col 82W (Greening)
218 Corporation Tax Act 2010 s 311 as enacted. More accurately, '6 accounting periods'.
219 Gammie (n 106) para 2.2.12
220 Michael P Devereux and Harold Freeman, '*A General Neutral Profits Tax*' (1991) 12 (3) Fiscal Studies 1, 3
221 Corporation Tax Act 2009 s 307 together with s 297. Note that financing costs are not deductible under the Supplementary Charge and the Petroleum Revenue Tax. See Chapter 3
222 Corporation Tax Act 2009 Part 5. Also see KPMG (n 179) 11.11
223 Corporation Tax Act 2010 s 286
224 Corporation Tax Act 2010 ss 286 and 287
225 Corporation Tax Act 2009 s 444. For the exceptions to this, see ss 441,442,445, 446, 486A and 522
226 Michael Haig, *'Corporation Tax'* in N Lee (ed) *Revenue Law: Principles and Practice* (21st Edition, Bloomsbury Professional Ltd 2013) 41.91; also see Musgrave and Musgrave (n 66) 377
227 United Nations Centre on Transnational Corporations (UNCTC), 'Financial and Fiscal Aspects of Petroleum Exploitation' (UNCTC Advisory Studies, Series B No 3, ST/CTC/SER.B/3, 1987) 17
228 See Section 2.4.4

229 Taxation (International and Other Provisions) Act 2010, Part 4, previously Income and Corporation Taxes Act 1988 Sch 28AA
230 HM Revenue & Customs, '*International Manual*' (Manual, HMRC 14 May 2015) INTM511015
231 HM Revenue & Customs, '*International Manual*' (n 230) INTM511015
232 Unlike some other jurisdictions. For example, in Australia from 2002, the 'safe harbour' for the debt:equity ratio is prescribed to be 3 to 1. This is also true for Japan since 2006. For Germany this figure used to be 1.5 to 1 until 2008. Then Germany limited the deductibility of interest to 30% of taxable income before interest, tax, depreciation and amortisation. For China, 'safe harbour' ratios are 5 to 1 for the financial sector, and 2 to 1 for non-financial sectors.
233 HM Revenue & Customs, '*International Manual*' (n 230) INTM511000
234 Taxation (International and Other Provisions) Act 2010 s 187 and Part 7. Under Income and Corporation Taxes Act 1988 s 209(2)(d) that excess was considered as 'distribution' to shareholders. This was however, affirmed as a 'restriction on freedom of establishment' and thus in breach of Article 43 of the Treaty Establishing the European Community – Consolidated Version [2002] OJ C 340/0173. *Test Claimants in the Thin Cap Group Litigation v Commissioners of Inland* Revenue (C-524/04) [2007] ECR I-02107 (Thin Cap Group Litigation), para 63
235 *Thin Cap Group Litigation* (n 234) 71–92.
236 Musgrave and Musgrave (n 66) 377
237 US Department of Treasury, *Integration of the Individual and Corporate Tax Systems: Taxing Business Income Once* (US Government Printing Office, Washington 1992) developed this approach.
238 It creates distortions as the cost of capital increases. See Alexander Klemm, '*Allowances for Corporate Equity in Practice*' (2007) 53 CESifo Economic Studies 2, 229–262, 231 and associated footnotes.
239 Although some commentators argue that governments can apply CBIT together with a lower profit tax rate. See Sijbren Cnossen, '*Taxing Capital Income in the Nordic Countries: A Model for the European Union?*' in S Cnossen (ed) *Taxing Capital Income in the European Union – Issues and Options for Reform* (OUP 2000) for example.
240 IRS, '*Foreign Tax Credit*' (2013) <http://www.irs.gov/Individuals/International-Taxpayers/Foreign-Tax-Credit> accessed 01 October 2014
241 (100–40) * 30% = 18
242 Tax liability would be 100 * 30% = 30. Please note that this example is for illustrative purposes. The rules are significantly more complex. The tax credit to be carried forward in the USA, for example, would be less than 10% as there are limits to allowable credit determined by the ratio of foreign income to the worldwide income.
243 The rules governing the tax credit are highly complex and multilayered. See, for example, 26 US Code § 901–989
244 See, for example 26 US Code § 901–909
245 26 US Code § 901–989. Also note that, in the USA, there are special rules on oil and gas income. 26 US Code § 907
246 Though not necessarily imposing a fixed figure. In Australia and Japan it is a fixed figure of 3:1, while in France and USA 1.5:1. In the UK, there isn't a fixed ratio. See HM Revenue & Customs, '*Thin Capitalisation: Practical guidance – comparison of lending in the UK with other countries: Thin capitalisation rules in different jurisdictions*' (Manual, HMRC 14 May 2014) INTM581010
247 The term ACE is coined by Devereux and Freeman (n 220) though theoretical foundations are based on the work of Robin Boadway and Neil Bruce, '*A General*

Proposition on the Design of a Neutral Business Tax' (1984) 24 Journal of Public Economics 2, 231–239
248 Boadway and Bruce (n 247) 231
249 Devereux and Freeman (n 220) 3
250 For the discussions in this chapter, cash-flow taxes would be the Brown Tax and the Resource Rent Tax, for example. Cash-flow taxation is also referred to as 'flow-of-funds' taxation. See Gammie (n 106)
251 J E Meade, 'The Structure and Reform of Direct Taxation' Report of a Committee chaired by Professor J. E. Meade, The Institute for Fiscal Studies (George Allen & Unwin Ltd 1978)
252 Note that this is different than the market valuation since the latter also includes expected profits or losses generated in the future. Gammie (n 106) para 2.2.14
253 Devereux and Freeman (n 220) 4. The original theoretical proposition by Boadway and Bruce (n 247) recommended a deduction for the interest cost of total assets while disallowing the interest deduction for debt financing. However, Devereux and Freeman's proposal achieves the same thing since the total assets effectively consist of total debt and equity. Also see the discussion in Klemm (n 238) 231
254 I.e. losses and gains are treated in an equal manner. Devereux and Freeman (n 220) 7–9
255 Klemm (n 238) 231. George Fane, *Neutral Taxation Under Uncertainty* (1987) 33 Journal of Public Economics 1, 95–105 treats this issue in depth.
256 Devereux and Freeman (n 220) 8
257 Klemm (n 238) 231–232
258 P Walton and W Aerts, *Global Financial Accounting and Reporting: Principles and Analysis* (2nd Ed, Cengage Learning 2009) Ch 5
259 Doina Maria Radulescu and Michael Stimmelmayr, '*ACE versus CBIT: Which is Better for Investment and Welfare?'* (2007) 53 CESifo Economic Studies 2, 294–328, 297–298
260 Klemm (n 238) 232
261 Isaac, J, *A Comment on the Viability of the Allowance for Corporate Equity* (1997) 18 Fiscal Studies 3, 303–318. This was also touched upon by Devereux and Freeman (n 219) who calculated that to replicate the tax revenues obtained between 1971 and 1990 in the UK the headline tax rate had to be 45% as opposed to the actual 35%.
262 Klemm (n 238) 232
263 Radulescu and Stimmelmayr (n 259) 298
264 Radulescu and Stimmelmayr (n 259) 298
265 It has been applied in one way or another in Croatia, Italy, Austria in the 90s and early 2000s, and in Brazil since late-90s. See Klemm (n 238)
266 Though, not as simple as royalty collection.
267 See the next Chapter for the changes introduced with the Fiscal Review.
268 See Section 2.1.1
269 Finance Act 2002 s 91
270 Corporation Tax Act 2010 s 330 as amended by Finance Act 2002 s 91
271 See the discussions in the previous Section above.
272 HC Deb 9 May 2002, vol 385, vols 359–361 (Ruth Kelly)
273 FOB stands for Free on Board whereby from the moment of Brent being loaded on to the ship, the costs of transportation, insurance, and offloading are borne by the buyer.
274 US Energy Information Agency, 'Petroleum & Other Liquids: Europe Brent Spot Price FOB' (US EIA 13 December 2015); All the oil prices in this Chapter are stated in nominal US Dollars unless otherwise stated.
275 US EIA (n 274)
276 HM Treasury (n 215) para 5.129

277 EES is the predecessor of RFES. See the discussion in Section 3.2.3.1.5, above
278 HC Deb (n 211) (Brown)
279 HM Treasury (n 215), para 5.130. Although this promise was kept, the industry did not benefit from a decrease in the corporation tax rate for the other industries, either.
280 Corporation Tax Act 2010 s 330 as amended by Finance Act 2011 s 7(1)
281 HC Deb 23 March 2011 vol 525, cols 964–965 (Osborne); Osborne was not specifically referring to Brent prices directly but Brent is one of the global benchmarks used in quoting oil prices.
282 US EIA (n 274)
283 HC Deb 23 March 2011 vol 525, cols 964–965; Also see HM Treasury (n 192) para 1.148
284 HM Revenue & Customs, *'Oil Taxation Manual'* (n 23) OT21219
285 Income and Corporation Taxes Act 1988 s 501A as inserted by Finance Act 2002 s 91. Also see Corporation Tax Act 2010 s 332
286 Corporation Tax Act 2010 s 332; previously, Income and Corporation Taxes Act 1988 s 501B(1) as inserted by Finance Act 2002 s 92(1)
287 Corporation Tax Act 2010 s 2(1) read together with s 4
288 Corporation Tax Act 2010 s 279
289 Corporation Tax Act 2010 s 330. Also see the Income and Corporation Taxes Act 1988 s 501A as inserted by Finance Act 2002 s 91
290 Corporation Tax Act 2010 ss 330–331. Also see the Income and Corporation Taxes Act 1988 s 501A as inserted by Finance Act 2002 s 91. The matters that are included in the calculation of debt finance are rather broad. For this, see Corporation Tax Act 2010 s 331
291 Finance Act 2009 Sch 44 s 18. Also, Corporation Tax Act 2010 s 351. Corporation Tax Act 2010 s 720 and Sch 3 repeal Finance Act 2009 Sch 44. The applicable legislation is instead Corporation Tax Act 2010 Part 8 Ch 7. Of course, if those new oil fields that receive a development consent on or after 22 April 2009 have been decommissioned, the allowance no longer applies. This has been legislated in Finance Act 2011 s 63 amending Corporation Tax Act 2010 s 337
292 Finance Act 2009, Sch 44, s 1. Also, Corporation Tax Act 2010, s 333. Note that the reduction is given until the profits are 0. Any remaining allowance can be carried forward. Corporation Tax Act 2010 ss 335–336
293 Finance Act 2009 Sch 44 s 24. Also, Corporation Tax Act 2010 s 356
294 Small Oil Field is defined as a field with oil reserves of 3.5 million tonnes or less. For the purposes of this definition, 1,100 m^3 of gas at 15 °C and at 1 atmospheric pressure is considered as 1 tonne of reserve. Finance Act 2009 Sch 44 s 21. Also, Corporation Tax Act 2010 s 353. However, for the small oil fields that received consent post-21 March 2012 the small oil field is defined as a field with oil reserves of 7 million or less. See the the Qualifying Oil Fields Order 2012, SI 3153
295 An ultra-heavy oil field is defined as a field that has oil at less than 18 °API and a viscosity higher than 50 centipoise at reservoir temperature and pressure. Finance Act 2009 Sch 44 s 22. Also, Corporation Tax Act 2010 s 354
296 An ultra-high pressure/high temperature field is defined as an oil field with a pressure higher than 1034 bar and a temperature of more than 176.67 °C in the reservoir formation. Finance Act 2009 Sch 44 s 23. Also, Corporation Tax Act 2010 s 355
297 Finance Act 2009 Sch 44 s 20. Also, Corporation Tax Act 2010 s 352
298 Finance Act 2009 Sch 44 s 24. Also, Corporation Tax Act 2010 s 356. The allowance is £75m for oil reserves up to 2.75 million tonnes. From then on the allowance declines geometrically until the allowance reaches £0 at 3.5 million tonnes of oil reserves. Finance Act 2009 Sch 44 s 24
299 Qualifying Oil Fields Order 2012 s 6(3)
300 Corporation Tax Act 2010 s 349A as inserted by Finance Act 2012 Sch 22

301 The authorisation for the project has to be on or after 21 March 2012. See The Qualifying Oil Fields Order 2012 SI 3153
302 Corporation Tax Act 2010 s 349A as inserted by Finance Act 2012 Sch 22
303 Corporation Tax Act 2010 s 349A as inserted by Finance Act 2012 Sch 22
304 Qualifying Oil Fields Order 2012, SI 3153
305 Additionally-developed Oil Fields Order 2013, SI 2910
306 Defined as an oil field that is located in more than 1,000 meters of water depth, received authorisation after 20 March 2012, and with oil reserves between 25 and 55 million tonnes. Corporation Tax Act 2010 s 355A as inserted by the Qualifying Oil Fields Order 2012 s 5
307 Defined as a field located in a water depth of less than 30 meters, received authorisation after 20 March 2012, with 95% of reserves consist of gas, and with total gas reserves between 10 and 25 billion m^3. Corporation Tax Act 2010 s 355B as inserted by the Qualifying Oil Fields Order 2012 s 5
308 Defined as a field that is located in more than 300 meters of water depth, with 75% of total reserves consisting of gas, and the planned pipelines carrying the gas from the field to a relevant infrastructure should stretch more than 60km. Corporation Tax Act 2010 s 355c as inserted by the Qualifying Oil Fields Order 2012 s 5
309 Department of Energy & Climate Change, '*Oil and Gas – Guidance: Oil and Gas: Fields and Field Development: Brown Field Allowances: Guidance*' (Guidance, DECC 22 January 2013, as updated on 29 December 2014)
310 Though, excepting those DECC-approved EOR projects that employ CO2 recovery. Additionally-developed Oil Fields Order 2013 s 2(7)
311 Corporation Tax Act 2010 s 356A as inserted Additionally-developed Oil Fields Order 2013 s 10. Please note that the upper ceiling is half a billion pounds for the PRT-liable fields. For a detailed discussion of the PRT system, please see the Section 3.4 below.
312 Additionally-developed Oil Fields Order 2013 s 2
313 HM Treasury (n 192) 1.149
314 Corporation Tax Act 2010 s 330C as inserted by the Finance Act 2012 Sch 21
315 Calculated as: Fraction= $\frac{\text{Supplementary Charge Rate} - 20\%}{\text{Supplementary Charge Rate}}$ which, at SC rate of 32%, would be equal to 37.5%, and at SC rate of 30%, would be 31.25%. Corporation Tax Act 2010 s 330A as inserted by the Finance Act 2012 Sch 2
316 Corporation Tax Act 2010 s 330A as inserted by the Finance Act 2012 Sch 21
317 See Section 2.2.1
318 Garnaut R and Ross A C, '*Uncertainty, Risk Aversion and the Taxing of Natural Resource Projects*' (1975) 85 The Economic Journal 338, 272–287
319 Garnaut and Ross (n 318) 279
320 Garnaut and Ross (n 318), Garnaut and Ross (n 113), Garnaut R and Ross A C, Taxation of Mineral Rents (Clarendon Press, 1983) all discuss this in detail.
321 Garnaut and Ross (n 318) 275
322 See Chapter 2
323 Kemp (n 111) 101
324 Oil Taxation Act 1975 s 1(2). Note that the definition and the determination of a field are given in Oil Taxation Act 1975 Sch. 1
325 Finance Act 1993 s 185. This is true with couple of exceptions: (1) From 1 July 2007 for those previously PRT-liable fields that have been decommissioned but subsequently have received a development consent (i.e. recommissioned) after 16 March 1993 will *not* be liable for PRT. Finance Act 1993 s 187(1) as amended by Finance Act 2007; (2) For those PRT-liable fields that are never likely to pay PRT can irrevocably opt-out from PRT liability. Finance Act 1993 s 185 as amended by Finance Act 2008 s 107 and Sch 20B
326 Hayllar & Pleasance (n 24) 15

327 HM Revenue & Customs, *'Oil Taxation Manual'* (n 23) OT03010. Oil Taxation Act 1975 as amended sets out the procedures for calculating this.
328 Charles J Wright and Rebecca A Gallun, *International Petroleum Accounting (PenWell 2005)* 22–26.
329 IFRS, '*Conceptual Framework for Financial Reporting: Chapter 1: The Objective of Financial Reporting*' (Agenda Paper 7A, IASB Meeting September 2007) OB2. The full definition of the objective is 'to provide financial information about the reporting entity that is useful to present and potential investors and creditors in making decisions in their capacity as capital providers.'
330 Wright and Gallun (n 328) 25
331 Wright and Gallun (n 328) 25
332 Oil Taxation Act 1975
333 Oil Taxation Act 1975 s 2
334 Oil Taxation Act 1975 ss 1, 7–8. Note that the terms 'oil allowance' and 'volume allowance' are used interchangeably in the literature, but, for the purposes of clarity, it is referred to as 'oil allowance' in this work.
335 Oil Taxation Act 1975 s 9
336 Oil Taxation Act 1975 s 2
337 Starting first with the most recent preceding period. If they cannot be relieved against preceding periods, then the losses are carried forward to the subsequent chargeable periods. Oil Taxation Act 1975 s 7. Also note that if a PRT-liable field is abandoned permanently then the losses from that field can be treated as expenditure in the participator's other PRT-liable field. Oil Taxation Act 1975 ss 2(9) and 6
338 Peat, Marwick, Mitchell & Co, '*A Guide to UK Oil & Gas Taxation*' (Peat, Marwick, Mitchell & Co 1986) para 4.1. Also reiterated in KPMG (n 179) para 4.1
339 Peat, Marwick, Mitchell & Co (n 338) para 4.1
340 See Section 3.2
341 Oil Taxation Act 1975 s 3(1) '…any expenditure (whether or not capital in nature)'.
342 See Table 3.4
343 Applies from the second half of 1982 and is inserted by the Oil Taxation Act 1983 s 7
344 Applies from the second half of 1982 and is inserted by the Oil Taxation Act 1983 s 6
345 Inserted by Finance Act 1981 s 118 in order to 'deal with refunds to licensees in respect of conveying and treating costs of royalties satisfied in kind.' Royalties have been abolished in their entirety in 2003. See the announcement Department for Trade and Industry, '*Outcome of Consultation Paper on Appropriate Timing of Abolition of North Sea Royalty*' (Consultation, DTI 2002)
346 Royalties have been abolished in their entirety in 2003 and therefore not discussed in this work. See the announcement Department for Trade and Industry (n 345)
347 Oil Taxation Act 1975 ss 2(4)-2(5) as amended by the Finance Act 1994 s 236 and Sch 23 and the Finance Act 2006 ss 146–147 Sch 18, and Sch 26. Also see HM Revenue & Customs, *'Oil Taxation Manual'* (n 23) OT05020
348 Usenmez (n 16) 6.31
349 HM Revenue & Customs, *'Oil Taxation Manual'* (n 23) OT17025
350 Oil Taxation Act 1975 s 8
351 There are three different oil allowances available depending on when and for which location a development consent has been granted. For those fields referred to as the 'relevant new fields' that received a development consent after 31 April 1982, the oil allowance is 10,000,000 tonnes with an allowance limit of 500,000 tonnes per period. However, for those relevant new fields that are either in the Southern Basin of the North Sea or onshore, the oil allowance is instead 2,500,000 tonnes with a limit of 125,000 tonnes for each period. Finally, those PRT-liable fields that are not

relevant new fields, the oil allowance is 5,000,000 tonnes with a ceiling of 250,000 tonnes per period. Though, note that the original amount in Oil Taxation Act 1975 s 8 was 500,000 tonnes per period with a total limit of 10,000,000 tonnes but with the Finance (No. 2) Act 1979 s 21 these figures were halved. HM Revenue & Customs, *'Oil Taxation Manual'* (n 23) OT17100 together with Oil Taxation Act 1975 s 8, Finance Act 1988 ss 36 and 138. Also note that under the original Oil Taxation Act 1975 s 8(7) 1 metric tonne of oil was equal to 40,000 cubic feet of gas but with the Finance (No. 2) Act 1979 s 21 this figure was changed to 1,100 cubic feet of gas at 150 °C and 1 atmospheric pressure. Finally, for clarification, note that the Southern Basin of the North Sea refers to the area to the East of United Kingdom between the latitudes 52° and 55° North.

352 The monetary value for a given chargeable period is calculated by the formula £ $= \frac{A \times B}{C}$ where A is the participant's gross profit in that period, B is the participant's share of the oil allowance in metric tonnes in that period, and C is the participant's share of the production in metric tonnes in that period. Oil Taxation Act 1975 s 8(3)

353 Oil Taxation Act 1975 s 2(5) and HM Revenue & Customs, *'Oil Taxation Manual'* (n 23) OT05016

354 Oil Taxation Act 1975 s 12 as amended by the Finance Act 1983 s 39

355 The categorisation of oil is introduced in Finance Act 2006 Part V and Sch 18

356 Oil Taxation (Market Value of Oil) Regulations 2006 s 3

357 Oil Taxation Act 1975 Sch 3 para 2(2AA) as inserted by the Finance Act 2006 s 146(5)

358 For a detailed explanation of the crude oil valuation for tax purposes see Box 3.4

359 Oil Taxation Act 1975 s 2(5C) as amended by Finance Act 2006 Sch 18. Also see HM Revenue & Customs, *'Oil Taxation Manual'* (Manual, HMRC 1 September 2016) OT05016

360 Oil Taxation Act 1975 Sch 3

361 Oil Taxation Act 1975 Sch 3 para 1

362 HM Revenue & Customs, *'Oil Taxation Manual'* (n 23) OT05025

363 This is only true since the amendments introduced under Finance Act 2006 came into force in 1 July 2006

364 This may be because the quality of the crude being sold may be higher than those involved in the Brent assessment

365 Price Reporting Agencies, such as Platts and Argus, are private entities that assess the prices of various benchmark crudes. A detailed discussion of the Price Reporting Agencies, however, is beyond the scope of this work. For further discussions see International Organization of Securities Commissions, '*Oil Price Reporting Agencies – Report by IEA, IEF, OPEC and IOSCO to G20 Finance Ministers*' (Report, IOSCO 14 November 2011) and the forthcoming paper Emre Usenmez, '*Formation of Oil Prices: The Commodity Futures Markets, the Role of Reporting Agencies and the Potential Ways Forward'* (unpublished, 2019)

366 Bill of Lading is a contract between a carrier and shipper of goods (in this case, oil) that specifies, among other things, the type and quantity of the crude and the destination. It legally demonstrates that a cargo has been loaded. Platts, '*Glossary'* (McGraw Hill Financial) <http://www.platts.com/glossary> accessed 16 November 2015. Thus, assessment of Brent around the date of Bill of Lading is used as the basis in this example.

367 This example is adopted from HM Revenue & Customs, *'Oil Taxation Manual'* (n 23) OT05025. For the discussions on the treatments of sales based on hedging strategies such as contracts for differences and other swaps, see HM Revenue & Customs, *'Oil Taxation* (n 23) OT05030

368 KPMG (n 179) para 4.5

369 KPMG (n 179) para 4.5
370 The separation of gas, referred to as 'light gases,' for tax purposes is introduced in Finance Act 1994 s 236 and Sch 23 amending Oil Taxation Act 1975
371 The categorisation of oil is introduced in Finance Act 2006 Part V and Sch 18
372 Oil Taxation Act 1975 Sch 3, para 2(1B) as inserted by Finance Act 2006 s 146(4)
373 HM Revenue & Customs, *'Oil Taxation Manual'* (n 23) OT05302. For tax purposes, HMRC accepts the following assessments by the Price Reporting Agencies: (1) 'Dated BFO' in the section entitled 'Atlantic Basin Crudes, London 16.30 hours, North Sea of the Argus Crude Report published by Argus Media Limited; (2) 'Dated BFO' in the North Sea 3rd Update of the Independent Chemical Information Services' World Crude Report published by Reed Elsevier Group plc, and (3) 'Brent (DTD)' in the International section of the Platts Oilgram report published by Platts, a division of McGraw-Hill Companies. Oil Taxation (Market Value of Oil) Regulations 2006, SI 3313 s 4. Note that the BFO forward contract assessments have been widened by the price reporting agencies to include Ekofisk in addition to Brent, Forties, and Oseberg in 2007. The regulations regarding the nominations on the forward contracts have been amended to reflect the change. See Oil Taxation (Nomination Scheme for Disposals) (Amendment) Regulations 2007, SI 1454. For a discussion of the underlying reasons of the expansion, please see Usenmez (n 365)
374 Oil Taxation (Market Value of Oil) Regulations 2006 s 3
375 HMRC publishes the daily values of Category 1 oils. See HM Revenue & Customs, *'LBS Oil and Gas Market Values for Category 1 crudes 2015'* (List, HMRC Large Business Service 2 June 2015)
376 Oil Taxation Act 1975 Sch 3 para 2(2) as amended by the Finance Act 2006 s 146(5)
377 Oil Taxation Act 1975 Sch 3 para 2(2) as amended by the Finance Act 2006 s 146(5)
378 Oil Taxation Act 1975 Sch 3 para 2(2) as amended by the Finance Act 2006 s 146(5)
379 Oil Taxation Act 1975 Sch 3 para 2(2) as amended by the Finance Act 2006 s 146(5)
380 Notional delivery day is the middle day of the three day loading period for offshore oil. Oil Taxation Act 1975 Sch 3 para 2(1A) as inserted by the Finance Act 2006 s 146(1)
381 Oil Taxation Act 1975 Sch 3 para 2(2AA) as inserted by the Finance Act 2006 s 146(5)
382 Oil Taxation Act 1975 Sch 3 para 2(2AA) as inserted by the Finance Act 2006 s 146(5)
383 Defined as methane, ethane or a combination of the two at 15 °C and at 1 atmospheric pressure. Oil Taxation Act 1975 s 12 as amended by the Finance Act 1994 s 236(4)
384 Oil Taxation Act 1975 Sch 3 para 3A as inserted by the Finance Act 1994 s 236 and Sch 23
385 Oil Taxation Act 1975 Sch 3 para 3A as inserted by the Finance Act 1994 s 236 and Sch 23
386 Oil Taxation Act 1975 Sch 3 para 3A as inserted by the Finance Act 1994 s 236 and Sch 23
387 Oil Taxation Act 1975 s 12 as amended by the Finance Act 1983 s 39
388 Oil Taxation Act 1975 s 12
389 Oil Taxation Act 1983 s 7
390 KPMG (n 179) 4.54
391 Oil Taxation Act 1983 s 7(5). If it is for the purposes of obtaining an interest the disposal would be subject to capital gains charge. A discussion on capital gains is beyond the scope of this work. For further information see the Taxation of Chargeable Gains Act 1992
392 Oil Taxation Act 1983 s 7(5). Also see HM Revenue & Customs, *'Oil Taxation Manual'* (n 23) OT015060. For the transfer of field Finance Act 1980, Sch 17

applies. Although a detailed discussion of this is beyond the scope of this work, the legislation essentially allows for the transfer of PRT allowances and liabilities to the new participator. Note that since the legislation refers to field transfers, proceeds from transfer of licences prior to establishing a field therewithin are not covered by this Schedule. Also see HM Revenue & Customs, *'Oil Taxation Manual'* (n 23) OT018020

393 Oil Taxation Act 1975 s 2. Please note that initial payment for the licence is excluded from this. However, these initial licence payments are allowable as an expenditure under Oil Taxation Act 1975 s 3(1); This provision used to also include a relief for the royalty payments under Oil Taxation Act 1975 s 2(7) though the significance of this has diminished after the abolition of royalty from 1 January 1983; see Department for Trade and Industry (n 345)

394 Finance Act 1981 s 118

395 Finance Act 1981 s 118. Also see KPMG (n 179) 4.60

396 See Section 2.1.1

397 Oil Taxation Act 1983 s 6

398 Oil Taxation Act 1983 s 6A

399 Oil Taxation Act 1983 s 6A; there are certain restriction to this exemption though, particularly for those relevant assets in connection with an existing field. For details, see HM Revenue & Customs, *'Oil Taxation Manual'* (n 23) OT15810

400 Qualifying assets are those long-term assets which, if mobile, are dedicated to that asset, Oil Taxation Act 1983 s 8; Long-term assets are defined as those assets whereby 'the useful life of which continues after the end of the claim period in which it is first used in connection with the oil field in question.' Oil Taxation Act 1983 s 3(8)

401 Oil Taxation Act 1983 s 6; These, however, do not include financing payments or payments for deballasting see Oil Taxation Act 1983 s 6(4)

402 Oil Taxation Act 1983 s 9

403 Oil Taxation Act 1983 s 9. Note that as a transition to bringing tariff charges within PRT computation, the TRA was 375,000 metric tonnes until 30 June 1987 for the contracts in place prior to 8 May 1982 Oil Taxation Act 1983 s 9(3)

404 Or, receivable

405 Oil Taxation Act 1983 Sch 3

406 I.e. the total amount of oil the tariff charge relates to.

407 User field is the field that has the hydrocarbons that require the use of the assets of another field in exchange for tariff payments.

408 Oil Taxation Act 1983 Sch 3 para 2(2)

409 And 375,000 metric tonnes until mid-1987. See (n 403) above.

410 Oil Taxation Act 1983 Sch 3 para 1(2)

411 *BP Oil Development Ltd v Commissioners of Inland Revenue* [1992] STC 28, 64 TC 498 (Ch D)

412 *BP v CIR* (n 411) 508.

413 *BP v CIR* (n 411) 498

414 *BP v CIR* (n 411) 503

415 *BP v CIR* (n 411) 498

416 *BP v CIR* (n 411) 503

417 *BP v CIR* (n 411) 498

418 *BP v CIR* (n 411) 498

419 *BP v CIR* (n 411) 505

420 *BP v CIR* (n 411) 506

421 *BP v CIR* (n 411) 508. The reasoning is twofold: First relates to the expenditures incurred on remote assets. The treatment of these under Oil Taxation Act 1983 Sch 1 is in plural form. Second, one concerns the treatment of 'straddling receipt' and the

'normal receipt' under Oil Taxation Act 1983 Sch 3 para 6. For a detailed discussion of these and the dissents see *BP v CIR* (n 411) 508–547

422 A detailed discussion on these issues are beyond the scope of this work. For a detailed discussion see Uisdean Vass, *'Access to Infrastructure,'* in G Gordon, J Paterson and E Usenmez (eds), Oil and Gas Law: Current Practice and Emerging Trends (2nd Ed, DUP 2011)

423 See the discussion in Section 2.1

424 See the discussion in Section 2.1

425 HM Revenue & Customs, *'Oil Taxation Manual'* (n 23) OT15675

426 Oil Taxation Act 1975 s 3(4)(a)

427 Oil Taxation Act 1975 ss 3(4)(b)-(c)

428 Oil Taxation Act 1975 s 3(4)(d). For example, royalty payments. 'The apparent purpose of these provisions is to simplify collection of the tax by ignoring fragmentation of profits which may arise under various royalty and other agreements.' Peat, Marwick, Mitchell & Co (n 338), Appendix II, para II.4

429 Excluding those payments to the Secretary of State for these purposes. Oil Taxation Act 1975 s 3(4)(e)

430 Oil Taxation Act 1975 3(4)(f) together with Finance Act 1973 Sch 15 para 4. The latter paragraph ensures that if the non-resident contractor does not pay its tax liability within 30 days, the onus falls on the licensee.

431 Defined as a 'contract under which a person (the guarantor) undertakes to make good any default by a participator in an oilfield (the relevant participator) in meeting the whole or any part of those liabilities of his which (a) arise under a relevant agreement relating to that field; and (b) are liabilities to contribute to field abandonment costs; and such a contract is an abandonment guarantee regardless of the form of the undertaking of the guarantor and, in particular, whether or not it is expressed as a guarantee or arises under a letter of credit, a performance bond or any other instrument.' Finance Act 1991 s 104

432 Finance Act 1991 s 105

433 See Section 3.2 above.

434 Oil Taxation Act 1975 s 3(1) '...any expenditure (whether or not capital in nature)'.

435 Oil Taxation Act 1975 ss 3 and 4

436 This is defined as those assets 'whose useful life continues after the end of the claim period in which it is first used in connection with the oil field in question.' Oil Taxation Act 1975 s 4(1) as amended by Oil Taxation Act 1983 s 3(8)

437 Oil Taxation Act 1983 ss 1 and 3, together with Oil Taxation Act 1975 s 4. The first claim period is defined in Oil Taxation Act 1975 Sch 5 para 1(1) as the period that ends on either 30 June or 31 December with a duration of 6 or 12 months of each subsequent periods. The choice of the dates and duration are left to the 'responsible person' to decide on. If the responsible person fails to provide a written choice, the default duration of a claim period is a year.

438 Oil Taxation Act 1975 s 4(3) and Oil Taxation Act 1983 ss 1–2

439 Oil Taxation Act 1983 ss 1 and 4 together with Finance Act 1993 s 190

440 Oil Taxation Act 1975 ss 3(1) and 12(2) These purposes include, exploring for oil either 'within the area,' or 5km beyond the boundaries, 'of the field' – though, 'the determining factor' whether expenditures are incurred in searching for oil for the PRT purposes is 'geographical' and not purposive, or 'geological.' In other words, they do not have to be 'incurred for a field purpose.' *Amerada Hess Ltd* v *Inland Revenue Commissioners* (2000) STC (SCD) 397; licence fee; 'ascertaining...the extent or characteristics of any oil-bearing area...or what the reserves of oil of any such oil-bearing area are;' 'winning oil' which essentially include the development and production costs; 'measuring the quantity of oil'; transporting the production to land including to those locations outwith the UK; 'initial treatment or initial storage'

of the production; sale of the production at an arm's length; 'obtaining an abandonment guarantee' which would typically include 'fees, commission or incidental costs' incurred in acquiring such a guarantee as explained in HM Revenue & Customs, *'Oil Taxation Manual'* (n 23) OT10300; 'closing down, decommissioning, abandoning or wholly or partially dismantling or removing any qualifying asset;' 'carrying out restoration work' subsequent to 'closing down of the field'; paying for a defaulter's decommissioning obligation; 'statutory redundancy payments'; and for obtaining tariff income. Oil Taxation Act 1973 s 3 together with Finance Act 1991 ss 103 and 107, Finance (No. 2) Act 1992 s 74 and Finance Act 2009 Sch 41

441 Finance (No. 2) Act 1979 s 19

442 Oil Taxation Act 1975 s 3(5)(a) together with HM Revenue & Customs, *'Oil Taxation Manual'* (n 23) OT12100 and OT12150. Note that for the E&A costs to qualify for the uplift such expenditures must be claimed under Oil Taxation Act 1975 Schs 5–6 and not Sch 7. See HM Revenue & Customs, *'Oil Taxation Manual'* (n 23) OT12150. Also see HM Revenue & Customs, *'Oil Taxation Manual'* (n 23) OT12200. For the treatment of appraisal costs, also see Oil Taxation Act 1975 s 3(5)(b) together with s 3(1)(c)

443 Oil Taxation Act 1975 s 3(5)(a) together with HM Revenue & Customs, *'Oil Taxation Manual'* (n 23) OT12100; In addition, the expenditures incurred in 'substantially improving' the production rate, and in 'providing any installation for the initial treatment or initial storage of oil won from the field' also qualify for the expenditure supplement. Oil Taxation Act 1975 s 3(5) together with HM Revenue & Customs, *'Oil Taxation Manual'* (n 23) OT12300 and OT12350

444 This means when the aggregate cash flow turns positive. For the discussion on the payback periods see Section 2.4.1.1

445 Oil Taxation Act 1975 s 3(4)(a)

446 HM Revenue & Customs, *'Oil Taxation Manual'* (n 23) OT12025. HMRC was sticking to this position as far back as 1986 in *Inland Revenue Commissioners v Mobil North Sea Ltd* [1986] 1 WLR 296, [1986] STC 45 at 60–61, 60 TC 310 (Ch D)

447 *IRC v Mobil North Sea Ltd* (n 446)

448 *IRC v Mobil North Sea Ltd* (n 446)

449 *Mobil North Sea Ltd v IRC* [1987] 1 WLR 1065, [1987] STC 458, 60 TC 310 (HL) at 1067. Note that the uplift before 1 January 1979 was 75% with a transitional rate of $66\frac{2}{3}\%$

450 Luckily the issues in identifying the purpose of the uplift did not have a bearing on the merits of the case. As High Court judge Harman J stated: 'I do not believe this makes any difference to the substance of the question I have to decide' *IRC v Mobil North Sea Ltd* (n 446)

451 In other words the government 'would end up with a lower share of economic rents than could have been obtained with full knowledge.' Kemp (n 111) 101

452 Kemp (n 111) 101

453 Garnaut and Clunies Ross (n 113) 195–199 and Kemp (n 111) 101–102

454 A detailed discussion on these non-field expenditure reliefs are beyond the scope of this work. See Peat, Marwick, Mitchell & Co (n 338) for a detailed information on these.

455 Oil Taxation Act 1975 s 5B inserted by the Finance Act 1987 s 64

456 Oil Taxation Act 1975 s 6 together with Finance Act 1984 s 113

457 Finance Act 1987 s 65 and Sch 14. Also see KPMG (n 179) 6.7–6.10

458 Oil Taxation Act 1975 s 9 and HM Revenue & Customs, *'Oil Taxation Manual'* (n 23) OT17525

459 See Section 3.4.1

460 HM Revenue & Customs, *'Oil Taxation Manual'* (n 23) OT17525

461 Oil Taxation Act 1975 s 9
462 As defined in Oil Taxation Act 1975 s 9(2). See also HM Revenue & Customs, *'Oil Taxation Manual'* (n 23) OT17560 for the adjustments.
463 Oil Taxation Act 1975 s 9
464 Oil Taxation Act 1975 s 9 as amended by the Finance Act 1981 s 114(1) 'Accumulated Capital Expenditure' is broadly the same expenditure that would also qualify for the uplift incurred up to and including the current period.
465 See the discussion in Section 2.4.1.1 for payback period. Also see Section 3.4.2 for its relevant application under uplift
466 Oil Taxation Act 1975 s9(1A) as amended by the Finance Act 1985 s 91(1)
467 See the discussion in Section 3.4.2
468 Corporation Tax Act 2010 s 299
469 Corporation Tax Act 2010 s 301
470 Additionally-developed Oil Fields Order 2013
471 To be eligible the expected capital cost per tonne of anticipated additional reserves have to exceed £60 in order to qualify.
472 Corporation Tax Act 2010 s 356A as inserted by Additionally-developed Oil Fields Order 2013 s 10
473 Corporation Tax Act 2010 s 356A as inserted by Additionally-developed Oil Fields Order 2013 s 10
474 Corporation Tax Act 2010 s 356A as inserted by Additionally-developed Oil Fields Order 2013 s 10
475 The PRT was levied at 50% but could be deducted for the RFCT purposes. The remaining half was charged at the rate of 30% + 32% (RFCT + SC rates) = 62%. Since the 62% is levied on one half, the rate is 31%. The total marginal tax rate is therefore 50% + 31% = 81%
476 RFCT + SC = 30% + 32% = 62%
477 See Section 3.2.3.1.1
478 See Section 3.2.3.1.2
479 See Section 3.2.3.1.3
480 See Section 3.2.3.1.4
481 See Section 3.2.3
482 For the discussion on discount rates and net present value calculations see Section 2.4.1
483 See Section 2.1
484 At least for the RFCT. See Section 3.2
485 See Section 3.2.3.1.5 above
486 Corporation Tax Act 2010 Part 8 Chapter 5
487 The legislation defines qualifying company as 'any company which…carries on a ring fence trade, or…is engaged in any activities with a view to carrying on a ring fence trade.' Corporation Tax Act 2010 s 309
488 This is precisely why the modelling in Chapter 5 will look at the effects of the existing regime on these two different investor types separately.
489 HM Treasury (n 192) 1.149
490 HM Treasury (n 192) 1.149
491 Either annual or semi-annual.
492 See Section 3.4.1
493 See Section 3.4
494 See Section 2.4 for the discussion on discount rates.
495 As there can be more than one discount rate per project to reflect the different risks at various points in the project
496 In Section 2.1 it has also been argued that unlike the investors the governments would not have to take into account sovereign risks, and as such, they can obtain

capital at lowers costs. This is further pronounced if the government is in receipt of concessional finance from international institutions. Therefore, the governments are likely to employ a lower discount rate than the investors. That is, at least in theory, 'benevolent governments' would apply a lower discount rate. In practice the discount rates employed by the governments may be higher, however, because the decision makers in the government face 'political risk in terms of their own longevity in office.' See Garnaut and Ross (n 320) Ch 5 and Boadway R and Keen M, 'Theoretical Perspectives on Resource Tax Design', in P Daniel, M Keen, and C McPherson (eds) The Taxation of Petroleum and Minerals: Principles, Problems and Practice (Routledge, 2010) 49. Boadway and Keen use the term 'benevolent' because for lower discount rate to hold governments would 'attach a high weight to the well-being of future generations, have relatively high income and slow prospective growth, are not strongly risk-averse and are able to diversify away the risks associated with resource extraction.'

497 Bryan C Land, *'Resource Rent Taxes: A Re-appraisal'* in P Daniel, M Keen, and C McPherson (eds) *The Taxation of Petroleum and Minerals: Principles, Problems and Practice* (Routledge 2010)

498 HM Treasury, *'Driving Investment: a plan to reform the oil and gas fiscal regime'* (Report, HM Treasury December 2014) 3.20, 3.28 and 3.29

4 The post-fiscal review reforms

4.1. The reforms

Thus far the discussions have focussed on the context within which the Fiscal Review has been published, and the analysis has been on the strength of the case the Treasury made for reforming the tax regime applicable to petroliferous trade. This chapter now looks at the changes that have been announced in the Fiscal Review and the ensuing reforms with the intention of analysing the extent of the current regime's[1] ability to capture economic rents and attain the objective set by the Fiscal Review.[2]

One of the Fiscal Review's immediate reforms concerned Supplementary Charge (SC). In recognition of investors' tendency to focus mainly on the marginal tax rates and not necessarily on the associated allowances and reliefs,[3] the applicable SC rate from the beginning of 2015 was reduced by 2% to 30%.[4] The effects of this on the marginal tax rates were a total decline of 1 percentage points for the Petroleum Revenue Tax (PRT)-liable fields, and 2 percentage points for all the other fields. Accordingly, the marginal taxes were 80% and 60%[5] respectively for PRT and non-PRT liable fields. Such a reduction was not too surprising given the government's promise in 2011 that if the oil price dropped below $75 they would reduce the SC rate.[6] The spot Free on Board (FOB) price of Brent dropped below that threshold from 28 November 2014 onwards,[7] so a reduction[8] was expected. However, it was surprising that the magnitude of that reduction was this small. Confidence would have been misplaced had there been an expectation for this particular fiscal concession to have a significant impact on investment levels. Perhaps this was why, in the first quarter of 2015, the industry was still expressing the heavy burden the fiscal regime was imposing on investors, including potential investors in the North Sea,[9] and calling for further reforms to be introduced in the next Budget.[10] These calls were particularly focussed on the need for a 'significant reduction in the supplementary charge', a simplified Investment Allowance mechanism[11] and a 'roadmap towards the ultimate elimination of petroleum revenue tax'.[12] The echo of these calls were also present in the OGA's first report, published in February 2015, which committed to further consultation with the industry when considering reforms to the fiscal regime.[13]

These pleas did not go unheeded. In the Budget that followed the Chancellor announced an additional set of changes to the fiscal regime[14] whereby from 1 January 2015[15] the SC rate was further reduced from 30% to 20%,[16] which effectively brought the SC rate back down to pre-March 2011 levels. Accordingly, the marginal tax rates for the PRT-liable fields were now 75%, and 50% for the non-PRT liable ones.[17]

Although these measures were welcomed by the industry,[18] it was clear in subsequent months that additional reductions were needed to weather the worsening circumstances as the oil prices continued to decline. The day Budget 2015 was announced Brent crude was trading at around $53.[19] By the time Budget 2016 was announced the price had declined by about 30% to approximately $37.[20] Therefore 'to help support the industry through the challenging commercial conditions' the Government announced a further reduction in the headline rate of the Supplementary Charge, this time to 10%.[21] In other words from 1 January 2016[22] the SC rate was now reset back to its initial position when it was introduced in 2002.[23] This reduction, in turn, effectively brought the marginal tax rate down to 40% for the non-PRT liable fields.

In addition to the SC headline rates, the Fiscal Review also announced changes to the allowance mechanisms within this fiscal pillar with a view to simplifying them.[24] This announcement was followed by a consultation,[25] then reiterated in Budget 2015,[26] and subsequently codified in the Finance Act 2015.[27]

These changes were such that from 1 April 2015 the existing set of allowances within the SC regime based on the field characteristics[28] no longer applied.[29] They were instead replaced by a basin-wide allowance mechanism. This new mechanism, called the Investment Allowance (IA), was designed to behave in a similar way as the previous set of allowances in that a certain portion of the profits would be exempted from the SC liability.[30] That exempted portion, however, was no longer determined based on the characteristics of an asset, as was the case in the previous allowances,[31] but instead on the relevant capital expenditures incurred.[32] An amount equal to 62.5% of those capital expenditures[33] incurred on qualifying oil fields[34] after the 31st of March 2015, were now relievable against adjusted ring fence profits prior to applying the SC rate.[35] For a company that incurred a total of £100 million qualifying capital expenditures in an accounting period, for example, this meant a reduction of £62.5 million from the adjusted ring fence profits. If such profits were less than £62.5 million in that accounting period, or in other words if there were any unrelieved Investment Allowances (IAs) left, then that leftover amount was to be carried forward into the next accounting period.[36] Since the SC was not a field-specific instrument, this allowance was not restricted to the particular field the qualifying expenditures incurred in, but could be relieved against the adjusted ring fence profits in its entirety for the SC purposes.

Replacing the multilayered nature of the allowances mechanism within the SC was certainly a positive development. It was likely to reduce both the administrative burden and the uncertainty concerning applicability of any of the sets of allowances.[37] Any additional administrative burden this new IA might create were, according to industry participants, 'manageable and proportionate to the benefits' this new mechanism was creating.[38] Yet, there was still a possibility that basing the allowance on capital expenditures could still create distortions in investment decisions since the system was generating incentives to favour capital-heavy arrangements,[39] which in turn meant that there was a possibility that small fields that were not particularly capital intensive could be adversely affected.[40]

Regardless, a capital expenditure-based allowance mechanism at a 62.5% rate was in place because during the relevant consultation it was shown that together with a reduction of the SC headline rate to 20%, an allowance at 62.5% could be sufficient enough to make a number of otherwise non-commercial projects commercial.[41]

It should be noted, though, going forward that the rate of new Investment Allowance could change from 62.5% because the Finance Act 2015 allowed the Treasury to promulgate regulations to change this rate.[42] Therefore, despite alleviating uncertainty by reducing the complexities surrounding the SC allowance system, this possibility of a change in the rate was inevitably adding back some degree of uncertainty.

Even though one of the goals was to simplify the SC allowance system, this pillar still contained more than one allowance mechanism going forward.[43] This was because the government had previously announced in 2014 its commitment to incentivise not only the ultra-High Pressure and High Temperature (uHP/HT) assets but also the 'nearby discoveries and prospects'[44] in the form of uHP/HT 'clusters'.[45] This commitment resulted in the Cluster Area Allowance (CAA) with a view to provide support for exploration and appraisal activities both in the existing and in nearby potential assets.[46] However, due to the responses to the consultation on the CAA,[47] the government decided to drop the inclusion of the uHP/HT element.[48] The respondents thought such an approach could be 'too restrictive.'[49]

The new approach was instead providing allowances for cluster areas regardless of whether any potential asset could be uHP/HT.[50] The 'cluster area' therefore was not necessarily defined by geological characteristics[51] but rather determined, from 3 December 2014 onwards,[52] by the Secretary of State,[53] with the possibility of input from the holders of the affected licences.[54] The sizes of the cluster areas were expected not to be extremely large as they would broadly be areas 'equivalent to 3 UK Continental Shelf blocks.'[55]

The mechanics of the CAA was very similar to those found under the new IA in that an amount equivalent to 62.5%[56] of qualifying capital expenditures[57] in a cluster area could be relieved against the adjusted ring fence profits before applying the SC rate.[58] Any unrelieved CAAs could then be carried forward.[59] Unsurprisingly, if an expenditure qualified for a CAA, then it could not qualify for the IA as otherwise it would have been equivalent to providing a double-relief on the same expenditure.[60]

As in the case of the IA, basing the CAA on capital expenditure[61] could also create inefficient behaviours on the part of the investors since the capital-heavy arrangements were likely to be favoured. As a result, this mechanism could have an adverse effect on the less capital intensive projects. Again similar to the IA, the allowance rate under the CAA was also not safe from future changes as the Secretary of State had the powers to promulgate regulations to change this rate.[62] Therefore, again there was some additional uncertainty going forward due to this possibility of changes in the allowances.

In addition to the changes to the SC pillar, a minor but important change to the Ring Fence Corporation Tax (RFCT) pillar was also introduced. Previously, in 2010, the Ring Fence Expenditure Supplement (RFES) mechanism within the RFCT regime was introduced to support those investors that were not yet in a taxpaying position.[63] With the modifications in 2012,[64] the RFES was providing a 10% uplift for 6 years to the oil extraction expenditures and losses.[65] Now, with the most recent changes, an extra 4 years were added to the offshore activities thereby bringing the total RFES claimable accounting periods to 10.[66] With this extension the system became slightly less complex since now the offshore and onshore RFES treatments mirrored each other.[67]

The RFES regime was in place to help the investors avoid being at a disadvantage due to the inability to use the allowances and reliefs immediately. This position was likely to arise either because the investors were not producing oil yet, or because their income from production could be less than their investments and costs.[68] In the absence of RFES, the real value of these allowances would have been increasingly lower the further in time the investor made use of them due to the time value of money concept.[69] Therefore, the RFES mechanism allowed for the regaining of this potential loss in the real value. This mechanism, however, could only be *neutral* if the rate of the RFES uplift was equal to the investors' cost of capital.[70] Thus, the 10% rate was unsurprising as it was assumed to be the typical rate for the cost of capital employed by the industry in their decision-making processes.[71]

The third fiscal pillar, the PRT, was also subject to a number of important changes.[72] From the beginning of 2015, the applicable headline PRT rate was reduced from 50% to 35%[73] in order to incentivise the extension of the life of 'key infrastructure' and to 'promote investment in incremental projects in older fields'.[74] This in turn brought the marginal tax rate for a PRT-liable field down to 67.5%.[75] This reduction, though, managed to last only one year. The next year the rate was reduced again, this time to 0%,[76] for periods ending after the last day of 2015 in order to 'increase the attractiveness of projects in the UKCS'.[77]

It should be noted that this 0% rate did not necessarily mean the PRT was abolished in its entirety because all the treatment of expenditures and losses in arriving at assessable profits continued to apply. It just meant, effectively, only the PRT liability was abolished.

Although the 0% PRT rate was a positive measure, it was unclear whether it could have a strong impact in achieving the objective of the MER UK. According to the most recent data approximately 85% of the fields in the UKCS were outside the PRT regime.[78] Only 61 fields[79] out of 404[80] were PRT-liable. By the end of 2014, only 24 out of those 61 fields[81] were actually profitable enough to pay any PRT.[82] Moreover, of those 24, only 9 fields generated enough profits to warrant a PRT of at least £10 million.[83] This corresponds to only about 2% of all the fields in the UKCS. With the current oil prices at less than half of the 2013 levels[84] the number of fields that were generating a noticeable PRT liability were expected to continue to decline anyway. It was not necessarily clear, therefore, to what extent effectively abolishing the PRT liability could sufficiently encourage investments, nor achieve the Fiscal Review objective.

In fact, the issue with the PRT, insofar as the *neutrality* was concerned, lay less with the headline rate and more with the 35% uplift.[85] This was because, as in the case of RFES, the rate needed to align with the investors' cost of capital. This, of course, did not mean setting the rate at the same level as RFES at 10% because, first and unlike RFES, PRT applied at the field level. Second, RFES was targeting those investors who were not generating any taxable profits as yet, while the reform measures for PRT were aimed at extending the field life and promoting incremental investment into the older assets. Therefore, investors would have had different investment profiles under these different fiscal measures and consequently different costs of capital. Unfortunately, it was virtually impossible to address the varying cost of capitals for each investor under the PRT regime with a single legislated rate, and as such it was always in a position to create non-neutrality for at least some of the investors.

Overall, with these reforms following the Fiscal Review the tax regime applicable to the upstream petroleum activities in the UKCS looked relatively simple despite preserving its multilayered nature. The 0% PRT rate meant that there was no longer a differentiation in the marginal tax rates between the PRT-liable and non-liable fields. At 10% SC, and 30% RFCT rates, the marginal tax rate was now 40% for both categories of fields.

The simplification of the tax regime by the post-Fiscal Review reforms was certainly a welcome development. Unfortunately, though, these reforms still did not address the non-neutral elements found within the tax regime. The fundamental issues highlighted in Chapter 3 regarding the inefficiencies including the segregated treatment of new entrants as compared to the existing taxpayers and the regressive elements that were not geared towards capturing the economic rents were still present.[86]

In order to be able to see this clearly, it is necessary to analyse the impact of the current tax regime on potential investment opportunities. As a group of the leading petroleum tax experts stated, 'a deeper understanding of the way the tax system actually functions cannot be obtained without analysing model fields.'[87] Therefore, the next section evaluates these post-Fiscal Review changes by analysing model fields in order to understand the behaviours of different investors in response to the current regime.

4.2. Model field analysis of the Fiscal Review reforms

The analysis of the model fields follows the guiding principles provided in the Fiscal Review, particularly the principles of taking costs and prices into account as well as flexibility.[88] Accordingly, the methodologies that take into account the full life cycle of a project with its cost, price and production dynamics can also be employed in assessing the reaction of investment behaviours to various fiscal tools. This is why the Net Present Value (NPV)[89] is treated as a particularly robust tool for analysing the behaviour of the current tax regime with its most recent modifications while conforming to the guiding principles of the Fiscal Review.

Such an analysis also inevitably follows the methodologies used in the theoretical evaluations of both pre- and post-Fiscal Review tax regimes.[90] This means the analysis focusses on identifying the sensitivities of the responses of the most recent UKCS fiscal regime to the changes in specific variables, namely the reserves,[91] oil prices and costs, in establishing the extent of their regressivity.[92] A fiscal mechanism is considered to have a regressive effect,[93] when it claims an increasingly larger amount of profits as the profitability declines, leaving lesser and lesser amounts to invest.[94] As discussed in Chapter 2, the presence of regressivity in the tax regime would mean inefficiency. It is expected, therefore, that the analysis of model fields will yield a set of conclusions that are consistent with those of the theoretical evaluations that shows the presence of regressivity. In other words, it is expected that the analysis will confirm that not only does the fiscal regime segregate a new entrant and an existing player, but that it is also inefficient.

Regarding the model on which the analysis is based, the operational conditions for the base case assume three model oil field scenarios at the post-exploration stage.[95] All scenarios are assumed to commence in 2018 with the expectation that the production is achievable within 3 years of a development decision. The reserve sizes for each of the base case scenarios are set at approximately 50, 20 and 10 MMbbls, respectively.[96] The average oil price is assumed to be $60 in constant and real terms for the life of the project. This price is not intended to reflect the market values but rather the values for investment screening. Prior to the relatively recent decline in the oil prices, the range of $65–$75 were commonly used by the banks in assessing applications for financing.[97] Therefore, the same approach is adopted here for the base case scenarios.

The development costs depend on a number of factors including the water depth and reservoir quality,[98] and, accordingly, are assumed to be a function of recoverable reserves with the values of $17.5, $20 and £22.5 per barrel for the large, medium and small fields respectively.[99] Table 4.1, above, provides these operational conditions. These assumptions reflect the high-cost environment of the UKCS. Also, in order to reflect the economies of scale, the smaller fields are designed with higher per barrel costs.

The development costs are specifically made up of both the development drilling expenditures and other capital expenditures. The drilling expenditures, as highlighted in Table 4.1, are modelled as 45% of the total development costs for large fields, and 50% for medium and small fields. The remaining portions of the total development costs are then made up of other capital expenditures, which include, among others, the costs of facilities, associated pipelines and construction.

Table 4.1 Operational conditions for the base case scenarios

Operational Conditions	*Field*		
	Large	*Medium*	*Small*
Oil Reserves (MMbbls)	50	20	10
Oil Price ($USD, real)	60	60	60
Total Development Costs ($/bbl)	17.5	20	22.5
of which Drilling Expenditures	45%	50%	50%
of which other Development Capital Expenditures	55%	50%	50%
Operating Costs (of *accumulated* development costs)	7.5%	8.25%	9%
Decommissioning Costs (of total development costs)	10%	10%	10%

Since the development costs are a function of the recoverable reserves, the phasing of the development costs under each scenario is also dependent on the size of the recoverable reserves. This phasing is carried out according to the schedule in Table 4.2 below.

The phasing of the drilling expenditures begins a year after the commencement of the development operations to reflect the delay in acquiring rigs and implementation of the development drilling programme. Similarly, the phasing of the other capital expenditures also depends on the size of the recoverable reserves, though the phasing begins immediately.

Similar to the development costs, the operating costs also increase as the fields get smaller due to the economies of scale. They are set at 7.5%, 8.25% and 9% of the *accumulated* development costs for large, medium and small fields, respectively. This approach simulates, for each field, the increase in the operating costs around the time when the development investments are concluding and when the project is already in its production phase.

Finally, the decommissioning costs are set at 10% of the total development costs with decommissioning assumed to be completed in a year. Given the relatively small sizes of the fields the duration is assumed to be a realistic expectation.[100]

Table 4.2 Phasing of the development cost components

	% of Total Other Capital Expenditures			*% of Total Development Drilling Expenditures*		
Year\Field	*Large*	*Medium*	*Small*	*Large*	*Medium*	*Small*
2018	10	30	50			
2019	27	30	50	15	40	20
2020	27	40		35	40	50
2021	26			30	20	30
2022	10			20		

The Table 4.1 above highlights all of these operational conditions for the base case scenarios.

The model is constructed based on the influence diagram below in Chart 4.1. The NPV[101] in the model is defined as the sum of the post-tax cash flows for each project discounted at the cost of capital of 10%. Cash flows are defined as the total revenues less the total costs for a given year. To reflect these definitions, the NPV in Chart 4.1 is influenced by its three main components: costs, revenues and tax. The cost component is made up of Development Costs, Operating Costs (Opex) and Decommissioning Costs. The Development Costs, in turn, are composed of Drilling and Other Capital Costs, including the costs of the facilities.

The Revenue in the model is a product of price and production in any given year. The price, as mentioned above, is set at a constant and real value of $60 to reflect the price commonly employed in investment screening.[102] The production profiles for each of the reserve scenarios are given in Charts 4.2a-c below. The values throughout the analyses are expressed based on the post-economic cut-off production profiles for each field. Economic cut-off is determined when cumulative Net Cash Flow (NCF) peaks and begins to tail off, or in other words, when the negative cash flow emerges later in the field life.[103] It is the point in time when technically continuing the production may, and often would, be possible but doing so would not be in the economic interest of the investor.

The tax component of the model is made up of the Ring Fence Corporation Tax (RFCT) charged at 30% and the Supplementary Charge (SC) levied at 10%.[104] Although, in reality there would be a lag in the tax payments, the model assumes no such lag in order to highlight the effects of the taxes.[105] The model further distinguishes the tax treatments of the existing taxpayers from those entering into the UKCS for the first time to assess whether the tax regime creates differing outcomes as argued under the theoretical evaluation.[106]

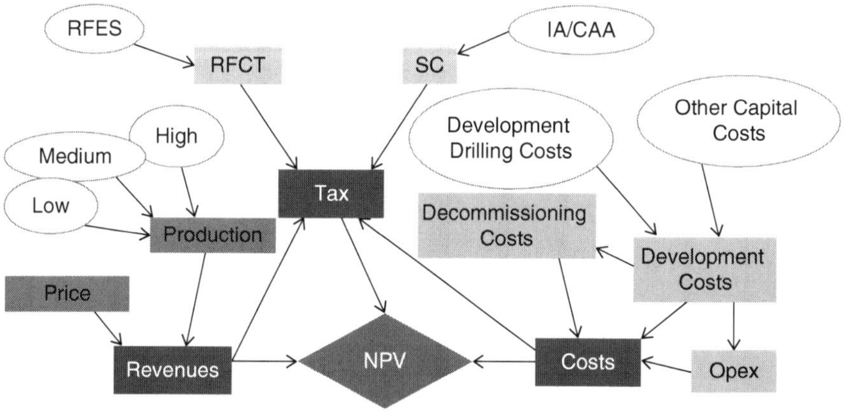

Chart 4.1 Influence diagram

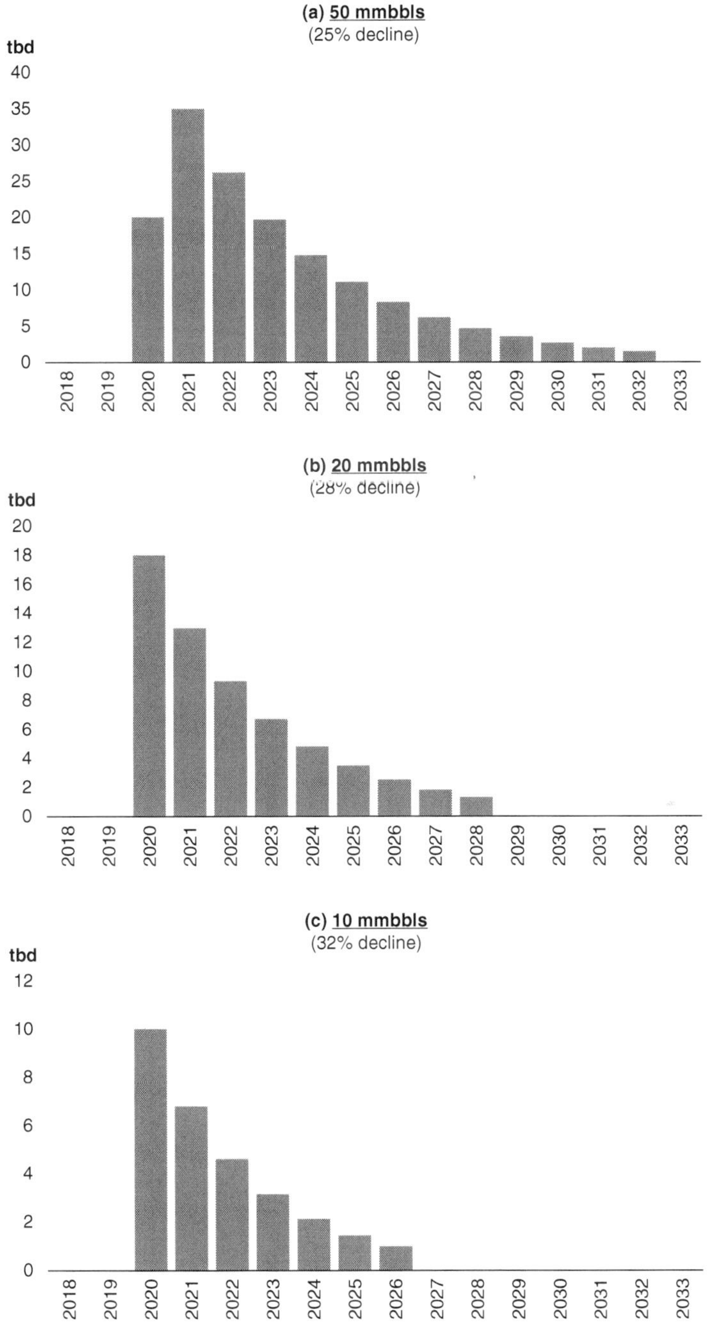

Chart 4.2 Annual average production profiles *(Post-economic cut-off, thousand barrels per day)*

The model is designed in accordance with the discussions on the RFCT in the preceding Chapter[107] so that all operating and capital expenditures, regardless of whether incurred at the development or decommissioning stages, are deductible in full the year they are incurred. For the existing taxpayers, it is assumed that the losses incurred during the pre-production phase are relieved in the same year against incomes from other ring fence projects. This assumption is explicitly accounted for in the model. For the new entrants, these initial losses are carried forward until the project begins generating an income. This relies on the Ring Fence Expenditure Supplement (RFES) mechanism,[108] which aims to alleviate the disadvantage the new entrants face of not being able to obtain tax reliefs – particularly at the pre-production stages – on the capital expenditures the year they are incurred.[109] Therefore, the model incorporates the RFES mechanism at 10% for the initial 10 years.[110]

Additionally, the model does not incorporate the Above the Line (ATL) credit[111] as it only applies to those expenditures that are revenue in nature and when the company is in an overall loss-making position.[112] Although the latter position is true for the new entrants, particularly at the development stage, the revenue expenditures during this period would be negligibly small compared to the capital expenditures. As such, incorporating this mechanism into the model would not have a material impact on determining the efficiency of the existing fiscal mechanism.

The model is also designed in accordance with the discussions in the previous chapter on the SC,[113] so that, for SC purposes, all capital expenditures are also deductible in full the year they are incurred. The losses are either carried forward for the new entrants, or they are relieved against incomes from other ring fence projects for the existing taxpayers. The current two allowance mechanisms under the SC, the Investment Allowance (IA) and the Cluster Area Allowance (CAA) are both provided at 62.5%.[114] Therefore, the model does not distinguish between the two and assumes that the investor utilises one or the other.

Based on these operational conditions, the model calculates the tax liabilities and the total Government tax takes. This is done in nominal terms in order to highlight the structural features of the fiscal components.[115] The results form the basis of the analyses of the tax behaviours in response to the changes in oil prices, reserve sizes and costs. The values for these variables change in accordance with the Table 4.3 below.

Table 4.3 Values of variables for sensitivity analyses

Variables	*High*	*Medium*	*Low*
Oil Price ($/bbl)	75	60	45
Development Costs ($/bbl)	22.5	20	17.5
Reserves (mmbbls)	50	20	10

Accordingly, if the tax take, measured as a percentage of the pre-tax Net Present Value (NPV),[116] increases as the oil prices or the reserves increase, or when the costs decline, then it is deemed to have a progressive effect. If it instead decreases in response to the same conditions, then it has a regressive effect. If, on the other hand, it remains the same, it is deemed as neutral.

Both the tax take and the pre-tax NPVs are calculated using a cost of capital of 10%,[117] and are treated as a measure of the economic rents expected from the project at the field development stage. The tax take, accordingly, measures the share of the economic rents captured by the Government.[118] This is the main measure the analysis is concerned with as it incorporates the cost of capital in its calculation.

4.2.1. Results of the model fields analysis: deterministic analysis

Prior to analysing the extent of the current tax regime's ability to capture economic rents it is important to first establish whether the base case scenarios would pass an investor's screening process. If they don't, then it would be a futile exercise to ascertain whether regressivity is present since it would be a moot point if the tax regime is discouraging investors that are not willing to invest in the first place.

To determine whether these base cases are investment worthy the post-tax returns to the investors are discussed in terms of payback,[119] maximum cash exposures,[120] the NPVs, the Internal Rate of Returns (IRRs)[121] and the Profit/Investment (P/I or NPV/I) ratios. Particularly the last method tends to be preferred by investors more frequently in screening and ranking investment opportunities. In fact, it is common among the investors to reject potential upstream projects at the development stage if the P/I ratios are less than 0.3.[122]

In order to calculate the P/I ratios for the base case scenarios the post-tax real NPV is divided by the pre-tax real Present Value (PV) of the field investment.[123] This is carried out for an existing taxpayer and for a new entrant separately. The approach of dividing *post-tax* NPV with *pre-tax* investment diverges from the one adopted academically where the common position is that the investment values should also be post-tax given the investment costs are tax deductible.[124] This work diverges from this position because the investors are known to allocate their capital on a pre-tax basis.[125] Therefore, in order to realistically simulate an investor's screening process, the pre-tax values of investments are employed here.

Accordingly, at the pre-tax level, payback is achieved in the year 2021 under the 50 mmbbls base case scenario, and in 2020 for the other two base case scenarios. This means, in 2 to 3 years' time the accumulated revenues would equal the investment expended under the three base case field scenarios.[126]

The maximum cash exposures, in nominal terms, are expected to be \$241m, \$203m and \$137m for the large, medium and small oil field base case scenarios, respectively. Together with the payback period, maximum cash exposures can aid the investor in the initial decisions concerning budget allocations. Based on these figures it can be concluded that all the base case scenarios are likely to cause not too heavy a burden on budgeting with monies allocated for these projects that will be available again in 2 to 3 years' time.

However, as highlighted in Section 2.4.1, the investors rather rely on the tools that incorporate the lives of the projects and the time value of money. This is why the NPV/I ratios and the IRRs tend to be employed more commonly since they are discounted at the cost of capital and thus take into account the time value of money.

The projected values for the P/I ratios and the IRRs for each of the investor types under the base case scenarios are illustrated in Chart 4.3 below. The IRRs indicate the average returns each of these base case opportunities was anticipated to earn. As expected, they decline for both of the investor types in tandem with the decline in the reserve value holding everything else constant. Yet it is already apparent that the system is treating the two types of investors differently. Despite the same scenarios the post-tax real IRRs are 9, 10 and 22% lower for a new entrant compared to an existing taxpayer for large, medium and small fields, respectively. This disparity is largely due to the mechanics of the RFES mechanism as the new entrant would not have any other income to set the early losses against.

Regardless, under both taxpayer positions the post-tax real P/I ratios are above the investment threshold of 0.3 for all the base case scenarios. Since this is the case, under these circumstances the investors would go ahead with their investment plans. Therefore, a sensitivity analysis can be carried out on all of the base case scenarios to ascertain the behaviour of the tax regime for each of the taxpayer positions.

Although Chart 4.3 makes it clear that the fiscal regime yields noticeably different results for existing taxpayers and new entrants who are considering an investment in the same assets, it does not provide information on whether the degree of regressivity that may be present in the tax regime, may also differ for

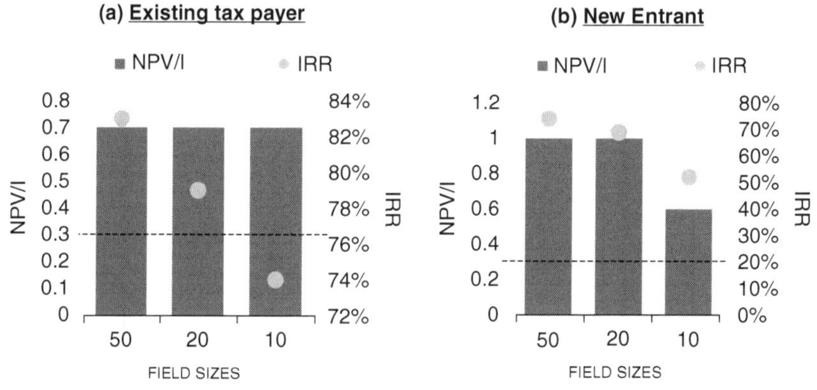

Chart 4.3 Post-tax real P/I ratios & real IRRs under the base case scenarios

these investor types. For that, sensitivity analysis is needed whereby a number of additional scenarios involving individual changes – while holding everything else as constant – in the costs, oil prices and the development costs are carried out to ascertain the behaviour of tax. Chart 4.4 below illustrates those sensitivities from the perspective of an existing taxpayer.

The Charts 4.4a-c show the ways in which the current tax regime behaves for an existing taxpayer in response to specific and individual changes in a number of variables. They illustrate that, whether at 50, 20 or 10 mmbbls, under all the reserve scenarios and for a given oil price of either $45, $60 or $75, the tax take of the government decreases as the costs increase.[127] Under the 50 mmbbls scenario (Chart 4.4a), for example, the government tax take at $45 oil price decreases from 33% to 21% as the costs increase from $17.5 per barrel to $22.5. Similarly, under the 10 mmbbls scenario (Chart 4.4c) the government tax take at $75 oil price decreases from 38% to 36% in response to the same cost increase. Therefore, it is possible to conclude that insofar as an existing taxpayer is concerned the fiscal regime responds to the changes in costs progressively. It is, however, observable that at higher oil price levels the *magnitude* of the progressivity decreases. For example, under the 20 mmbbls scenario (Chart 4.4b), as the per barrel costs increase the government take decreases from 33% to 22% at $45. At $75 the decline is considerably smaller under the same circumstances from 38% to 36%. This demonstrates the natural interdependency between the oil price and the costs in terms of the cash flow.

Since there is such interdependency, it is not surprising that a similar observation emerges for the changes in oil prices. In all three reserve scenarios, and for any given level of costs, the tax take of the government increases as the oil prices increase. Under the 20 MMbbls scenario (Chart 4.4b), for example, the government tax take at $20 per barrel cost[128] increases from 29% to 37% as the oil prices move from $45 to $75. It is again possible to conclude, therefore, that for an existing taxpayer the tax system responds progressively to the changes in oil prices. As in the case of changes in costs, it is also possible to observe an increasing *magnitude* of progressivity at higher development cost levels. This again demonstrates the natural dependency regarding the cash flow between the oil price and the costs.

Interestingly, a similar pattern does not emerge for changes in the reserve sizes[129] for any given levels of oil prices or costs. Instead, the government take remains at the same levels as the reserve size changes. At $45 oil price and at $17.5 cost per barrel, for example, the government take is at 33% for all the reserve scenarios (Chart 4.4a-c).[130] Similarly, at $60 oil price and at $20 per barrel cost the government take is at 35% for all the reserve scenarios.[131] It is, therefore, possible to conclude that insofar as the existing taxpayer is concerned, the fiscal regime responds proportionally to the changes in reserve sizes. In other words, it captures the same portion of profits for a given cost and oil price levels regardless of the field size.

Comparing these results to those for a new entrant it becomes evident that the current tax regime does not behave the same way as it does for an existing taxpayer. Chart 4.5 illustrates these different behaviours. The modelling shows, interestingly, that the response of the tax regime to the changes in costs is not as consistent for a new

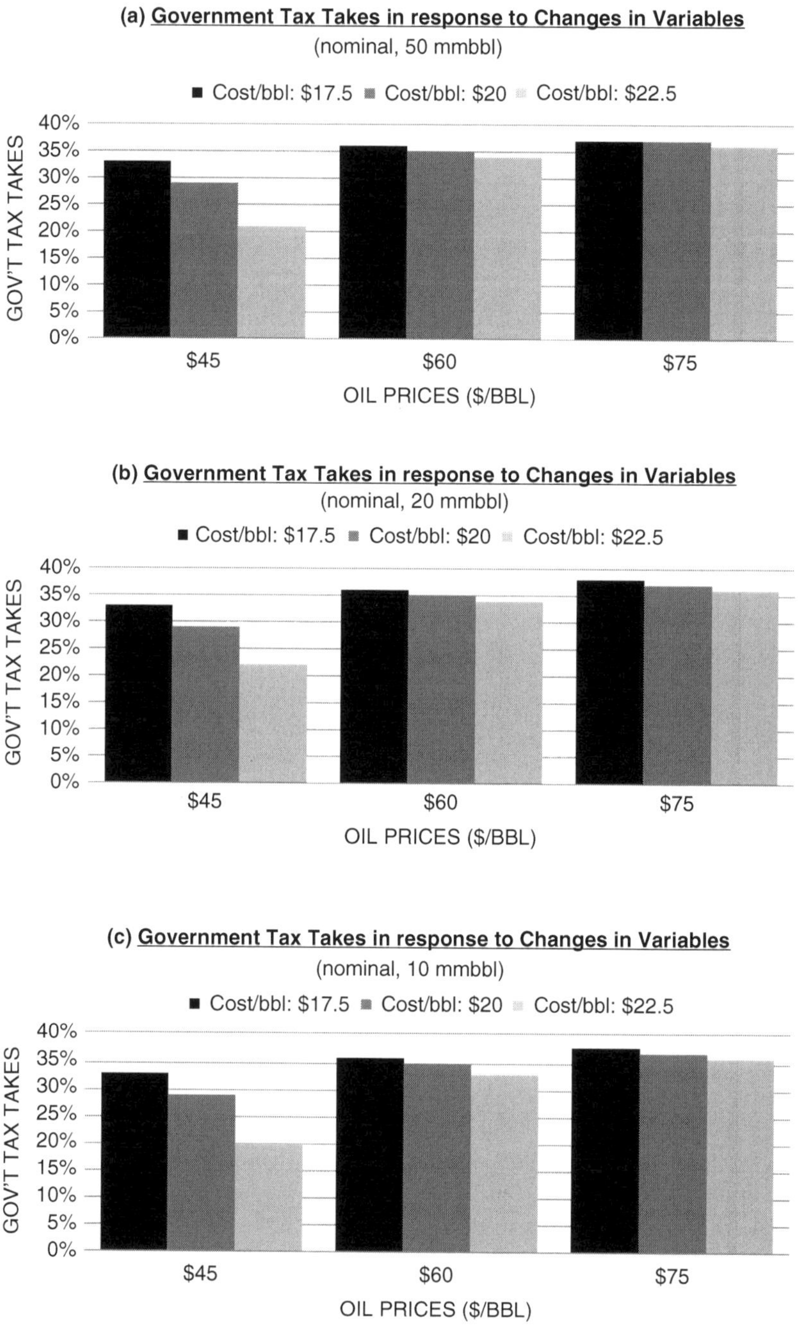

Chart 4.4 Response of the UKCS tax regime: existing taxpayer

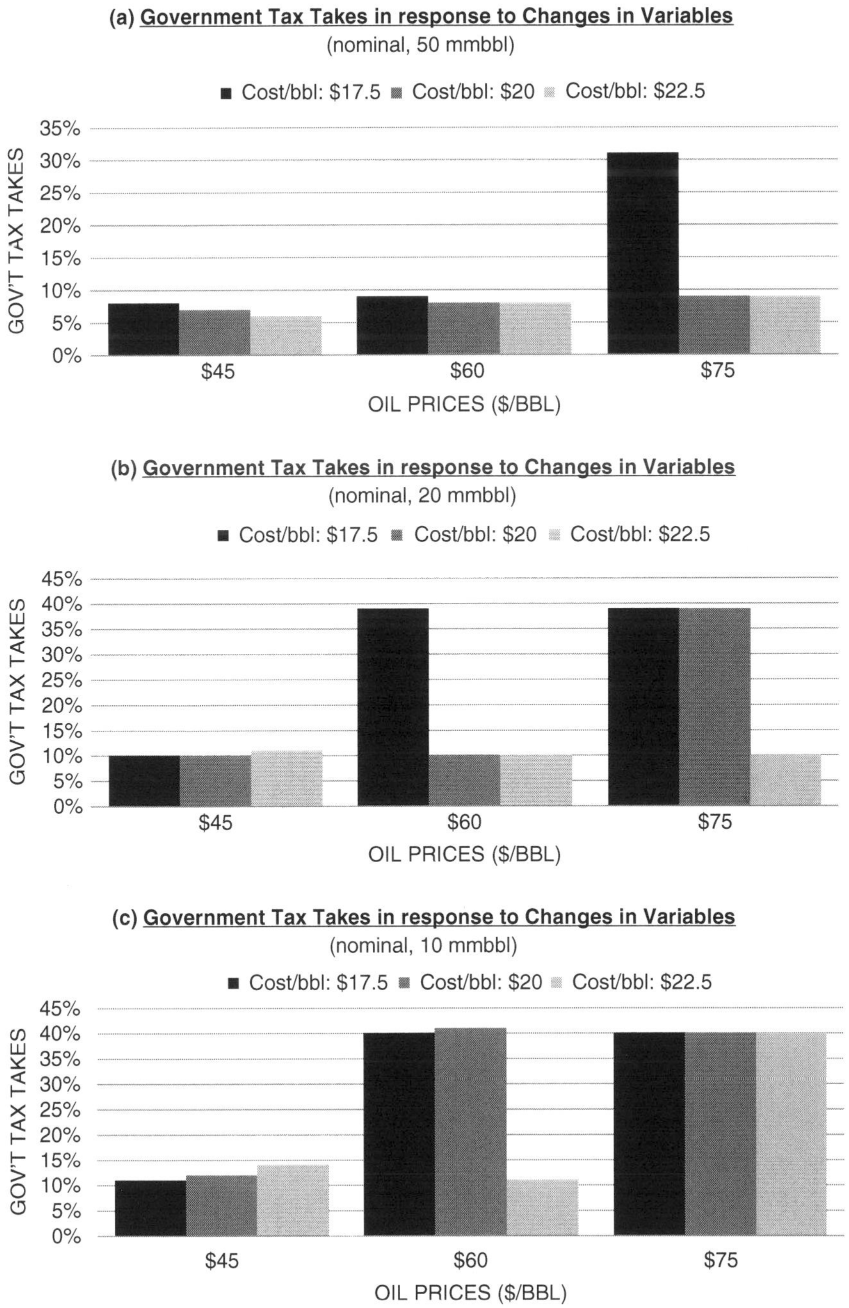

Chart 4.5 Response of the UKCS tax regime: new entrant

entrant as it is for an existing taxpayer. For example, at $45 oil price the response of the tax regime to the changes in costs is progressive under the 50 MMbbl scenario. Yet this turns to a slightly regressive response under the 20 MMbbl scenario, and even more regressive under the 10 MMbbl one. At higher oil price levels, however, the response of the tax regime to the same changes is instead proportional.

This behaviour of the tax regime is largely due to both a new entrant's inability to utilise the losses immediately against another ring fence income and the combined impacts of the Ring Fence Expenditure Supplement and the Investment or Cluster Area Allowances. This means, unless the taxable profit is large enough due to lower costs or higher income, the RFCT liability will arise only later in the field life, if at all. This is why the government take can jump from 14% under the highest cost and lowest reserve and oil prices scenario[132] to 31% under the opposite scenario.[133]

A similar mixed pattern is also observed with respect to changes in oil prices where the behaviour of the tax regime oscillates between being progressive and regressive. The regressivity becomes more pronounced with respect to changes in the reserve sizes. For example, the government take at the base case scenario of $60 oil price and $20 per barrel cost increases from 8% to 41% as the reserve size reduces from 50 to 10 mmbbl. This behaviour of increasing tax claim as the field gets smaller is consistent across all levels of oil prices and costs modelled.

At first the outcomes of the sensitivity analysis may come across as surprising since the theoretical discussion on the regressive response of the reformed tax regime is present only in certain circumstances for a new entrant and non-existent for an investor with tax history. However, a closer examination reveals that the magnitude of the progressivity, particularly in the case of an existing taxpayer, seems to decline as the relevant values of the variables change. This, in turn, reveals the limitation of the sensitivity analysis carried out here. The analysis reveals the behaviour of the tax regime only in specific circumstances without taking account of the entire possible outcomes. It gives a good indication as to how the tax system can behave but not how it behaves when all the possibilities are considered. This is why the next section carries out stochastic analysis. Such an approach will assist in deriving a robust conclusion as it takes into account all of the possible outcomes for each variable.

4.2.2. Results of the model fields analysis: stochastic analysis

In ascertaining the extent of neutrality and efficiency of the existing tax regime the deterministic analysis[134] above relies on establishing progressivity and regressivity. The stochastic approach on the other hand relies on measuring the degree of risks the current tax regime creates in establishing the degree of neutrality and efficiency. In carrying out the latter approach and, consequently, obtaining a better understanding of the tax regimes' impact on risk-sharing,[135] a more sophisticated analytical method using Monte Carlo simulation modelling[136] is employed in this Section. The fundamental aspect of this type of modelling is

Table 4.4 Base values of variables for Monte Carlo analysis

Stochastic Variables	*Values*				*Probability Distribution*	*Chapter Subsection*
	Mean	*St. Dev.*	*Min*	*Max*		
Oil Price ($USD)	60	25%	5	150	BetaPERT, Mean Reverting	4.2.1.1.1
Reserves (million barrels)	20	15	0	∞	Lognormal	4.2.1.1.2
Development Costs ($ per barrel)	20	10%	6	34	Normal	4.2.1.1.3
Operating Costs (% of accumulated development costs)	8.25	1.25%	1%	∞	Normal	4.2.1.1.4

its ability to take all the possible outcomes of each of the variables into consideration.

Accordingly, the values for the base case scenario for the Monte Carlo simulations are as per Table 4.4 which assumes – as has been the case under the deterministic analyses – that the investment potential is at the development stage. The analysis is carried out on the variables in Table 4.4 separately for an existing taxpayer and a new entrant.

For the simulations each one of the oil prices, reserves, development costs and operating costs are initially treated as stochastic separately while holding others constant at their mean values. They are then simulated as stochastic at the same time in order to incorporate extreme but highly improbably possibilities.[137]

When the oil price is modelled stochastically the subsequent analysis of the existing tax system behaves in a non-neutral pattern. The results show that the tax regimes reduce the mean expected return by 43% for an existing taxpayer, and 54% for a new entrant, indicating that a new entrant faces a higher degree of risk than an existing taxpayer as a direct consequence of the tax regime.[138] The simulation also shows that the fiscal regime increases the chances of turning positive pre-tax NCF to a negative one, with a more pronounced effect for a new entrant. What these reveal is that the existing fiscal regime can cause non-development of fields which are otherwise viable before tax, particularly if the investor is a new entrant. In other words, the current tax system is not neutral, and as such, is less than efficient when the oil prices are simulated as stochastic, particularly so for a new entrant.

The results of stochastic reserves analysis also corroborates the finding that a new entrant faces a different treatment than an existing taxpayer. However, what is interesting here is that when reserves are modelled as stochastic it is observed that the tax regime considerably reduces the risks for both types of investors, and even more so for a new entrant. As surprising as this conclusion may be it is not necessarily inexplicable since the state, as argued above in Section 4.2.2.1, shares some of the risks via the tax regime. Particularly, the loss deductions, carry-forward and the RFES and other allowance mechanisms can explain this outcome. In other words, it may be that the fiscal regime captures the same portion of profits for given cost and oil price levels regardless of the field size. Therefore, insofar as the reserve sizes are concerned, the tax regime may be neutral. Yet, when the risks in this simulation are further analysed based on investment thresholds it is observed that the tax regime may still create some risks for a new entrant that may impact its investment decisions. Therefore, it can be concluded that under the stochastic reserves modelling the existing system is mostly proportional and, thus, neutral, though it has some regressive elements which adversely impacts the investment decisions. Although the magnitude of such regressivity is considerably smaller compared to the case of stochastic oil price analysis, the degree of risks the current tax system creates is higher for a new entrant than an existing taxpayer. This can again translate into non-development of fields that are viable pre-tax, particularly if it is a new entrant that is assessing the investment potential.[139]

The results of the third and fourth Monte Carlo simulations, modelling development costs and operating costs as stochastic, respectively, suggest a risk dynamic of the tax system that is closer to the behaviour under the stochastic reserve size modelling than the conclusions reached under the deterministic analysis. That is, the tax regime seems to be neutral for the most part, though there is evidence of some degree of increased risk for a new entrant.[140]

What these four simulations show is that the current tax regime creates varying magnitudes of risk exposures on the same project for an existing taxpayer and a new entrant. It also shows that the behaviour of the current tax regime is different depending on which variable is treated independently and individually stochastic. When the oil prices are modelled, for example, the tax regime has a clear, non-neutral impact on the investment opportunity. Yet this is not necessarily the case when either the development or operating costs are modelled stochastically. This discrepancy can only be resolved by identifying the magnitudes of the impacts of each of the variables on the post-tax expected return for each taxpayer position.

Therefore the fifth, and final, simulation runs all the variables simultaneously and independently stochastic while additionally carrying out a tornado analysis. The former analysis includes scenarios that incorporate extreme positions with miniscule probabilities of occurring in order to take account of all possibilities. The latter method is employed in ranking the magnitudes of the impacts of each of the variables on the overall behaviour of the tax regime.

The results of the final Monte Carlo simulation show, as expected, that there is a risk differential between the two investor types since the increases in risk are not uniform between them. The existing fiscal regime poses a higher risk for a new entrant than it does for an existing taxpayer, having a stronger negative impact on the investment decisions by a new entrant. This conclusion is expected following the theoretical analysis and largely confirms the similar findings of the deterministic approach in Section 4.2.1.

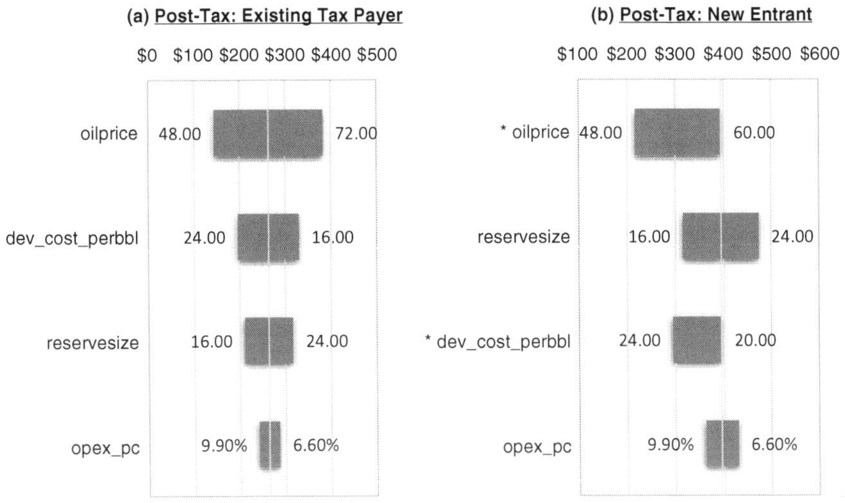

Chart 4.6 Tornado diagrams

The tornado diagrams in Chart 4.6 show the relative sensitivities of the taxpayer positions to changes in each of the variables and ranks them from the most impactful to the least. Each of the variables are modelled with a testing range ±20% deviations from the base case scenario. Within this range the tornado simulation chooses values at random in calculating the NPVs. The diagrams then present the variable that changes the NPV the most at the top and the least at the bottom. The range of NPVs are presented horizontally while the minimum and maximum values employed for each of the variables are provided next to each bar in Chart 4.6.

Accordingly, Chart 4.6 shows that the variability in oil prices have the highest impact on the overall returns for both taxpayer positions. However, the second highest impact is not the same for the investors. For an existing taxpayer the development costs have a larger impact on the overall expected returns than the size of the reserves. For a new entrant the reverse is true. This confirms that the mechanisms within the current tax regime does, in fact, segregate the two taxpayer positions. This segregation is specifically caused by the fact that an existing taxpayer can deduct the development costs in the year incurred while a new entrant is not able to, but instead has to carry forward at a 10% RFES rate. Such segregation as illustrated in the tornado charts shows that the size of the reserves, and consequently the production levels, have a larger impact for a new entrant as it determines the speed at which those development costs can be recovered. The tornado analysis, therefore, not only indicates how much weight the conclusions of the simulations that modelled the individual variables stochastically ought to be given for each taxpayer position but also emphasises the different behaviour patterns emerging for each investor as a result of the existing tax regime.

4.3. The Way Forward

The foregoing theoretical and quantitative analysis makes it clear beyond a doubt that the ensuing reforms following the Fiscal Review have fallen short of their own objective. The analysis shows that the current tax regime with its most recent modifications is still not efficient enough to capture the economic rents. Given the strong and real volatility of the oil prices[141] this non-neutrality of the current fiscal regime could still become a considerable threat against the MER UK strategy[142] as it evidently could continue to cause the non-development of some of the fields that are viable pre-tax.

There is, however, a way to reform the fiscal system so that it is more robust than these recent modifications which can alleviate the problem of non-neutrality and ensure efficient collection of economic rent in conformity with the aims of MER UK. The following Chapter discusses this new proposed reform.

Notes

1 Current at the time of writing.
2 See Chapter 2
3 HM Treasury, *'Driving Investment: a plan to reform the oil and gas fiscal regime'* (Report, HM Treasury December 2014) 4.5
4 HM Treasury (n 3) 4.6. Also see HM Treasury, *'Autumn Statement 2014'* (Statement, HM Treasury December 2014) 1.125
5 RFCT + SC = 30% + 30% = 60% for the non-PRT fields; and PRT + (half of RFCT + SC) = 50% + 30% = 80% for the PRT paying fields.
6 HC Deb 23 March 2011 vol 525, cols 964–965 (Osborne); Also see HM Treasury, *'Budget 2011'* (Report, HM Treasury 23 March 2011) para 1.148 Also see Section 3.3
7 US Energy Information Agency, 'Petroleum & Other Liquids: Europe Brent Spot Price FOB' (US EIA 13 December 2015)
8 HM Revenue & Customs, 'Finance Bill 2015: *Corporation Tax: Oil and Gas Taxation and the Reduction in Supplementary Charge'* (Policy Paper, HMRC 10 December 2014)
9 Oil & Gas UK, 'Activity Survey 2015' (Report, Oil & Gas UK 2015); Also see Oil & Gas UK, '*Report paints bleak picture of high-potential industry but the solution is clear, says Oil & Gas UK'* (Press Release, Oil & Gas UK 24 February 2015)
10 Oil & Gas UK, '*Oil & Gas UK meeting with Chancellor George Osborne'* (Press Release, Oil & Gas UK 25 February 2015)
11 See Section 3.3.1 for the Investment Allowance mechanisms then in place.
12 Oil & Gas UK (n 10)
13 Oil & Gas Authority, '*Call to Action: The Oil and Gas Authority Commission 2015'* (Report, the OGA Commission 25 February 2015)
14 HM Treasury, 'Budget 2015' (Report, HM Treasury 18 March 2015)
15 Finance Act 2015 s 48
16 Finance Act 2015 s 48. Also see HM Treasury (n 14) 2.142

17 RFCT + SC = 30% + 20% = 50% for the non-PRT fields; and PRT + (half of RFCT + SC) = 50% + 25% = 75% for the PRT paying fields.
18 Oil & Gas UK, *'Budget Lays Strong Foundations for Regeneration of the UK North Sea'* (Press Release, Oil & Gas UK 18 March 2015)
19 US Energy Information Agency (n 7)
20 US Energy Information Agency (n 7)
21 HM Treasury, 'Budget 2016' (Report, HM Treasury 16 March 2016) 1.269
22 Finance Act 2016 s 58
23 See Section 3.3
24 HM Treasury (n 3) 4.8
25 HM Treasury, *'Fiscal reform of the UK Continental Shelf: response to the consultation on an investment allowance'* (Consultation, HM Treasury March 2015)
26 HM Treasury (n 14) 1.129
27 Finance Act 2015 s 49 Sch 12, 14
28 See Section 3.3
29 Finance Act 2015 Sch 14
30 HM Treasury (n 14) 2.1–2.3
31 See Section 3.3
32 Although please note that at the time of writing the Treasury, under its Finance Act 2016 s 60 and 63 powers, proposed a regulation to expand the allowance to include certain operating expenditures, including tariff expenditures, and leasing expenditures as well. The proposed regulation is titled The Investment Allowance and Cluster Area Allowance (Investment Expenditure) Regulations 2016. This proposal, however, has not been laid before the Parliament yet. The Government is planning to do so after the Parliament's summer recess, though at the time of writing this is yet to be laid before the Parliament. HC WQ&A 06 June 2016, WQ 38,238 and 38,364
33 And other qualifying expenditures that may be regulated by the Treasury. Finance Act 2015 Sch 12 s 2 inserts s 332BA into Corporation Tax Act 2010
34 Defined as an 'oil field that is not wholly or partly included in a cluster area' Finance Act 2015 Sch 12 12 s 2 inserts s 332B into Corporation Tax Act 2010, The term 'cluster area' is further defined at Corporation Tax Act 2010 s 356JD as inserted by Finance Act 2015 Sch 13 s 2
35 Finance Act 2015 Sch 12 s 2 332B
36 Finance Act 2015 Sch 12 s 2 332EA
37 HM Treasury (n 25) 2.37
38 HM Treasury (n 25) 2.38
39 HM Treasury (n 25) 2.17
40 HM Treasury (n 25) 2.44
41 HM Treasury (n 25) 2.44
42 Finance Act 2015 Sch 12 s 2 332JA
43 There is also the Onshore Allowance, though it is outside the scope of this work. See Corporation Tax Act 2010 Part 8 Chapter 8
44 HM Treasury, *'Maximising economic recovery: consultation on a cluster allowance'* (Consultation, HM Treasury July 2014) 3.2
45 HM Treasury, 'Budget 2014' (Report, HM Treasury 19 March 2014) 1.114
46 HM Treasury (n 44) 3.2
47 HM Treasury, *'Maximising economic recovery – consultation on a cluster area allowance: summary of responses'* (Consultation, HM Treasury December 2014)
48 HM Treasury (n 47) 2.22–2.26
49 HM Treasury (n 47) 2.34
50 HM Treasury (n 47) 2.4
51 HM Treasury (n 47) 2.22

52 Finance Act 2015 Sch 13 s 5
53 Currently of the DECC though it will eventually transfer to OGA. HM Treasury (n 47) 2.24
54 Finance Act 2015 Sch 13 s 2 356JD. Note that investors can also exclude certain assets from the designation. See Finance Act 2015 Sch 13 s 6
55 HM Treasury (n 47) Box 2.C
56 Finance Act 2015 Sch 13 s 2 356JF
57 Though there may be other types of expenditures that could also qualify if the Treasury promulgates regulations to that effect. Finance Act 2015 Sch 13 s 2 356JE
58 Finance Act 2015 s 50 and Sch 13, 14
59 Finance Act 2015 Sch 13 s 2 356JGA
60 Finance Act 2015 Sch 12 s 2 332B
61 Although this may change with the introduction of the new proposed regulations. See (n 32) above.
62 Finance Act 2015 Sch 13 s 2 356JMA
63 See Section 3.2.3.1.5 above.
64 Corporation Tax Act 2010 s 310 as enacted.
65 See Section 3.2.3.1.5 above.
66 Finance Act 2015 s 47 and Sch 11
67 HM Treasury (n 14) 4.10–4.12. Note that the RFES provides for interest at 10% for 10 years for expenditures incurred from 5 December 2013 on onshore activities. Finance Act 2014 Sch 14. However, a detailed discussion of the onshore treatment is beyond the scope of this work.
68 HM Treasury (n 14) 4.10
69 See Section 2.4.1.3.2 above.
70 See the discussion in Section 2.4.1.3.1 for the rationale behind this.
71 HC Deb 5 July 2011, vol 530, col 82W (Greening)
72 The Government also announced in addition to changes to the fiscal pillars a one-off £20m funding support for seismic surveys. HM Treasury (n 14) 1.129
73 Finance Act 2015 s 52
74 HM Treasury (n 14) 1.129
75 PRT+(((1-PRT)*RFCT)+(1-PRT*SC)) = 35%+(65%*30%)+(65%*20%) = 35% + 19.5% + 13% = 67.5%
76 Finance Act 2016 s 140
77 HM Revenue & Customs, '*Oil and Gas Taxation: Reduction in Petroleum Revenue Tax and Supplementary Charge*' (Policy Paper, HMRC 16 March 2016)
78 As at the time of writing.
79 HM Revenue & Customs, '*Number of oil and gas fields with different PRT liabilities*' (Table, HMRC 30 June 2015)
80 Department of Energy and Climate Change, '*UKCS Field Information*' (DECC, 03 August 2015) <https://www.og.decc.gov.uk/fields/fields_index.htm> accessed 21 October 2016
81 As of 31 December 2014, most recent data available at the time of writing.
82 HM Revenue & Customs (n 79)
83 HM Revenue & Customs (n 79)
84 See Appendix I
85 See Section 3.4 above.
86 See Section 3.5
87 Petter Osmundsen, Magne Emhjellen, Thore Jensen, Alexander Kemp, and Christian Riis, '*Petroleum Taxation Contingent on Counter-factual Investment Behaviour*' (September 2015) 36 The Energy Journal 1
88 See Section 2.5

89 See Section 2.4.1.3 for discussions on NPV.
90 See Chapter 2
91 Or, production profiles
92 See Chapter 2
93 There is a difference between *design* and *effect* insofar as the regressivity and progressivity is concerned. Please see Chapter 2 for a detailed discussion on this.
94 See Chapter 2
95 The intention of the dissertation is to ascertain the responsiveness of the fiscal regime. By assuming the oil field discovered, it creates the opportunity to carry out the assessment on the projected cash flow without introducing the uncertainty of exploration. For an explanation of the impact of exploration see Section 2.4.3. This approach of excluding exploration in analyses is consistent with the academic practice. See, for example, Alexander G Kemp, D Rose and L Stephen, *'Petroleum Investment and Taxation: The North Sea and the Far East*' (1995) North Sea Study Occasional Paper No. 49, Wemmys Otman, *'The Petroleum Development Investment Risks and Returns in Libya: a Monte Carlo Study of the Current Contractual Terms (EPSA IV)'* (2004) North Sea Study Occasional Paper No. 94, Alexander G Kemp and B Macdonald, *'The UK and Norwegian Fiscal Systems: A Comparative Study of Their Impacts on New Field Investments'* (1992) North Sea Occasional Papers No. 38
96 The model data employed in this work is consistent with the most recent industry data. See Oil and Gas UK, *'Activity Survey 2016'* (Report, 2016 Oil & Gas UK) 58. The data is also consistent with those employed in the most recent NSSO Papers (ISSN 0143-022X) which are not only accepted within the REF Framework but also feed directly into policy making in the UK and have demonstrable REF impact. See, for example, Alexander G Kemp and Linda Stephen, *'The Investment Allowance in the Wider Context of the UK Continental Shelf in 2015: A Response to the Treasury Consultation'* (February 2015) North Sea Occasional Paper No. 132, and Alexander G Kemp, *'Maximising Economic Recovery from the UK Continental Shelf: A Response to the Draft DECC Consulting Strategy'* (January 2016) North Sea Occasional Paper No. 135
97 Alexander G Kemp and Linda Stephen, *'Price Sensitivity, Capital Rationing and Future Activity in the UK Continental Shelf after the Wood Review'* (November 2014) North Sea Study Occasional Paper 130
98 The levels of permeability and porosity, among other factors, directly affect the quality of the reservoir and, in turn, the cost of development. Alexander G Kemp and D Rose, *'Fiscal Aspects of Investment Opportunities in the UKCS and Norway, Denmark, the Netherlands, Australia, China, Alaska (North and South) and the US Outer Continental Shelf'* (1993) North Sea Occasional Paper No. 43
99 The model data employed in this work is consistent with the most recent industry data. See (n 96)
100 Alexander G Kemp, *'Petroleum Exploitation in North West Europe and the Atlantic Margin: Tax and Government Takes and Investor Returns'* (August 2012) Unpublished work. This is also consistent with the NSSO Papers (ISSN 0143-022X). See (n 96).
101 See Section 2.4.1.3 for a discussion on the NPVs.
102 Kemp and Stephen (n 97)
103 Alexander G Kemp and David Reading, *'The Economics of Incremental Investments in Mature Oil Fields in the UK Continental Shelf'* (1991) North Sea Study Occasional Paper No. 36 and Alexander G Kemp and Linda Stephen, *'Prospective Activity Levels in the Regions of the UKCS Under Different Oil and Gas Prices: An Application of the Monte Carlo Technique'* (1999) North Sea Study Occasional Paper No. 71

104 Since the PRT was abolished in 1993 and applied at 0% for the pre-1993 fields it is not applicable to these projects
105 Alexander G Kemp and David Reading, *'The Impact of Petroleum Fiscal Systems in Mature Field Life: A Comparative Study of the UK, Norway, Indonesia, China, Egypt, Nigeria and United States Federal Offshore'* (1991) North Sea Study Occasional Paper No. 32
106 See Section 3.5
107 See Section 3.2
108 See Section 3.2.3.1.5
109 This is because compared to the existing tax payers, the new entrants would not have other UKCS incomes to utilise the reliefs against.
110 Although the 10-year period under the RFES mechanism is not necessarily consecutive, for modelling purposes it is assumed to be consecutive from the first year of the project.
111 See Section 3.2.3.1.3
112 Corporation Tax Act 2009, ss 104C-104N as inserted by the Finance Act 2013, Sch 15
113 See Section 3.2
114 See Section 4.1
115 This is also the approach adopted in Kemp (n 100)
116 See Section 2.4.1.3 for a detailed discussion on the NPV concept.
117 See Section 2.4.1.3.2 for a detailed discussion on the concept of cost of capital.
118 Alexander G Kemp and David Reading, *'A Comparative Analysis of the Impact of the UK and Norwegian Petroleum Tax Regimes on Different Oil Fields'* (1990) North Sea Study Occasional Paper No. 31. Also see, Kemp and Macdonald (n 95)
119 For a detailed discussion on the payback period, see Section 2.4.1.1
120 For a detailed discussion on the payback period, see Section 2.4.1.1
121 See Section 2.4.1.5 for a detailed discussion on IRR.
122 Kemp and Stephen (n 97) 9–10
123 Both calculated at the 10% discount rate.
124 Kemp and Stephen (n 97) 10
125 Kemp and Stephen (n 97) 10
126 For the 20 and 10 mmbbls field scenarios it is 2 years' time, and for the 50 mmbbls it is 3 years' time.
127 The changes in the costs include those changes in the development costs, associated operating costs, the decommissioning costs and the phasing of the development costs. See Tables 4.1 and 4.2
128 Depicted in orange columns in Chart 4.4b
129 And, by definition, to the production profiles and volumes.
130 Depicted in the first blue column of each chart.
131 Depicted in the second orange column in each chart.
132 Depicted as the first green column in Chart 4.5c
133 Depicted as the last blue column in Chart 4.5a
134 Which is based on discrete values for each of the variables.
135 Alexander G Kemp and Kathleen Masson, '*Taxation and Project Risk Sharing with Special Reference to the UKCS*' (1998) North Sea Study Occasional Paper No. 66; Alexander G Kemp and Kathleen Masson, '*Oil and Gas Exploration and Development in the UKCS: A Monte Carlo Analysis of the Risks and Returns*' (1998) North Sea Study Occasional Paper No.69; and Alexander G Kemp and David Reading, '*Economic and Fiscal Aspects of Field Abandonment with Special Reference to the UK Continental Shelf*' (1991) North Sea Study Occasional Paper No. 34

136 See Section 4.2 for a detailed discussion of this simulation.
137 For the sake of brevity, however, the pre- and post-tax results are provided in the website where both statistics tables and frequency charts can be found for interpretation purposes as well as a detailed explanation.
138 Please see the discussion on the website for the details.
139 Please see the discussion on the website for the details.
140 Please see the discussion on the website for the details.
141 As illustrated in Appendix I
142 See Section 3.5 for a detailed discussion on this strategy.

5 The new UKCS fiscal regime

A proposal for reform

5.1. Reforming the UKCS fiscal regime

This work proposes a new system for the UK's petroleum tax regime that takes the guiding principles of the Fiscal Review to their natural conclusion. In order to reach that natural conclusion the proposal first envisages a single-pillared tax regime. A consequence of this single-pillared approach is the inevitable abolition of the existing Ring Fence Corporation Tax (RFCT) and Supplementary Charge (SC) pillars. Of course, in this new system the Petroleum Revenue Tax (PRT) would naturally continue to apply to pre-1993 fields since the proposed reforms would not apply retrospectively. Retrospective application is undesirable[1] because it would increase the fiscal instability for which the investors would attach a higher risk premium, thus requiring a higher return for investing into the UKCS. This would run contrary to the objectives of both the Wood Report and Fiscal Review. In order to avoid this, therefore, the new system would apply only to those licences that are granted on, or after, this new fiscal system comes into force. The fields existing prior to such time would still be subject to the fiscal regime currently in place.[2]

The approach of this system is certainly distinctive in that it illustrates the real possibility of establishing a cash-flow tax regime in the UK. In broad terms, the proposed reform uniquely modifies the cash-flow-based tax regime put forward by E C Brown in 1948[3] (Brown Tax, see Box 5.1) while incorporating some of the existing rules of the PRT pillar. It is the characteristics of neutrality, efficiency and simplicity that makes the Brown Tax a perfect base to build the new system upon. Taking this theoretical model as a starting point therefore, the new system modifies it to adapt to the realities of the petroliferous trade in the UK.

As the subsequent discussions will demonstrate this new system would indeed satisfy the objectives and the principles of the Fiscal Review. The ensuing theoretical and quantitative analysis will reveal that the proposed system is not only considerably simpler than the existing regime but also behaves in a perfectly neutral and efficient manner. All this, while complying with the Fiscal Review guiding principles. Thus, the analysis will show that the proposed tax reform would completely align with the Treasury's objective of a simpler tax regime that can capturing economic rents.

Box 5.1 The fiscal regime of E C Brown

The simplest form of resource rent[4] tax, at least theoretically, was posited in 1948 by E C Brown[5] and referred to either as Brown Tax, R-based cash-flow tax[6] or as pure rent tax.[7] Brown originally proposed this tax as an alternative to the standard tax on profits whereby a fixed rate would apply to cash flows.[8] Accordingly, all the expenditures regardless of their nature would be 100% recoverable in the year they are incurred.[9] This is with the exception of interest payments and other financing costs which would not be separately allowable.[10] Under Brown's system, if the assets were sold at a later date the proceeds from those sales would be subject to corporation tax as opposed to capital gains tax.[11]

For any given year, the deduction of costs from a company's proceeds would give the cash flow for that year. Under the Brown Tax system, if that cash flow is positive the government would receive the tax receipts at the fixed tax rate, just as it would under the standard corporate tax mechanism. If, on the other hand, it is negative, and there are no other existing incomes to set it against, the government would then reimburse the company the value equal to the negative tax liability. The amount of reimbursement would not be equal to the entire loss, or the negative cash flow, but rather a share of that loss equal to the fixed tax rate. Chart 5.1 illustrates this at an arbitrarily chosen 40% fixed tax rate. In that Chart, at year 0, the government reimburses the investor 40% of the £100m loss. At year 4, the government collects 40% tax, or £8m, in tax revenue from a total profit of £20m. This means, effectively, the government becomes an equity partner with the company – albeit without the benefits and liabilities of an actual equity partner – equally sharing the upside and downside with that company.

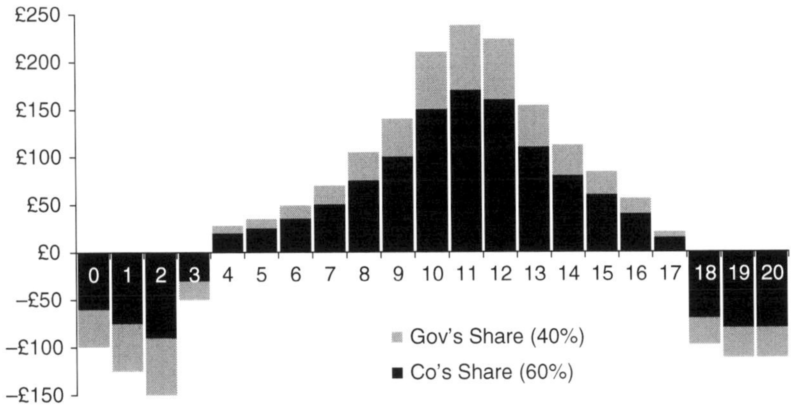

Chart 5.1 Brown tax

Chart 5.1 reveals that the Brown Tax is perfectly proportional[12] in that, regardless of the magnitude of the cash flow, the same 40% rate applies proportionally. The design of it also makes it very simple and certain. It is a tax applied on the cash flow of each period, and all the expenditures are allowable in full immediately. This means there is not any need for complex carry-forward rules. As such, it would be 'unnecessary for the authority to estimate the investor's discount rate.'[13] The government can avoid creating complexities in the tax law and simply set the rate and both parties can reasonably predict what the tax liability would be for each period.

This does not mean the state would not receive any tax income at all. On the contrary, from a company's perspective the post-tax returns would naturally be less than the pre-tax values, as the state's tax share would make up the difference. What it does mean is that the Brown Tax would not induce any artificial influence on the investor's decision-making. This is because the Brown Tax would, in effect, make the government an equity partner via the fiscal mechanisms.

Even though the post-tax *values* would be lower the post-tax *rates of return* would not be less than the pre-tax rates of return since both the negative and positive cash flows would be reduced by the same tax rate.[14] Thus, the Brown Tax is completely neutral, and as a result can directly target economic rents. It is also quite simple since it would not require investors' cost of capitals to be known in order to determine the economic rents.[15] As such, the headline tax rate can be set at 'very high' levels 'without deterring any projects.'[16]

5.2. The new system

Just like the theoretical Brown Tax the new fiscal system advocated here would have a fixed percentage headline tax rate. However, the new fiscal regime would deviate from the theoretical Brown Tax when it comes to determining the tax base. The deviation would come about because the tax base under the Brown Tax system is the corporate profits. Whereas under the proposed new regime the tax base would be the cash flow of a project. This is an important distinction because, as it has been previously argued[17] the corporate income as a base would make it rather difficult to capture the economic rents arising from different projects as the effects of such a fiscal mechanism on individual projects would vary. This is why it is important to build a mechanism that focusses on each project's cash flow instead.

A project's cash flow in any given period is determined by that project's income after deducting the relevant costs associated with that project. An oil project's income is predominantly determined by the sales of production and the tariff receipts. In the proposed system the determination of the value of production would largely follow the existing rules within the PRT pillar,[18] albeit with some minor but important variations. The PRT mechanism would be an excellent guide in this respect as it is also based on project cash flows. Additionally, relying on the valuation mechanisms of the PRT pillar would also leverage the existing expertise on the PRT administration both in the Treasury and in the industry. This would, in turn, avoid creating additional administrative burdens.

Accordingly, under the new regime the rules for an arm's length sale would equally be strict as they are under the current PRT system with the powers for the HMRC to adjust the sale price if it is deemed that a given sale is not at an arm's length. This would be in place to prevent the pricing of a crude sale being influenced away from the market fundamentals by pre-existing commercial relationships between the relevant parties.[19]

The valuation of non-arm's length sales[20] would also follow the existing PRT rules[21] whereby the crude oils would be divided into the same two categories present under the PRT regime with the first category including the Brent, Ekofisk, Flotta, Forties blends and the Statfjord oil. The reason for this separation would be due to the trading volumes. These are the blends that contribute to the global benchmark of Dated Brent,[22] and as a result they tend to be traded at a considerably higher frequency. This, in turn, can make the price discovery relatively easier than other crudes that are not sold as frequently.

The price for the non-arm's length crude sales would be determined by the arm's length sale of the same crude on the same date. For the crude oils in Category 1, this would be determined by the sale price of a single cargo, of the same crude, under the standard terms and conditions of the relevant terminal on the same loading date. For the Category 2 oils, the dating of the arm's length sale price would be more flexible[23] reflecting the reduced frequency of their physical trade.

Sale of crude oil is not the only possible avenue of generating income. Another income for a given project may be generated from the tariff payments. The tariff receipts would also be defined the same way as they are under the PRT system and would include all the payments that are paid in exchange for the use of a project's assets and for employing the relevant services associated with the use.[24]

The new regime would also either explicitly exclude the tariff incomes from the tax calculations, or, possibly because it would still be deemed as 'income,' provide a mechanism similar to that of a Tariff Receipt Allowance (TRA)[25] found under the PRT mechanism. Either approach would nonetheless behave as a protection from the tax liability for the tariff incomes.

From the outset, the introduction of such a mechanism may seem counter-intuitive as it not only introduces a layer of complexity – particularly in the form of a TRA-like mechanism – but can also have the potential to distort behaviour by artificially incentivising tariff contracts. However, as discussed in Chapter 2, the methods employed by the investors in assessing an investment potential in an upstream opportunity involves a number of variables including prices, costs and production, but not tariff incomes. That is, at least theoretically, tariff income could be completely taxed away without impacting an investor's investment decision process since the presence, or lack thereof, of that form of income does not directly influence the ultimate decision to invest.

Yet, a complete taxation of the tariff income is not advocated here. This is because the tax-exempt tariff income can create clear incentives for the asset holders to allow for third-party access for petroleum throughput.[26] Of course, this incentive in the form of a TRA-like mechanism can only be appropriate if the poor drafting[27] of the original legislation[28] can be avoided and clear allowances can be given for each separate use of assets even if the separate uses originate from a single field. This way, an asset owner can receive allowances for each of the separately charged third-party access activities.[29] Given that the third-party access is one of the primary issues identified in the Wood Report in preventing the realisation of the MER UK objective[30] this approach can go some way towards addressing this issue.[31] Therefore, even though the government may lose certain tax income as a result of these allowances in the short-term, this would be countered by the very likely larger tax incomes in the future from those smaller fields that can now produce due to the access to the existing third-party assets.

Compared to the treatment of a project's income, the treatment of the costs would not adopt the complexities of the PRT regime. Instead, any expenditure regardless of capital in nature or not, and irrespective of whether it is for a long-term asset or not,[32] would simply be deductible in full the year they are incurred, as long as they are incurred in relation to the project. As a result, the costs of buying land and constructing structures onshore, for example, would be excluded from the allowable costs.[33]

The treatment of the financing costs can possibly follow either the path provided within the systems of Allowance for Corporate Equity (ACE)[34] or of the Comprehensive Business Income Tax (CBIT).[35] Both of these mechanisms are designed to address the imbalance created between the treatment of the costs of debt and of equity in financing a project.[36] The former addresses this imbalance by allowing deductions both for the interest payments as costs of debt and for the opportunity cost of tying up equity in a particular project. The latter does not allow any deduction for either of them. This work advocates the adoption of the latter[37] for two reasons. First, the administrative burden and the difficulty in determining equity costs is large enough to discourage policymakers towards simpler alternatives.[38] Second, and perhaps more importantly, although the individual projects of the investors would be subject to the new fiscal regime promoted here, the investors would nonetheless also be subject to the rules under the standard corporation tax system applicable to all the companies registered in the UK. Under the current general corporation tax rules the interest payments incurred as a cost of financing which were obtained for the purposes of a company's trade are treated as an expense and deducted in full immediately.[39] As a result, allowing the same under the proposed mechanism would result in investors obtaining reliefs twice for the same costs incurred.

The interaction between the general corporation tax and the system advocated here would not be limited to the financing costs either. The tax payments under the new proposed system would be deductible for the standard corporation tax purposes in order to prevent the same income getting taxed twice. This is not unlike the current regime in place whereby the PRT payments are deductible for the RFCT purposes.[40] Additionally, similar to the currently existing regime, any reimbursements from the Treasury as a result of this new regime would also be treated as income for the general corporation tax calculations.[41]

When a project's cash flow for a given period is determined based on the methods described above, the mechanisms found in the theoretical Brown Tax would subsequently be applied. This is also the point where the proposed regime would fundamentally deviate from the PRT regime.

Accordingly, once the relevant cash flow of a given period is known the fixed tax rate would apply regardless of whether it is in a profit or a loss position. If it is in profit, the tax liability arising from that project would be the share of the positive cash flow equal to the fixed tax rate. If it is in a loss position in that period, then the investor would receive a reimbursement from the Treasury. The reimbursement would also be equal to the fixed tax rate portion of the negative cash flow.

In addition, if a given investor has multiple assets in the UKCS, the negative and positive tax liabilities from different upstream assets would be aggregated before determining the final liability for that period and the direction of the payment between the Treasury and the investor. This would not mean the costs from one field could be set against the other, but instead the aggregation would take place only after the tax liabilities are determined for each project separately. This is an important procedural distinction not only because the fixed tax rates may differ for each project[42] but also such an approach would prevent unique project dynamics from impacting other projects with different sets of parameters.

When taken holistically, this new system would certainly satisfy the Fiscal Review's objective of simplifying the existing fiscal regime.[43] Given that the proposed system would apply to the cash flow of each period, and that all the relevant costs are deductible in full immediately, it would not require any complex carry-forward or carry-back rules. As a consequence, it would be 'unnecessary for the authority to estimate the investor's discount rate.'[44] Therefore, the government can avoid creating complexities in the tax law. It would only have to set the definitions and rules for the tax rate, the components of the project cash flow – specifically, the project income and relevant expenditures, the rules governing the tariff allowances, and the rules for pooling together the tax liabilities of multiple projects. That is it.

This proposed new regime would not need to be designed on a blank page either. A good portion of these rules are already robustly present in the PRT regime. Relying on some of these existing rules would further reduce the administrative costs of developing the regime and of the relevant training of the staff. Furthermore, the simplicity of this regime would mean both the government and the investors can reasonably anticipate and predict the tax liability for each period, satisfying the 'fiscal stability' requirement of the Fiscal Review.[45]

This new system would also satisfy the 'fair return' objective of the Fiscal Review. This objective requires the state to retain a share of the economic rent while ensuring that the 'returns on the private investment needed to exploit these resources is sufficient to make extraction activity commercially attractive.'[46] Such a balance, then, is achieved with a system that adopts the guiding principles of a flexible fiscal mechanism that reduces the tax burden in tandem with maturity, and that takes into account the 'competitiveness,' 'prices and costs.'[47]

The proposed system certainly takes into account the prices and costs associated with a given upstream project. In fact, since it is a tax on the cash flows these are almost exclusively what it considers.[48] Furthermore, given that it directly targets the profitability of a project, it is extremely responsive to variations in oil prices, costs, field sizes and production profiles. As the profitability decreases, perhaps due to rising costs, declining prices, declining production, or any combination of these factors, the government's tax take, in absolute terms, would equally decrease and become negative as the profitability turns into loss. In the opposite circumstances, the government's tax take, in absolute terms, would increase. Therefore, it can unequivocally be concluded that this new regime would satisfy the requirements of the Fiscal Review's guiding principles and its objective of adapting to the 'changing economics of the UKCS.'[49] This means this new tax can apply equally robustly throughout the lifecycle of an upstream project from exploration and appraisal, through development and production, to decommissioning. In other words, by applying these same underpinning principles to each project the new system advocated here would do away with the need to have parallel fiscal regimes catering to mature fields and new assets separately with its multilayered complexity. Thus, additionally satisfying Sir Ian Wood's recommendation of a holistic approach that views exploration, development and production in unison.[50]

The proposed system behaves proportionally and therefore completely neutral. As such, it targets the economic rents, 'no more and no less.'[51] It behaves proportionally, and thus neutral, because the after tax rate of returns from a project would not be less than the pre-tax rate of returns since both the negative and positive cash flows are impacted by the same tax rate. Of course, this does not mean the government does not receive any tax. From the investor's perspective the new regime would certainly reduce the post-tax Net Present Values (NPVs) compared to their pre-tax values.[52] However, this would not induce any artificial influence on the investor's decisions by, for example, reordering the pre-tax rankings of the projects an investor may be considering and making one particular project suddenly more attractive over another after tax. This is because the new system would put the government in a position that is effectively similar to an equity partner. Although, it is important to note that this equity partnership position would not be of a company as would be under the theoretical Brown Tax but of individual projects instead. In this sense, the government would behave via the proposed tax regime as an equity partner in an upstream project answering a cash call in one period and retaining a share of the profits equivalent to tax rate in another.

It is readily acknowledged that the proposed regime is controversial. The controversy arises not least because the government can effectively be an equity partner without the legal rights to the decision-making process throughout the life of a project. This is because these legal rights are predominantly governed by private contractual arrangements called Joint Operating Agreements (JOAs)[53] to which the government is not a party. However, with the implementation of the Wood Review[54] this position of the government is now less clear-cut.

On the back of the Wood Review's recommendations,[55] the Oil and Gas Authority (OGA) as the new regulator,[56] is now able to not only require data from the investors[57] but also attend their meetings[58] as long as those meetings either 'relate to activities carried out under an offshore licence,' or more broadly, 'are relevant to the fulfilment' of the MER UK objective.[59] This means, as the Wood Review recommended,[60] the OGA can now attend the meetings of Operating Committees and the Technical Management Committees of the licence consortia. In other words, the OGA can now take part in the meetings that determine the course of actions to take with regard to a licenced asset.[61] Although such participation is without voting rights,[62] the OGA representative would presumably still be able to influence the outcomes of these meetings since the legislation obligates the OGA representative to 'participate' as opposed to observe.[63] Even if the OGA's participation was limited to an observatory role, its power to impose sanctions on the non-compliant entities[64] would nonetheless result in those meetings being inevitably influenced by the presence of the OGA.

Therefore, the new fiscal regime proposed herein, that in effect makes the government an equity partner to a project, does not jeopardise the government's position but rather compliments it. Through the OGA, the government is already positioning itself to act as an indirect equity partner in an upstream venture. The proposed regime merely supports this position by aligning the tax regime with this behaviour.

A related controversial issue concerns the payment made by the Treasury to the investor when the cash flow is in a negative position for a given period. This is certainly deemed as 'difficult to "sell" politically.'[65] Albeit important, this book does not concern itself with the associated political dimensions and solely focusses on the legal and economic aspects of the UKCS fiscal regime. Within these boundaries, it is important to highlight that the provisions for the government to pay the upstream investors under certain circumstances already exists. Under the Above the Line (ATL) mechanism, for example,[66] an investor can receive a certain amount as a direct payment from the HMRC if it is in an overall loss position and cannot reduce its corporation tax liability.[67] Similarly, under the Decommissioning Relief Deeds (DRDs),[68] the Treasury is obligated to reimburse the investor the difference, in each period, should the future fiscal position adversely change from the time of signing the DRD.[69] Therefore, it can be safely concluded that there are strong and recent precedents of the Treasury committing itself to pay, rebate or reimburse an investor in the petroleum sector. The proposed regime would remove the fragmented nature of this commitment and simplify it by applying it universally over the life of an upstream project in the UKCS.

In fact, the DRDs can be a successful model in alleviating the issue of investor confidence – or, lack thereof – in the government reimbursing a portion of losses in periods that are later in the field life while currently collecting a high share of the profits.[70] A contractual tool modelled after the DRDs can be instrumental in resolving this investor confidence problem because, as standardised contracts, the DRDs have been developed ‘to provide assurance’ to the investors on the reliefs they would receive when decommissioning.[71] The assurance would come from the fact that a DRD is a legally enforceable contract and as such an investor would have a judicial redress in the event of a breach of that contract by the government.[72]

Therefore, in order to provide assurances to the investors that the government will continue to honour its obligations under the proposed fiscal system, a contractual mechanism akin to the DRDs ought to be employed. Unlike the DRDs, however, it would not be limited to the decommissioning expenditures. It would instead provide for both the investor and the government to pay each other within a specific time frame[73] with the direction of the payments determined by each period’s cash flow. This would be in addition to the government’s commitment in the same contract to reimburse the difference if the future fiscal regime changes adversely. Such an approach would further support the ‘fiscal stability’ objective of the Fiscal Review.[74]

In this sense these mechanics of the proposed contractual arrangement of fiscal payments, and certainly of the DRDs, resemble a stand-alone contractual version of stabilisation clauses commonly found in economic development agreements, including the production sharing agreements used in the natural resources sectors.[75] These types of clauses aim to bring stability to the legal and regulatory environment surrounding such long-duration agreements.[76] Specifically, a variant referred to as ‘stabilisation clause *stricto sensu*’[77] aims to create this stable environment by preventing and/or precluding the applicability of future changes in the laws of the contracting State,[78] thereby freezing the existing laws and regulations in place at the time of the agreement.[79]

This concept of stabilisation was defined in an arbitration tribunal in 1988 as a ‘contract language which freezes the provisions of a national system of law chosen as the law of the contract as of the date of the contract, in order to prevent the application to the contract of any future alterations of this system.’[80] Viewed from this perspective, it becomes apparent that both the proposed contractual arrangement and the DRDs also share this aim. The latter effectively freezes the relevant specific allowances that are available for decommissioning as of 17 July 2013 when the Finance Act 2013 entered into force.[81] The former does the same but for both parties' cash-flow based tax payment commitments instead. Under both contractual arrangements any future adverse legislative changes result in reimbursements regardless.

However, these contractual arrangements raise the issue of sovereignty. Sovereignty may be an issue because freezing the relevant applicable laws at the time of the contract may be viewed as curtailing the future governments' legislative powers.[82] Yet, a number of international tribunal decisions consistently confirmed that the problem of incompatibility between the state sovereignty, on the one hand, and contractual limitations to it on the other, did not exist. As early as 1958, in the *Saudi Arabia v Aramco*[83] arbitration award it was stated that:

> By reason of its very sovereignty within its territorial domain, the State possesses the legal power to grant rights which it forbids itself to withdraw before the end of the [Agreement], with the reservation of the Clauses of the...Agreement relating to its revocation. Nothing can prevent a State, in the exercise of its sovereignty, from binding itself irrevocably by the provisions of [an Agreement] and from granting to the [counterparty] irretractable rights. Such rights have the character of acquired rights.[84]

Though this tribunal did not specifically comment on the compatibility of stabilisation clauses, it nonetheless highlighted that a State also exercises its sovereign rights in binding itself via a contract.

Such contractual arrangements are not limited to the natural resources sector either. Government bonds also have a similar sovereignty-limiting effect. This was expressed in the delivery of the *Revere Copper v Overseas Private Investment Corporation*[85] arbitral decision:

> Inevitably, in order to meet the aspirations of its people, the Government may for certain periods of time impose limits on the sovereign powers of the State, just as it does when it embarks on international financing by issuing long term government bonds on foreign markets...To suggest that for the purposes of obtaining foreign capital the Government could only issue contracts that were non-binding would be meaningless.[86]

The underlying point of this is that a State relies on its sovereignty when entering into a contractual relationship which may curb its future legislative powers just as much as it does when attempting to annul the same contract when the curtailment of those powers are actually realised. Therefore, as long as a government freely enters into such agreements, not obliging with its terms and commitments would not be acceptable under international investment law. This line of reasoning was emphasised in the delivery of the *Texaco v Libya*[87] award:

> There is no need to dwell at any great length on the existence and value of the principle under which a State may, within the framework of its sovereignty,

> undertake international commitments with respect to a private party. This rule results from the discretionary competence of the State in this area...
>
> [T]he State, by entering into an...agreement with any partner whatsoever, exercises its sovereignty whenever the State is not subject to duress and where the State has freely committed itself through an untainted consent.
>
> The result is that a State cannot invoke its sovereignty to disregard commitments freely undertaken through the exercise of this same sovereignty and cannot, through measures belonging to its internal order, make null and void the rights of the contracting party which has performed its various obligations under the contract.
>
> One should conclude that a sovereign State...cannot disregard the commitments undertaken by the Contracting State: to decide otherwise would in fact recognize that all contractual commitments undertaken by a State have been undertaken under a purely permissive condition on its part and are therefore lacking of any legal force and any binding effect...such a solution would gravely harm the credibility of States since it would mean that contracts signed by them did not bind them; it would introduce in such contracts a fundamental imbalance because in these contracts only one party – the party contracting with the State – would be bound. In law, such an outcome would go directly against the most elementary principle of good faith and for this reason it cannot be accepted.[88]

Therefore, it can be safely said that the stabilisation clauses are compatible with state sovereignty and do provide at least some protection for long-term investments.[89]

As a separate but interesting point, it was an accepted view among some scholars that despite removing the uncertainties for investors to a certain extent these types of clauses were not to be found in the developed Western world, presumably due to the differentials in the negotiation strengths of the parties.[90] Faber and Brown, for example, stated that,

> Once agreement has been reached on royalties, taxes, customs duties and related matters, much skill and ingenuity goes into drafting clauses to ensure that, in terms of the contract, no scrap of residual power is left to the government to increase its share of any available surplus by new fiscal measures not contemplated by the agreement... it has to be recognized that such contracts cannot be negotiated with any of the industrialized countries of the West. A mining or oil company would get short shrift if it sought from the British Government contractual guarantees binding Parliament for the future in terms, of a specific fiscal package.[91]

It must be surprising, not least to those commentators, therefore, that the UK is now using stand-alone contracts, the DRDs, which give the same effect as stabilisation clauses. From the international investment perspective, these contracts, and the ones proposed in this Chapter, seem to be compatible with the sovereignty of the British Parliament insofar as they emulate the stabilisation clauses.

However, there is also the public law dimensions that ought to be considered. Fortunately, the public law dimensions of this issue also support the position established by the international arbitration.

The relevant key aspect of public law concerns the contractual liability of the Crown. Since 1948,[92] there has been an avenue for obtaining judicial redress under a contract entered into with the Crown.[93] Contracting parties now have the possibility of suing the relevant government department[94] 'by ordinary process either in the High Court or in a county court.'[95] In such an event, the government departments, ministers and civil servants, in their capacity as the agents of the Crown,[96] would not be liable personally, as the liability would lie with the Crown.[97]

There are, of course, certain unique characteristics of the government as a contracting party that are different than private contracting parties, namely that the government also has a public duty. This means the government cannot enter into contracts that restrains the exercise of its public powers or restricts itself from carrying out its public duties.[98] This has been affirmed in the Queen's Bench in 1983,[99] and upheld in the House of Lords in 1985[100]:

> the Crown cannot put itself in a position where it is prevented from performing its public duty... If it seeks to make an agreement which has that consequence, that agreements is of no effect.[101]

This principle is rooted in a landmark decision by the King's Bench in 1921.[102] In order to understand why the proposed contractual arrangements, and by corollary the DRDs, don't fall within this restriction and how these arrangements differ in the ways in which the executive functions may be limited, a brief discussion on the facts of this landmark case is required.

During the First World War, ships from neutral countries could be detained in the ports of Britain. A steamship company from Sweden, a neutral country, obtained written assurances from the British government that their ship, *Amphitrite*, would not be detained when it brought approved cargo to the UK.[103] However, after unloading its cargo, and while loading a new cargo bound for Sweden at a different British port, the ship was detained.[104] The company subsequently sold the ship to avoid further losses, and sought damages from the Crown for breach of contract.[105] The judgment emphasised that because the 'welfare of the State' was at stake, the undertaking obtained was not a contract, and as such breach of contract would not be present:

> No doubt the Government can bind itself through its officers by a commercial contract, and if it does so it must perform it like anybody else or pay for damages for the breach. But this was not a commercial contract; it was an arrangement whereby the Government purported to give an assurance as to what its executive action would be in the future in relation to a particular ship in the event of her coming to this country with a particular kind of cargo. And that is, to my mind, not a contract for the breach of which damages can be sued for in a Court of law. It was merely an expression of intention to act in a particular

> way in a certain event. My main reason for so thinking is that it is not competent for the Government to fetter its future executive action, which must necessarily be determined by the needs of the community when the question arises. It cannot by contract hamper its freedom of action in matters which concern the welfare of the State.[106]

Viewed from this perspective, the proposed contractual arrangements[107] can also be seen as 'an expression of intention to act in a particular way in a certain event' – in this case, an adverse change in tax laws. However, the mechanisms of the proposed contracts, and of the DRDs, do not necessarily limit the future executive action, at least not in the same way as the assurances provided in the *Amphitrite* case. These contracts do not limit the future parliaments from enacting new tax legislation. Nor do they limit the scope of those future legislations since they still apply to the oil companies. These contractual arrangements instead add another set of prescribed actions rather than curbing any future laws or their application. That is, if any of the future tax legislations adversely affect the taxpayer compared to the position at the time of signing,[108] the contracts initiate a set of procedures that eventually lead to the reimbursement of the difference between two tax positions.

Furthermore, the application of this 'executive necessity' rule is not without its limits. This particular defence only 'avails the Crown where there is an implied term to that effect or that is the true meaning of the contract.'[109] This limitation has been affirmed by the Court of Appeal in 1976:[110]

> a public body, which is entrusted by Parliament with the exercise of powers for the public good, cannot fetter itself in the exercise of them. It cannot be estopped from doing its public duty. But that is subject to the qualification that it must not misuse its powers: and it is a misuse of power for it to act unfairly or unjustly towards a private citizen when there is no overriding public interest to warrant it.[111]

This means, the only way a future parliament can rescind on these contracts would be to raise the 'executive necessity' rule. However, it would be quite difficult to demonstrate an overriding public interest when the investors would still pay their tax liabilities under the new tax rules enacted in the future. Additionally, the reimbursements they subsequently may receive would not mean the net effect would be tax-free conduct of activities but rather a tax-paying position based on the rules in place at the time of signing the contract. Such a tax-paying position may consequently undermine any 'overriding public interest' test.

Legally, therefore, these proposed contractual arrangements – just like the DRDs – would be compatible with the sovereignty of the UK, and as such enforceable. This means, the investors would have a judicial redress in the event of a breach of this proposed contract by the government. Thus, these contracts would provide the certainty highly needed by the investors.

The only possible caveat to this may concern the source of the money for the reimbursements. Under the Crown's contracts, any payments due are paid from money provided by the Parliament.[112] If, exceptionally, the parliament disapproves a payment or otherwise does not provide funds for the payment, such payments, under certain circumstances, may not be enforced.[113] These circumstances are provided in *Churchward v R.*[114]

In the *Churchward* case the Lord Commissioners of the Admiralty, as agents of the Crown, covenanted with Joseph George Churchward to have vessels ready to carry mail between Dover, Calais and Ostend, if and when required, in exchange for an annual sum 'out of money to be provided by parliament.'[115] However, the Parliament did not provide funds for the payment,[116] nor had it authorised the Admiralty to enter into such an agreement in the first place.[117] Given that the 'Commissioners of the Admiralty could not possibly bind her Majesty by contracts inconsistent with, nor can her Majesty possibly do right to her subjects, in violation of the express provisions of an act of parliament,'[118] there was not an enforceable contract between the parties.[119]

What can be derived from this case is that unless the legislature approves from the outset[120] or it is provided for in a statute,[121] a contract involving the provisioning of funds by the Parliament will not have legal validity.[122]

Such a caveat, however, is not necessarily applicable to the circumstances of the DRDs. This is because not only the right for the Government to enter into such contracts is legislated[123] but also the obligation to pay investors the liabilities arising out of the DRDs.[124] Therefore, a similar legislation would be required to underpin the proposed contractual arrangements for the cash-flow-based tax payments.

With this caveat of dependency on underpinning legislation, the proposed contractual mechanism does provide a greater certainty than the frequent tinkering the tax regime has been undergoing. With this type of contract in place, the investors would have strong and legally enforceable assurances that they will receive negative taxes, particularly in later periods of a field life.

A final issue regarding the proposed tax reform concerns setting the appropriate tax rate. Given that the proposed system completely targets the economic rents, and therefore, targets that portion of the profits that are above what is required to entice the investor to continue to invest,[125] taxing that away, theoretically, should not artificially alter investment decisions and deter investments. As such, the tax rate can be set at 'very high' levels 'without deterring any projects.'[126] Thus, it can be inferred that the decision of the tax rate is largely a function of the extent of the desire on the government's part to be an equity partner.

Given that the desire for the government to be an equity partner may vary for each project, the proposed contractual arrangements can also be the vehicle for setting the tax rate rather than legislating it. This approach would provide the flexibility for the government to choose the degree of equity exposure it would like to be in for each individual project. This approach may be less simple than having a fixed legislated single rate but the flexibility it would provide for the government would outweigh the additional, albeit little, complexity multiple tax rates would create. Under this approach the government would no longer behave like an equity partner at the same rate for all of the projects but can choose its exposure based on the risk dynamics of each project. For higher risk projects, for example, the government can limit its exposure by agreeing to a lower tax rate, and vice versa.

Therefore, the reforms proposed herein would provide flexibility not only in terms of responsiveness to the changes in oil prices and costs but also in its tax rates applicable to each project. It would still be significantly simpler than the current regime in place while continuing to satisfy the Treasury's objective of capturing the economic rents.

Although what is being proposed herein is unique, it certainly is not the first time a tax regime has been proposed that has attempted to adopt a modified version of the system put forward by E C Brown. Both Australia and Norway have considered mechanisms based on the Brown Tax, though their versions were significantly different than the one proposed in this work.

5.2.1. The Australian approach

The Australian government announced in its 2010–2011 Budget its proposal for introducing Resource Super Profits Tax (RSPT)[127] applicable to upstream resource extraction projects from 1 July 2012.[128] This was in response to the report by the then Secretary to the Treasury, Dr Ken Henry (the Henry Review) presenting 138 recommendations to the overall Australian tax system.[129] The proposal, however, was shelved due to a backlash particularly from the mining industry.[130]

Had it been implemented, the proposal would have seen the RSPT replacing the existing tax regime, Petroleum Resource Rent Tax (PRRT). Under this new tax scheme, a 40% flat rate tax would have been applicable to 'super profits' arising from projects.[131]

The Henry Review described the recommended tax as:

> A uniform resource rent tax [that] should be set at 40 per cent. It would use an allowance for corporate capital system, with taxable profit associated with a resource project equal to net income less an allowance for undeducted expenses or unused losses. The allowance rate would be set by the long-term government bond rate, as the government would share in the risks of projects by providing a loss refund if the tax value of expenditure is otherwise unable to be used.[132]

The scheme proposed in the subsequent Budget largely adopted this recommendation. The proposed regime allowed for exploration expenditures to be deductible in full the year they were incurred while the capital expenditures were subject to declining balance depreciation.[133] Any losses arising from a project in a given financial year were to be first offset against the RSPT profits from that project, then against the RSPT profits from other projects the same company was involved in.[134] If any losses remained, then they would have been carried forward at the risk-free interest rate[135] to be offset against the future incomes. If at the end of the project there losses still remained, the Australian Government guaranteed to 'credit firms for the tax value of their extraction and exploitation costs' and would 'even refund that credit when a project winds up.'[136] The uplift of the carried-forward expenses at the risk-free rate would effectively have made the producer a lender to the government at the long-term government bond rate, though the loan would certainly have been under a wholly different legal framework than the bond market.

The treatment of losses under the RSPT intended to address the structural issues present in the existing PRRT regime.[137] Under the PRRT system, the applicable tax rate on project profits was also 40%. Capital expenditures, regardless of whether they were incurred for exploration, development or production, were deductible 100% first-year[138] basis.[139] Losses were also carried forward with an uplift factor varying between 5% and 15% over the Long-Term Borrowing Rate (LTBR). These, however, did not apply to losses arising from abandonment costs – though the latter was still subject to credit.[140]

At the time there were 10 different classes of deductible expenditures, though broadly speaking the undeducted exploration expenditures were being carried forward with an uplift of LTBR+15%, and the undeducted development and operating expenditures at LTBR+5%.[141] Therefore, the 15 and 5 percentages could be viewed as risk premiums attached over the LTBR.[142] However, the risk premiums could inevitably vary from project to project as a function of the likelihoods of sufficient future profits to cover the losses carried forward. Therefore, there was a possibility that such fixed risk premiums could be either under- or over-sufficient in taking account of this uncertainty.

It is this structural issue that was being addressed by the RSPT via full guarantee of reimbursements at the end of the field life. Thanks to this feature, the uplift rate set at the long-term government bond rate, and only at that rate, was deemed appropriate because the deductions were 'certain to be received by the firm at some point in time with guaranteed full compensation for any delay in receiving them.'[143] Of course, this was only true to the extent that the Australian government would have stayed true to its commitment by the time the end of field life was reached. Otherwise, this was introducing a sovereign risk that was not necessarily being captured by the long-term borrowing rate.[144] Having said that, it would have been questionable to what extent such sovereign risk may have materialised given that the 40% rate under PRRT was introduced in 1987[145] and had not changed since.

The proposed RSPT was claimed to be built on the Brown Tax as its theoretical foundation.[146] However, a closer inspection revealed that the reimbursements under the RSPT did not happen annually as would have been the case under the Brown Tax, but rather at the end of the project life. Until then, the negative tax liabilities were instead proposed to be carried forward at the LTBR. In this sense, therefore, the RSPT was closer to the theoretical Resource Rent Tax

(RRT)[147] under which the negative cash flows were also carried forward at a specific threshold rate.[148] This threshold rate, though, would have been set not at the LTBR but at the investor's discount rate to avoid disincentivisation.[149] It is therefore evident that despite the claims that the proposed RSPT was built on the theoretical Brown Tax,[150] it was significantly closer in resemblance to the RRT instead.

5.2.2. The Norwegian approach

A similar approach was also observable in Norway. At the turn of the millennium, the Norwegian Ministry of Finance released a report on the country's petroleum tax regime.[151] Some of the reforms that were proposed in that report were then duly passed in the subsequent year.[152] Although the report was advocating a neutral cash-flow-based tax system like the Brown Tax it nonetheless did not recommend payments of negative taxes to the investors.[153] Instead, it proposed a regime very close to the RRT system[154] albeit without the immediate deduction for capital costs. As a result, the proposed regime was not exactly the application of the RRT regime either as it was recommending the depreciation of those costs together with an uplift.[155] Consequently, the development costs, for example, could be depreciated at a maximum of 16.67% per year.[156]

In 2013, the Norwegian government further modified the uplift, cutting it from 7.5% to 5.5% over four years.[157] As previously discussed in Section 3.4.2.3 unless the uplift rate is aligned with the investor's discount rate there would inevitably be distortions.[158] Regardless, what is important for the purposes of the discussions in this work is that both the Australian government and the Norwegian government did consider a neutral cash-flow-based tax system loosely modelled on the Brown Tax. Yet, they both decided to adopt regimes far closer to the RRT instead, not least because of the political pressures, particularly in the case of Australia. For Norway, an additional reasoning was given as the possibility of the cash-flow tax not constituting a creditable foreign tax for the US investors.[159] Mechanisms that allow receiving a tax credit as opposed to a tax deduction at an investor's home jurisdiction can also be an important determinant in investment decision. Therefore, presence of such mechanisms would be an important consideration in fiscal system design in order to avoid disincentivisation.

This avoidance of disincentivisation can particularly be acute for the US investors as obtaining a tax credit can be quite advantageous at home, though the US rules governing creditability are complex and multilayered.[160] Therefore, it is understandable that rather than creating a possible disincentive the Norwegians erred on the side of caution and adopted a regime that instead resembled the RRT together with a form of Allowance for Corporate Equity (ACE).[161]

5.2.3. The new system without the Australian and Norwegian issues

These issues that forced the modification of both the Australian and Norwegian proposals closer towards the RRT mechanism are less of a concern for the proposed reforms for the UK's tax regime. This is because the rules of the proposed new system builds on those of the existing PRT regime. The US Tax Court has already held that the PRT payments in the UK are creditable in the US as it satisfies the US income tax and creditability requirements.[162] Specifically the Court stated that

> The purpose, administration, and structure of PRT indicate that PRT constitutes an income or excess profits tax in the US sense. The provisions of PRT include in the tax base, with limited exceptions, income earned from North Sea-related activity and permit allowances, reliefs, and exemptions that effectively compensate for nondeductibility of certain oil company expenses, particularly interest.

Although a deduction is not allowed for interest expenses related to North Sea operations, uplift, oil, safeguard and tariff receipts allowances provide sufficient relief to offset for the nonallowance of a deduction for interest expense.[163]

Although these latter measures may be viewed as 'crude' in substituting for, or even mimicking interest payments, the Court has rejected 'these labels as merely argumentative and as without merit.'[164] Therefore, the mechanism similar to a TRA-allowance advocated for the new regime can then also be viewed as a substitute for not allowing interest payments regardless of how 'crude' that substitution is. Therefore, it can be argued that the proposed new regime would fall within the tax creditability regime in the US.[165]

The political pressures concerning the payments to investors by the UK would not be a major issue either. This is because there is already an established commitment of the Treasury to pay the upstream investors under certain circumstances. The proposed fiscal system in this Chapter just simplifies and broadens those circumstances, and as such is not necessarily as controversial as it first appears. The government, via the OGA, has already been mandated to join in the decision-making process of the investors in developing upstream assets. It is therefore complimentary to this position that the fiscal regime aligns the government with the other equity partners.

Moreover, the commitment of the government through the proposed contractual mechanism, as it already does under the DRDs, would provide both the assurances to the investors and the flexibility to the government to decide for each project the level of equity partnership it wants to commit itself to. All this, without jeopardising the UK's sovereignty.

The proposed fiscal reform, therefore, would certainly satisfy the objectives set out in the Fiscal Review without falling foul of the parliamentary sovereignty. At least theoretically, the assessment confirms that the proposed regime would be proportional and neutral, thus targeting the economic rents. However, as was pointed out in the preceding Chapter,[166] 'a deeper understanding of the way the tax system actually functions cannot be obtained without analysing model fields.'[167] The next section, therefore, analyses model fields in its evaluation of the proposed reforms to the UK's tax regime applicable to the petroliferious trade.

5.3. Model field analysis of the proposed new system

As was the case in the preceding Chapter, the evaluation of the proposed new regime also follows the guiding principles provided in the Fiscal Review. Consequently, the analysis employs the same set of assumptions and the same suite of model fields and associated variables that reflect the typical operating conditions in the UKCS as those that were used in the preceding Chapter. This approach not only ensures consistency but also allows for comparison. For simplicity, the analysis in this Section uses one fixed tax rate of 60% and it specifically employs the discounted cash-flow method, or DCF, that is commonly used both by the industry in assessing investment,[168] and by the arbitrators in determining the value of assets for arbitral awards.[169] As was the case in Chapter 4, this method relies both on deterministic and stochastic approaches.

Since the assumptions and the operational conditions for the suite of models employed are the same as those in Chapter 4, the payback period[170] at the pre-tax level will also naturally be the same. That is, for a project that commences its development programme in 2018 the payback is achieved in 2021 under the 50 mmbbls base case scenario, and in 2020 for the other two base case scenarios. This means, in 2 to 3 years' time the accumulated revenues would equal the investment expended under the three field scenarios.[171]

Similarly, the maximum cash exposures, in nominal terms, are expected to be \$241m, \$203m and \$137m for the large, medium and small oil field base case scenarios, respectively. The projected values for the IRRs and the P/I ratios for the base case scenario are illustrated in Chart 5.2 below. The IRRs indicate the average returns expected to be generated by each of these base case opportunities. As anticipated, they decline in a linear fashion in tandem with the decline in the reserves holding everything else constant. Also as expected, the P/I ratios

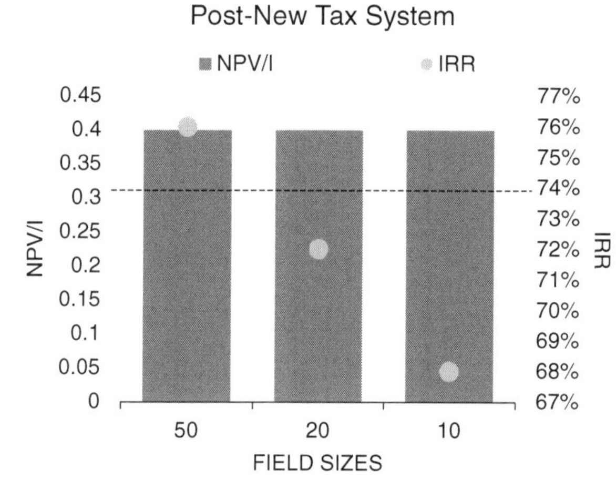

Chart 5.2 Post-new tax system real P/I ratios & real IRRs under the base case scenario

are uniform at 0.4 across all three field sizes. That is, at 60% tax rate an investor would expect to make 4 pence for each pound invested in these projects. Since it is above 0.3, under all the base case scenarios the investors would go ahead with their investment plans. This means, the sensitivity analyses can be carried out on all of the base case scenarios to ascertain the behaviour of the tax regime.

Chart 5.2 makes it clear that the proposed fiscal regime seems to generate the same level of returns for each pound invested regardless of the size of the fields. However, it does not provide information whether there is any regressivity present with respect to oil prices or costs. To ascertain this therefore Chart 5.3 below illustrates the results of the sensitivity analysis.

It is evident from the Charts 5.3a–c in each of the reserve sizes modelled, at all three oil price levels and for each per barrel cost levels the government's tax take remains fixed at 60%. This means, the headline rate becomes the actual tax take of the government. Thus, the proposed new regime is perfectly proportional. That is, the tax captures the same portion of the profits regardless of the changes in oil prices, costs or field sizes *ceteris paribus*.

At first this result may seem puzzling, given that the results in the previous Chapter have largely been concerned with regressive and progressive elements in ascertaining the extent of the alignment of the existing fiscal regime with capturing economic rents.[172] However, a careful examination of the criteria laid out in Section 2.5 will reveal that the real concern is the avoidance of regressive *effect*, specifically the attainment of economic efficiency, and the associated concept of neutrality. For a fiscal mechanism to be economically efficient, and therefore target economic rents, it ought to be sensitive broadly to the variations in field sizes, oil prices and costs.[173] As such, it will not alter the investment decisions, or the rankings of the investment opportunities, and thus be neutral. Thus, it is the proportional *effect* that ensures the neutrality.

It is important to emphasise that the proposed regime is not only proportional in terms of the fixed rate it imposes but it also has a proportional *effect*. That is, unlike the VAT, for example, where the fixed rate has a regressive effect as it claims a larger portion of income from those who earn less,[174] the proposed regime maintains its proportionality for all income levels, including losses. This is precisely because of the built-in reimbursement mechanism that effectively makes the government an equity partner. By sharing both the upside and the downside of the annual cash flow, the government aligns itself perfectly with the project dynamics which particularly include the uncertainties and the changes in the oil prices, costs and field sizes. As a result, the government's position via the fiscal regime becomes proportional irrespective of the changes to these variables. Hence the perfect proportionality results of the deterministic modelling of the proposed regime.

This position is also supported when all the possible outcomes for each variable are taken into account. This stochastic analysis employs the Monte Carlo method thereby incorporating the chances of occurrence for each value of each variable. The stochastic analyses are carried out on the same variables as in the previous Chapter. As was the case there, initially each of the variables were treated separately as stochastic while holding the others constant at their mean values. This is done in

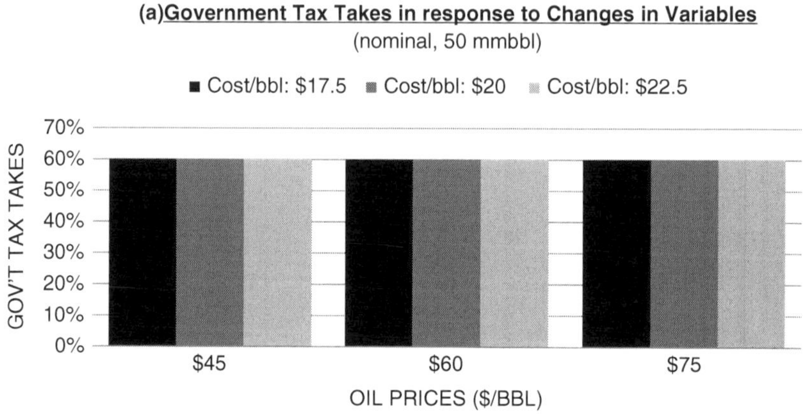

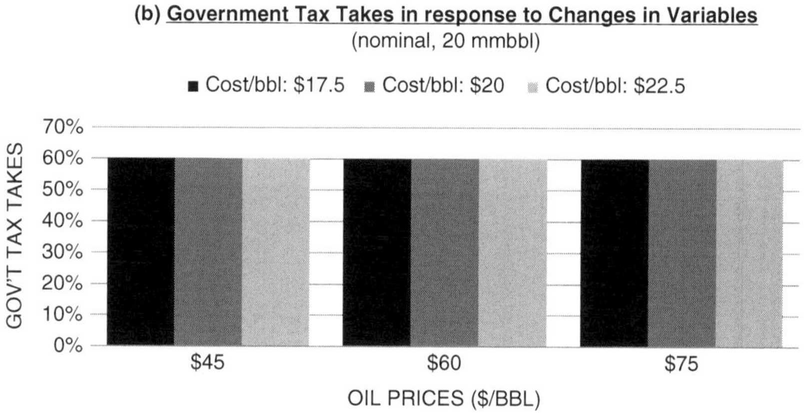

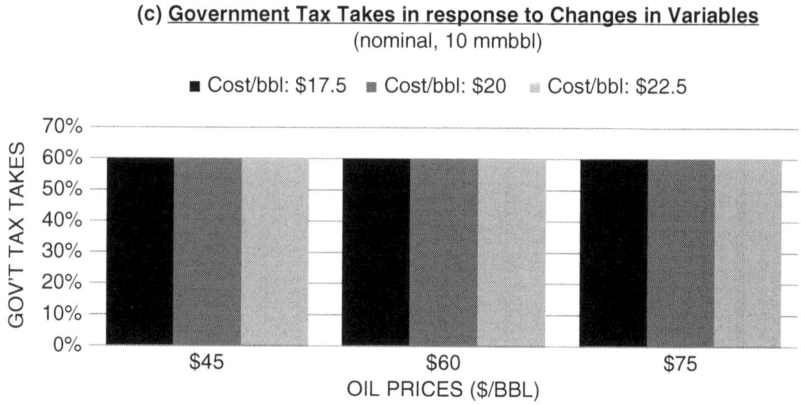

Chart 5.3 Response of the proposed tax regime

order to tease out the degree of risks the proposed new tax system creates with respect to each variable. This is then followed by a simulation where all the variables are stochastic simultaneously which incorporates the extreme possibilities with the smallest probabilities to ascertain the relevant magnitudes of the impacts of all the variables.

Accordingly, the statistics of the pre- and post-tax returns at 10% cost of capital when oil prices are stochastic are shown in Table 5.1.[175]

The statistics in Table 5.1 show that under the mean-reverting oil price modelling [176] the tax regime reduces the mean expected return by about 60%[177] from a pre-tax mean expected return of $525 million[178] to a post-tax mean expected return of $219 million. This is a clear indication towards confirming the preceding conclusions of both the theoretical and deterministic analysis that the proposed new tax regime reduces the expected returns for all investors at the headline rate. Since the proposed new regime is effectively making the state an equity partner in the modelled project, it is expected that the simulation would conclude that the state and the investor would share the risks at a level roughly equal to the headline tax rate.

The extent of this risk sharing between the investor and the state can be measured through the widths of the probability distributions.[179] The post-tax range of outcomes – measured as the total values between the minimum and maximum in Table 5.1 – is about 40%[180] of pre-tax range, confirming the expectations. This means, the proposed regime reduces the risks for the investor as much as the tax rate, very much like any other equity partner's share albeit the share is determined by the tax rate instead. As has been argued in Chapter 4, the current regime in place shares the upside and downside of petroliferous trade in a rather convoluted way via the loss deduction, carry-forward and allowance mechanisms. The proposed regime instead clarifies this position by making it simple, transparent and predictable.

This risk sharing position can also be seen via an alternative measure of risk. As discussed in the preceding Chapter, the coefficient of variability[181] is another measure of risk that allows for comparison between two distributions with different

Table 5.1 Monte Carlo results for stochastic oil prices

	Pre-Tax	*Post-Tax*
Trials	10,000	10,000
Base Case	$438	$175
Mean	$549	$219
Standard Deviation	$439	$176
Variance	$192,895	$30,863
Coeff. of Variation	0.8005	0.8005
Minimum	'-$445	'-$178
Maximum	$1,811	$724

NPV @ 10% Discount Rate, $million, nominal.

means.[182] As was the case in the analysis in Chapter 4, the pre- and post-tax distributions do have different means so this measure of risk may be more appropriate in this analysis. Based on the coefficients of variability in Table 5.1, there is not a risk differential between pre-tax and post-tax positions. This uniformity of coefficient levels at 0.8005 indicates a proportional taxation effect. That is, the tax regime does not at all impact the overall risks of the project. Thus, the state only shares the risks to the extent of the tax rate without impacting the project's risk profile. This certainly confirms the arguments laid out in this Chapter that this new tax regime is completely neutral.

It may be argued though that this confirmation derived from Table 5.1[183] may hold at least insofar as the oil prices are concerned. Yet the above conclusions hold true for all the variables when they are modelled individually stochastic.[184] To avoid repetition of the arguments, therefore, the subsequent discussion instead looks at the modelling results when all the variables are stochastic. Accordingly, the statistics of the pre- and post-tax returns at 10% cost of capital when all the variables are stochastic are shown in Table 5.2.[185]

The results derived from the set of statistics in Table 5.2 mirror those derived from Table 5.1 in that the proposed tax regime reduces the mean expected return also by about 60%[186] from a pre-tax mean expected return of $694 million[187] to a post-tax of $278 million.

This result is certainly expected particularly because the proposed new regime is effectively making the state an equity partner in the project. As a result, the expected outcome of the simulation would be that the state and the investors would share the risks at levels equal to the headline tax rate. The extent of the risk sharing in Table 5.2 confirms these expectations as it shows that the range of post-tax outcomes is again 40%[188] of the pre-tax range. This means, the proposed regime reduces the risks for the investor as much as the headline tax rate.

The other measure of risks also reveals a similar result. Based on the coefficients of variability in Table 5.2 there is again not a risk differential between pre-tax and post-tax positions. This uniformity of coefficient levels, at 1.08, indicates a

Table 5.2 Monte Carlo results for all variables stochastic

	Pre-Tax	*Post-Tax*
Trials	10,000	10,000
Base Case	$438	$175
Mean	$694	$278
Standard Deviation	$760	$304
Variance	$577,292	$92,367
Coeff. of Variation	1.09	1.09
Minimum	'-$755	'-$302
Maximum	$9,766	$3,906

NPV @ 10% Discount Rate, $million, nominal.

proportional taxation effect. That is, the tax regime does not impact the overall risks of the project. Thus, the state only shares the risks to the extent of the tax rate without impacting the project's risk profile at all. This is true even when all the variables are modelled as stochastic, incorporating even the most extreme circumstances with the lowest chances of occurrences.

When viewed from the risk perspective, the Monte Carlo analysis reveals that the regime responds in the same way to the changes in oil prices, costs and reserve sizes separately and simultaneously: the state shares the risks of a given project at the tax rate without increasing or decreasing the overall project risk. This means, irrespective of a given project's inherent risks, the tax regime does not introduce a new set of risks or artificially favours a specific type of projects over others by changing their risk dynamics. Thus, it is completely neutral.

This Chapter therefore advocates a new tax regime that allows the principles of the Fiscal Review to guide its design in achieving the Treasury's objective of capturing the economic rents. For the Treasury, implementation of this proposal can be a correction of a missed opportunity. This missed opportunity has risen despite correctly identifying the criteria and the principles required to establish a robust fiscal regime for the UK's petroliferous trade. Unfortunately, it has not recommended a reform that complied with those principles and the criteria. This new regime proposed herein addresses that deficiency directly and proposes a system that takes those criteria and principles to their natural conclusion. In order to realise the MER UK objective the Treasury requires a robust fiscal reform that targets the economic rents. This Chapter puts forward that reform.

Notes

1 Though please note that retrospective application is possible in the UK but there is a presumption against retrospective effect. This presumption is well established in the criminal law – see, for example, Article 7 of European Convention of Human Rights and Fundamental Freedoms [1953]. This presumption can also be found in tort – see *Phillips v Eyre* (1870) LR 6 QB 1 at 23: 'The court will not ascribe retrospective force to new laws affecting rights unless by express words necessary implication that such was the intention of the legislature.' For the new tax regime put forward in this chapter, retrospective effect would not be the intention for the reasons given above.

2 See Section 4.1 for a discussion of the current system in place.

3 E Carry Brown, '*Business-Income Taxation and Investment Incentives*' in L A Metzler (ed), *Income, Employment and Public Policy: Essay in Honor of Alvin H. Hansen* (New York, W W Norton & Co, Inc 1948)

4 Please note 'resource rents' and 'economic rents' are used interchangeably in the literature.

5 Brown (n 3)

6 James Edward Meade, '*The Structure and Reform of Direct Taxation*' Report of a Committee chaired by Professor J. E. Meade, The Institute for Fiscal Studies (George Allen & Unwin Ltd 1978) Ch 12

7 These terms are used interchangeably throughout this work.

8 Original proposal by Brown (n 3) and Meade (n 6) were for the tax regime to apply to corporate income and not at a project level.

9 Alexander G Kemp, *Petroleum Rent Collection around the World* (The Institute for Research on Public Policy 1987) Ch 4
10 These costs would not be allowable because doing so would amount to a double deduction since all the costs are already allowable immediately in full. See Boadway R and Keen M, 'Theoretical perspectives on resource tax design' in P Daniel, M Keen, and C McPherson (eds) The Taxation of Petroleum and Minerals: Principles, Problems and Practice (Routledge 2010) 32
11 Meade (n 6) Ch 12; a discussion on capital gains is beyond the scope of this work.
12 See the discussion in Chapter 2 for proportionality.
13 R Garnaut and A C Ross, *Taxation of Mineral Rents* (Clarendon Press 1983) Ch 7
14 Kemp (n 9) Ch 4
15 Garnaut and Ross (n 13) Ch 7, and Kemp (n 9) Ch 4
16 Garnaut and Ross (n 13) Ch 7, 100
17 See Sections 2.3, 3.2 and 3.5
18 See Section 3.4
19 This is also the case under the PRT regime. See Section 3.4
20 Which would include 'appropriation' as it does under the PRT regime.
21 See Section 3.4.2.1 and Box 3.4
22 This is a 'benchmark assessment of the price of physical, light North Sea crude oil. The term "Dated Brent" refers to physical cargoes of crude oil in the North Sea that have been assigned specific dates…It is a critical component of the Brent Complex, which includes the trading of physically delivered oil like Dated Brent and cash BFOE (Brent-Forties-Oseberg-Ekofisk), as well as financially settled derivatives like Brent Futures, Contracts for Differences (CfDs), Dated-to-Frontlines (DFLs) and a variety of other derivatives.' Platts, '*Dated Brent*' (McGraw Hill Financial 2015) <http://www.platts.com/price-assessments/oil/dated-brent> accessed 17 August 2015
23 As is the case under the PRT regime. See Section 3.4.2.1 and Box 3.4
24 These would exclude the financing and deballasting costs just as the PRT system does. Oil Taxation Act 1983, s 6 provide the relevant provisions for the PRT system.
25 See Section 3.4.2.2
26 See the discussion under Section 3.4 for the concept of petroleum throughput and the Oil Taxation Act 1983, Sch 3 para 1(2) for the legal definition.
27 See *BP Oil Development Ltd v Commissioners of Inland Revenue [1992] STC 28, 64 TC 498 (Ch D)* for the issues surrounding the poor definition of 'throughput'.
28 Oil Taxation Act 1983, Sch 3
29 In *BP v CIR* (n 27) for example, transportation from the originating field to the asset and temporary storage was charged separately than various processing activities, which were, in turn, themselves were charged separately.
30 See Section 2.1
31 In fact, this reasoning is also behind the drive to include the tariff expenditures within the Investment Allowance and Cluster Allowance mechanisms found within the current Supplementary Charge pillar. See the proposed regulations: The Investment Allowance and Cluster Area Allowance (Investment Expenditure) Regulations 2016
32 Oil Taxation Act 1975 s 4 together with Oil Taxation Act 1983 ss 1 and 3 make this distinction. For the details of the relevant treatments under the PRT regime see Section 3.4.2.3 above.
33 This is also the case under the PRT system. See Oil Taxation Act 1975, s 3(4)(b)–(c)
34 A detailed discussion of the ACE system is beyond the scope of this paper. For a brief treatment see Box 3.2
35 A detailed discussion of the CBIT system is beyond the scope of this paper. For a brief treatment see Box 3.2
36 See Box 3.2 for a detailed discussion on this imbalance.
37 This is also the case under the PRT system. See Oil Taxation Act 1975, s 3(4)(b)–(c)

38 Michael P Devereux and Harold Freeman, '*A General Neutral Profits Tax*' (1991) 12 (3) Fiscal Studies 1, 3
39 Corporation Tax Act 2009, s 307 together with s 297
40 Corporation Tax Act 2010, s 299
41 This is also similar to the existing PRT-RFCT interaction under Corporation Tax Act 2010, s 301. For a detailed discussion of the interaction between the existing pillars see Section 3.5
42 The issue of setting an 'appropriate' tax rate is discussed further below.
43 This was also emphasised by the Chancellor Osborne in his Budget 2014 speech. See George Osborne, 'Chancellor George Osborne's Budget 2014 Speech' (Speech, HM Treasury, 2014)
44 Garnaut and Ross (n 13) Ch 7
45 HM Treasury, '*Driving Investment: a plan to reform the oil and gas fiscal* regime' (Report, HM Treasury December 2014) and Osborne (n 43)
46 HM Treasury (n 45) Box 4.A
47 HM Treasury (n 45) Box 4.A
48 In addition to the prices and costs it also takes into account the production levels.
49 HM Treasury (n 45) and Osborne (n 43)
50 Sir Ian Wood, '*UKCS Maximising Recovery Review: Final Report*' (Report, 25 February 2014)
51 Garnaut and Ross (n 13) Ch 7 p 100
52 Though not the rate of returns. For a discussion on the difference between the NPV and the rate of return see Section 2.4.1.6
53 A detailed discussion on the Joint Operating Agreements, and on their legal status, is beyond the scope of this work. However, for a succinct explanation and analyses see Scott Styles, '*Joint Operating Agreements*' in G Gordon, J Paterson and E Usenmez (eds), *Oil and Gas Law: Current Practice and Emerging Trends* (2nd Ed, DUP 2011)
54 Wood (n 50) See Section 3.5 for a detailed discussion on the Wood Review.
55 Wood (n 50) 3.3 Recommendation 3.iv Operating and Technical Management Committees are established within the Joint Operating Agreements for the management of the project and the relationship between the JOA parties. A detailed discussion on these Committees, however, is beyond the scope of this work. For a discussion on these see Styles (n 53)
56 HC Deb 6 November 2014 vol 587, cols 52–53WS (Davey). Oil and Gas Authority Limited, Registered in England and Wales Company Number: 09666504. 100% of the shares are owned by the Secretary of State for Energy and Climate Change. The sole director of the Company is Stephen John Charles Speed, an employee of DECC, and the Company Secretary is Quayseco Limited, a law firm.
57 Energy Act 2016 s 34
58 Energy Act 2016 s 39
59 Energy Act 2016 s 37
60 Energy Act 2016 s 39 as recommended in the Wood Report.
61 Energy Act 2016 s 39
62 Energy Act 2016 s 39 does not allow for the OGA representative to vote.
63 The wording in the Energy Act 2016 s 39 is 'participate'.
64 Energy Act 2016 s 39(4) together with Chapter 5
65 Garnaut and Ross (n 13) Ch 7 p 100
66 See Section 3.2.3.1.3 for a detailed discussion on this mechanism.
67 Corporation Tax Act 2009, s 104N as inserted by Finance Act 2013, Sch 15
68 See Section 3.2.3.1.4
69 Finance Act 2013, s 80 read together with Cl 5 of DRD. A copy of a model DRD (hereinafter, Model Decommissioning Relief Deed) can be obtained from HM

Treasury, '*Decommissioning Relief Deeds: increasing tax certainty for oil and gas investment in the UK continental shelf*' (Consultation, HM Treasury 9 July 2012)
70 Garnaut and Ross (n 13) Ch 7
71 HM Treasury, 'Budget 2012' (Report, HM Treasury 21 March 2012) 2.125
72 Finance Act 2013 Part 2
73 Under the DRDs the payments are to take place within 60 or 120 days depending on whether the relevant field is a PRT-liable one or not.
74 HM Treasury (n 45) and Osborne (n 43)
75 Timothy B Hansen, '*The Legal Effect Given Stabilization Clauses in Economic Development Agreements*' (1987–1988) 28 Virginia Journal of International Law 1015
76 Bertrand Montembault, 'The Stabilisation of State Contracts Using the Example of Oil Contracts. A return of the Gods of Olympia?' (2003) 6 International Business Law Journal 593, 596
77 A F M Maniruzzaman, 'Some reflections on stabilisation techniques in international petroleum, gas and mineral agreements' (2005) 4 International Energy Law & Taxation Review 96, 97
78 Talal A Q Al-Emadi, '*Stabilisation clauses in international joint venture agreements*' (2010) 3 International Energy Law Review 54
79 Thomas W Waelde and George Ndi, '*Stabilizing International Investment Commitments: International Law Versus Contract Interpretation*, (1996) 31 Texas International Law Journal 215
80 *Amoco International Finance Corporation v Islamic Republic of Iran* (1988) 27 ILM 1314 (United States Claims Tribunal, Partial Award)
81 Model Decommissioning Relief Deed Cl 1.1
82 George R Delaume, *'The Proper Law of State Contracts Revisited'* (Spring 1997) 12 ICSID Review-FILJ 25
83 *Saudi Arabia v Arabian American Oil Company (Aramco) Arbitration Tribunal* (23 August 1958) 27 ILR 117–233
84 *Saudi Arabia v Aramco* (n 83) 168
85 *Revere Copper and Brass, Incorporated v Overseas Private Investment Corporation* (American Arbitration Association, 24 August 1978) 17 ILM 1321–1383
86 *Revere Copper and Brass* (n 85) 1342–1343
87 *Texaco Overseas Petroleum Company / California Asiatic Oil Company v Government of the Libyan Arab Republic* (1978) 17 ILM 1–37
88 *Texaco v Libya* (n 87) 23–24, 31. A similar views were held in other Tribunals as well. See, for example, *Revere Copper and Brass* (n 85); *AGIP Company v Popular Republic of the Congo* (International Centre for Settlement of Investment Disputes, 30 November 1979) 21 ILM 726–739; and *The Government of the State of Kuwait v The American Independent Oil Company (Aminoil)* (The Arbitration Tribunal, 24 March 1982) 21 ILM 976–1052
89 Please note that a detailed discussion on the variants of stabilisation clauses and an analysis of the extent of which such clauses are effective in providing investment protection are beyond the scope of this work.
90 Wolfgang Peter, *'Stabilization Clauses in State Contracts'* (1998) 8 International Business Law Journal 875, 887
91 Mike Faber and Roland Brown, 'Changing the Rules of the Game: Political Risk, Instability and Fairplay in Mineral Concession Contracts,' (Jan 1980) 2 Third World Quarterly 100
92 With the Crown Proceedings Act 1947 coming into force.
93 Crown Proceedings Act 1947 s 1
94 Or, in the event that there is not a department named, the Attorney-General.
95 Anthony Bradley and Keith Ewing, *Constitutional and Administrative Law* (13th ed, Pearson 2013) 771

96 This was affirmed in *Town Investments Ltd v Department of the Environment* [1978] AC 359 (HL) at 381
97 *Macbeth v Haldimand* (1786) 1 Term Rep 172, 99 ER 1036 (KB)
98 Colin Turpin and Adam Tomkins, *British Government and the Constitution* (7th ed, Cambridge University Press 2011)
99 *R v IRC, ex p Preston* [1983] 2 All ER 300 (QB)
100 *Preston, Re sub nom R v IRC, ex p Preston* [1985] AC 835, [1985] 2 All ER 327, [1985] 2 WLR 836 (HL) at 862
101 *R v IRC, ex p Preston* (n 99) 306g
102 *Rederiaktiebolaget Apmhitrite v R* [1921] 3 KB 500 (KBD)
103 *Rederiaktiebolaget v R* (n 102) 501
104 *Rederiaktiebolaget v R* (n 102) 501
105 *Rederiaktiebolaget v R* (n 102) 501–502
106 *Rederiaktiebolaget v R* (n 102) 503 Rowlatt J
107 And the DRDs for that matter.
108 Or as at July 2013 for the DRDs
109 *Robertson v Minister of Pensions* [1949] 1 KB 227 at 237 (KB) (Denning J)
110 *H.T.V. Ltd v Price Commission* [1976] ICR 170 (CA)
111 *H.T.V. Ltd v Price Commission* (n 110) 185 (Lord Denning)
112 Bradley and Ewing (n 95) 771
113 *Churchward v R* (1865) LR 1 QB 173 (pre-SCJA 1873)
114 *Churchward v R* (n 113) 173
115 *Churchward v R* (n 113) 174, 176–177, 211
116 *Churchward v R* (n 113) 185–186, 199
117 *Churchward v R* (n 113) 210
118 *Churchward v R* (n 113) 210 (Shee, J)
119 *Churchward v R* (n 113) 210–212 (Lush, J)
120 *Commercial Cable Co v Government of Newfoundland* (1916) 2 AC 610, *Auckland Harbour Board v The King* (1924) AC 318, and *A-G v Great Southern and Western Rly Co of Ireland* (1925) AC 754
121 *Mackay v A-G for British Columbia* (1922) 1 AC 457
122 *Mackay v A-G* (n 121) 461
123 Finance Act 2013 Part 2
124 Finance Act 2013 s 80
125 See Section 2.3.1 for a detailed discussion of this point.
126 Garnaut and Ross (n 13) Ch 7 p 100
127 Kevin Rudd and Wayne Swan, '*Stronger, fairer, simpler: a tax plan for the future*' (Commonwealth of Australia the Treasury Media Release 2 May 2010) <http://ministers.treasury.gov.au/DisplayDocs.aspx?doc=pressreleases/2010/028.htm&pageID=003&min=wms&Year> accessed 26 March 2017
128 Parliament of Australia, '*Budget Measures: Budget Paper No. 2: 2010–2011*' (Budget Paper, Commonwealth of Australia 2010)
129 Ken Henry, Jeff Harmer, John Piggott, Heather Ridout, and Greg Smith, '*Australia's Future Tax System: Report to the Treasurer*' (Commonwealth of Australia The Treasury, December 2009)
130 See Australian Financial Review, '*Rio Joins BHP in Suspending RSPT ads*' (Article, AFR 24 June 2010) and Dennis Shanahan, '*Kevin Rudd to Backflip on Mining Tax Rate*' (The Australian 27 May 2010)
131 Parliament of Australia, '*Taxation – Resource super profits tax*' (Budget Review, Commonwealth of Australia 2010)
132 Henry et al (n 129) 48
133 During the initial few years from the commencement of RSPT whereby the transition from the existing system to RSPT would occur, the Government proposed an

accelerated depreciation rates whereby the starting base would be written-off across 5 years with 36% in the first year, 24% in the second year, 15% in the third and fourth years, and 10% in the fifth year The Treasury, '*The Resource Super Profits Tax: a Fair Return to the Nation*' (Commonwealth of Australia The Treasury 2010)

134 Parliament of Australia (n 131) and KPMG, *'The Treasury: CGE Analysis of Part of the Government's AFTSR Response'* (Report, KPMG 2010)

135 i.e. at a long-term government bond rate.

136 The Treasury (n 133) v

137 Note that this regime did not apply to the Joint Development Area in the Timor Sea, to onshore projects and to the North West Shelf Project – which includes the Cossack, Wannaea, Lambert and Hermes fields. See North West Shelf Gas, '*North West Shelf Project: Overview*' (2014) <http://www.nwsg.com.au/projects/overview> accessed 26 March 2017, and Woodside Petroleum, '*North West Shelf Project*' (Woodside Petroleum) <http://www.woodside.com.au/Our-Business/Producing/Pages/North-West-Shelf.aspx> accessed 26 March 2017 – until 2012 when it was extended to include the latter two. The Joint Development Area is still subject to royalty and excise, see Australian Taxation Office, *'Guide to Depreciating Assets 2013'* (Guide 1996–06, ATO 2013)

138 Plant and machinery were allowable at 25% declining balance prior to 1 July 2001. However, under the uniform capital allowance system this is no longer the case. Such capital expenditures are now allowable 100% at the year they are incurred, Australian Taxation Office (n 137)

139 Although, only the exploration expenditure is allowed to be set against income from other fields.

140 The abandonment credit is the lesser of (a) '40% of the excess expenditure' and (b) the total amount of PRRT paid or payable in relation to the petroleum project in previous years, reduced by any previously allowable credits in relation to the petroleum project" Australian Tax Office, '*Petroleum Resource Rent Tax'* (Guide, ATO 2016)

141 Australian Tax Office (n 140)

142 KPMG (n 134)

143 S Bond and M P Devereux, *'Generalised R-based and S-based Taxes Under Uncertainty'* (IFS Working Paper W99/9, Institute of Fiscal Studies 1999)

144 R Boadway and M Keen, *'Theoretical perspectives on resource tax design'* Queen's Economics Department Working Paper No 1206, Queen's University 2009)

145 Petroleum Resource Rent Tax Assessment Act 1987 as amended by Tax Laws Amendment (2013 Measures No. 2) Act 2013

146 Henry et al (n 129)

147 See Section 3.4

148 The RRT was also the theoretical foundation for the Australia's PRRT regime.

149 See Section 3.4

150 Henry et al (n 129)

151 Norwegian Ministry of Finance, *'Skattlegging av petroleumsvirksomhet'* (Norwegian Official Report 2000:18 Norwegian Ministry of Finance 2000)

152 Norwegian Ministry of Finance, Ot.prp. nr. 86 (2000–2001) The details of the reforms is outside of the scope of this work as it does not impact the arguments presented in this work.

153 Norwegian Ministry of Finance (n 151)

154 Diderik Lund, *'Petroleum Tax Reform Proposals in Norway and Denmark'* 23(4) Energy Journal 37

155 Norwegian Ministry of Finance (n 151)

156 A detailed discussion on the depreciation schedule is outside of the scope of this work as it does not impact the arguments presented in this work.

157 Norwegian Ministry of Finance, '*Riktige beregninger fra Finansdepartementet*' (Norwegian Ministry of Finance 2013)
158 See Section 3.4 for a detailed discussions on the potential distortions a rigid uplift can create. Also see Petter Osmundsen, Magne Emhjellen, Thore Jensen, Alexander Kemp and Christian Riis, '*Petroleum Taxation Contingent on Counter-factual Investment Behaviour*' 36 Energy Journal 1, for a criticism of these changes.
159 Lund (n 154)
160 26 US Code § 901–989. Also note that, in the USA, there are special rules on oil and gas income. 26 US Code § 907
161 Norwegians termed it Capital Return Allowance as it applied to the whole investment and not only the equity finance as it would be under ACE. As mentioned in Chapter 3, a detailed discussion on ACE is beyond the scope of this work. For a detailed discussion on ACE see Box 3.2
162 *Exxon Corporation and Affiliated Companies v Commissioner of Internal Revenue* 113 US TC 24 (1999)
163 *Exxon v CIR* (n 162) 32–33
164 *Exxon v CIR* (n 162) 34
165 The creditability of the R-based tax has also been argued by the leading academics. See Charles E McLure, Jr, Jack Mintz, George R Zodrow, *US Supreme Court Unanimously Chooses Substance over Form in Foreign Tax Credit Case: Implications of the PPL Decision for the Creditability of Cash-flow Taxes*' (Centre for Business Taxation WP 14/11, Oxford University August 2014)
166 See Section 4.1
167 Osmundsen et. al. (n 158)
168 See Chapter 2
169 William H Knull, III, Scott T Jones, Timothy J Tyler and Richard D Deutsch, '*Accounting for Uncertainty in Discounted Cash Flow Valuation of Upstream Oil and Gas Investments*' (August 2007) 25 Journal of Energy and Natural Resources Law 3
170 For a detailed discussion on the payback period, see Section 2.4.1.1
171 For the 20 and 10 mmbbls field scenarios it is 2 years' time, and for the 50 mmbbls it is 3
172 See Chapter 4
173 See Section 2.3
174 See Section 2.3
175 For their distributions see Website.
176 This means for the entire field life the modelling relies on the same mean value for the oil price. This is in contrast to time-dependent modelling whereby the stochastic value randomly assigned in the first period is treated as the mean value for the probability distribution in the second period. This is repeated throughout the field life. The effect is that the latter type of modelling introduces a higher volatility into the oil price. However, this work models the oil price as mean-reverting in ascertaining the risk-sharing features of the tax regime.
177 The exact figure is 60.1%
178 Please note that the numbers for pre-tax mean expected NPV will differ from those in Chapter 4 even though the simulation is based on the same model, data and assumptions. This is due to the random value selection for the oil price variable in each repetition.
179 See Section 4.3
180 (724+(-178)) / (1811+(-441)) = 0.399, or 39.9%
181 See Chapter 4
182 Alexander G Kemp and Kathleen Masson, '*Taxation and Project Risk Sharing with Special Reference to the UKCS*' (1998) North Sea Study Occasional Paper No. 66;

Alexander G Kemp and Kathleen Masson, '*Oil and Gas Exploration and Development in the UKCS: A Monte Carlo Analysis of the Risks and Returns*' (1998) North Sea Study Occasional Paper No. 69; and Alexander G Kemp and David Reading, '*Economic and Fiscal Aspects of Field Abandonment with Special Reference to the UK Continental Shelf*' (1991) North Sea Study Occasional Paper No. 34

183 And from the distributions in website

184 See the website for the results of the other variables individually stochastic.

185 Their distributions are presented in website

186 The exact figure is 49.93%

187 Please note that the numbers for pre-tax mean expected NPV will differ from those in Chapter 4 even though the simulation is based on the same model, data and assumptions. This is due to the random value selection for the oil price variable in each repetition.

188 (3906+(-302)) / (9766+(-755)) = 0.3999, or 39.99%

6 Conclusion

The fiscal regime applicable to the upstream petroleum sector in the UK still needs to be reformed. Unfortunately, the recent reforms introduced by the government have been inadequate. This book puts forward a reform policy and recommends a new fiscal regime underpinned by contractual arrangements between investors and the state. The result of the new regime is to align the UK government with the equity partners in individual petroliferous projects. With this new policy framework the proposed fiscal regime can achieve its mandate of strongly supporting the Maximising Economic Recovery (MER UK) objectives.

It certainly is evident that with comparatively lower returns, higher costs, increased complexities and the associated uncertainties the time is, and has been, appropriate for reforming the fiscal regime. The Treasury also argued so. In its Fiscal Review it set the objective of the reform as supporting the MER UK goal while ensuring a 'fair return' for the UK in the form of 'rent'.[1] This objective itself was supported by three guiding principles. The first principle highlighted the need for the levels of tax takes to fluctuate in parallel with the levels of maturity, or the need for flexibility. The second, the need for fiscal policies to consider 'wider economic benefits of oil & gas production'.[2] The third principle provided the guidance on 'fair return', in that, the concept of 'fair return' had to 'take account of both prices and costs'.[3] Consequently, this work adopted the Fiscal Review objective as its own goal in developing a new fiscal regime for the UKCS and relied on the same guiding principles.

However, the Fiscal Review did not provide any explanation as to what exactly was meant by its objective of ensuring 'rent' nor by its principles. In order to clarify and understand the Fiscal Review objective and its principles, this work relied on petroleum tax theory and the methodologies employed by investors in evaluating potential investments in the upstream petroleum sector. Accordingly, this work showed that it was the Ricardian rent the Fiscal Review objective was referring to. Capturing this was therefore also the objective of the new fiscal system proposed in this work. This was then supplemented by a clear understanding of the Treasury's principles regarding how prices and costs could be taken into account, and how flexibility could be achieved. This, in turn, provided the opportunity to develop a set of objective criteria to assess the fiscal reforms. Both the ensuing reforms following the Fiscal Review and the reforms proposed in this work were assessed on their abilities to capture economic rents.

The criteria of efficiency, flexibility and neutrality adopted in this work were in conformity with the guiding principles of the Fiscal Review. Its first principle alluded to the concept of flexibility, while the third principle to the concepts of efficiency and neutrality.[4] Therefore, it was evident that the objective and the guiding principles established by the Treasury were firmly grounded in tax theory. Yet the measures introduced by the government in response were largely insufficient since they did not follow the Fiscal Review's own guiding principles.

In order to understand why these reforms introduced by the Treasury were unsatisfactory a discussion was needed on what exactly the Treasury was reforming. This was because only with the discussion on the then existing tax regime was it possible to understand the nature of the reforms introduced by the Treasury and the extent of their inadequacy in attaining the Fiscal Review objective.

Therefore, Chapter 3 laid out the then existing fiscal regime to highlight what was being reformed and why such reform was needed. It discussed the three pillars, the Ring Fence Corporation Tax (RFCT), the Supplementary Charge (SC) and the Petroleum Revenue Tax (PRT) that together make up the fiscal regime, and showed their complexity. When taken together, the marginal tax rates at the time of the Fiscal Review were as high as 81% for the PRT-liable fields and 62% for the others. Worse, as a whole the system was far from achieving the objective set out in the Fiscal Review. When set against the criteria of efficiency, neutrality and flexibility the system was performing poorly.

Thus, it was evident why the tax regime in place at the time of the Fiscal Review was inefficient and in desperate need of reform. Yet the reforms that followed were far short of the Fiscal Review objective and quite divergent of its guiding principles. The initial reform measures reduced the headline Supplementary Charge (SC) rate by 2%.[5] This reduction in the headline rate effectively reduced the marginal tax rates from 81% to 80% for the PRT-liable fields, and from 62% to 60% for all other fields.

It was not likely that such a small change in the marginal tax rates would have been sufficient enough to have a considerable impact on the investment levels. This view was supported both by the industry[6] and by the new regulator, the Oil and Gas Authority (OGA).[7] Both entities believed that the measures were not robust enough to support the MER UK objectives. In response the government further reduced the applicable SC rate by another 10% a few months later,[8] and then by another 10% a year later.[9] These initial measures also simplified the complex and fragmented allowance mechanisms, replacing them with two umbrella mechanisms called Investment Allowance[10] and Cluster Area Allowance.[11]

In addition to the changes in the SC pillar, the Treasury's reforms also introduced important changes to the other two fiscal pillars. The RFCT pillar was amended by extending the application of its RFES mechanism from 6 years to 10 while the PRT pillar was subject to a number of successive changes.

The PRT headline rate was first reduced from 50% to 35% in 2015,[12] bringing down the marginal tax rate for a PRT-liable field to 67.5%. This rate, however, was in place only for one year. From 2016, the rate was reduced to 0%.[13] This latter measure, of courses, did not abolish the PRT pillar, it only abolished the PRT liability since all the treatments of expenditures and losses in arriving at assessable profits continued to apply. These measures resulted simply in assessable profits no longer generating PRT liability.

This work therefore argued that although some of the reform measures were positive, they did not necessarily follow the guiding principles of the Fiscal Review and subsequently fell short of its objective. Specifically, when taken as a whole the reform measures did not address the non-neutral elements of the UKCS tax regime. The inefficiencies and regressive elements continued to be present. To see how these reforms fell short of the Fiscal Review objective this work subsequently analysed the impact of the current, post-reform tax regime on potential investment opportunities. This analysis in Chapter 4 utilised model oil fields while following the guiding principles of the Fiscal Review.

Accordingly, the deterministic analysis concluded that for an existing taxpayer the current tax regime following the most recent reforms responded progressively to the changes in overall per barrel costs and oil prices, and proportionally to the changes in reserve sizes. This initially seemed like a positive and unexpected outcome. It seemed positive because it avoided regressivity, and it was unexpected because it seemed to be yielding a result different than the theoretical analysis. Yet, a closer examination revealed that the magnitude of the progressivity seemed to decline in tandem with the changes in the variable values.

The outcomes of the deterministic and theoretical analysis were more in alignment when the model field analysis was carried out on the new entrant. Despite the presence of certain non-regressivity, the system was showing some strong regressive behaviours for a new entrant which were largely due to new entrant's inability to utilise initial losses or allowances.

This, in turn, revealed the limitations of the deterministic approach in that it identified the behaviours of the tax regime only under specific circumstances. It provided a good indication as to how the tax regime might behave but not how it would behave when all the possibilities were taken into account. This is why a stochastic approach in the form of a Monte Carlo analysis was additionally carried out.

The results of the Monte Carlo analysis showed that the fiscal regime was certainly non-neutral for both investor types, particularly when the oil prices were modelled as stochastic. This meant that the tax regime was increasing the chances of turning a cash flow that was positive pre-tax to a negative one after tax. Worse, this was more likely for a new entrant.

Thus, the quantitative analysis supported the conclusion of the theoretical analysis that the Fiscal Review reforms fell short of its own objective. The results showed that the regime with the most recent reforms was still not efficient in capturing the economic rents.

It was therefore posited that given the volatility in the oil prices, and its disproportionate impact on the behaviour of the fiscal regime, this non-neutrality could still become a considerable threat to the MER UK strategy. Without further reforms, the regime could still cause the non-development of some fields that would be viable pre-tax. This work, therefore, argued in Chapter 5 what those reforms ought to be like.

The first step in reforming the fiscal regime had to be the abolition of both the RFCT and the SC for all new projects. This was because these fiscal pillars by design could not target economic rents and thus could neither achieve the Fiscal Review objective nor support the MER UK strategy. The policy recommendation of this work was the replacement of these pillars by the new regime.

The new regime put forward in this work had its origins both in the Brown Tax and the PRT with appropriate modifications to suit the unique nature of the upstream petroleum sector in the UK. Like the PRT, and unlike the Brown Tax, it was advocated that the new regime would apply to individual project cash flows. The use of individual cash flows as the tax base would mean that the tax rate would apply not only to profits but also, like the Brown Tax, to losses in each tax period. For investors with multiple projects, the tax liabilities would be aggregated after they are determined separately for each project. Finally, unlike either the PRT or the Brown Tax, the headline tax rate would be determined contractually for each project. This new tax regime would not only be considerably simpler than the current regime but also in perfect conformity with the Fiscal Review's guiding principles, thus achieving the Fiscal Review objective.

It was also advocated that the regime would include a mechanism similar to the TRAs that exempt the tariff incomes. Although the tariff incomes did not come within the economic rent calculations and therefore could be taxed away in its entirety, making them tax-exempt could avoid creating disincentives for granting third-party access by the asset owners. This could then further support the MER UK strategy.

It was further shown that the new regime would satisfy the theoretical criteria of neutrality and efficiency. The neutrality would be maintained since the rankings of the attractiveness of various potential projects at the pre-tax level would be preserved and not get reordered when viewed after tax. Thus, it was argued that the regime would directly target the economic rents arising from the projects.

It was readily acknowledged that the proposed regime would be controversial. One of the strongest controversies concerned the fact that the state would effectively become an equity partner via the tax regime without the legal rights to participate in decisions regarding the running of the projects. However, the strength of this controversy subsided following the Wood Review since the new regulator, the OGA, was now able to participate in the decision-making process of investors. Although this participation was without voting rights, the powers of the OGA to impose sanctions on the investors nonetheless placed the new regulator in a highly influential position. The proposed tax regime, therefore, was simply complementing this position fiscally and financially.

Another strong controversy concerned the fact that the state would have to pay the investor an amount equivalent to the negative tax liability when the cash flow for that tax period is negative. Yet there were already precedents for this in the current regime. Under both the DRD and the ATL mechanisms, the Treasury was obligated to pay the investors. Instead of this current fragmented approach, the new regime proposed to apply this obligation uniformly throughout the lives of the projects.

This approach, however, then led to a separate but related issue. It was argued that under this approach the state would have decreasing incentives to comply with the obligation to pay the investors towards the end of the projects' lives. This issue, however, was addressed by putting forward a contractual mechanism that was broader than but similar to the DRDs. It was broader than the DRDs because it was not restricted to decommissioning but covered the entire lives of the projects. On the other hand, it was similar to the DRDs, because, like the DRDs, the proposed contractual arrangement resembled a stand-alone version of stabilisation clauses, specifically the *strictu sensu* variant, commonly found in economic development agreements.

Although, it was subsequently argued, this contractual arrangement could ensure the state would comply with its obligations throughout the lives of the projects, it could also be viewed as a restriction on the legislative powers of future governments. Yet the proposed contractual arrangement, as well as the DRDs, were and would be compatible with the UK's sovereignty. This was affirmed both by the domestic courts and by the international tribunals. Therefore, it was shown that these contracts would be legally enforceable, providing assurances to the investors that the negative taxes would be paid.

These contracts, it was argued, would also be the platform for determining the headline rate. This would resolve the problem of predetermining an umbrella tax rate for all projects irrespective of their risks. By individualising the tax rate within these contracts the state could determine separately the degree of its exposures to the risks of each project. In other words, the state would effectively have the option to decide the extent of its equity partnership for each project. Therefore, the proposed regime would target the economic rents arising from individual projects while incorporating flexibility into the level of risk exposures for the state.

Chapter 5 also noted that this new fiscal framework is not the first to find its origins in the Brown Tax. Previously, both Australia and Norway proposed reforms that were built on the theoretical Brown Tax. However, the Australian proposal was modified to the degree that it resembled more the theoretical Resource Rent Tax (RRT) than the Brown Tax. The Norwegian proposal, on the other hand, was comparatively closer to the Brown Tax in resemblance. Yet, political palatability and the potential inability of the US investors to claim tax credit at home resulted in a regime that was also much closer to the theoretical RRT regime instead.

Yet these proposals in Australia and Norway were significantly different than what has been proposed in this work. None of the issues that were present in those jurisdictions were a barrier to the new regime put forward for the UK. This was because not only was there already, in the current post-Fiscal Review regime, the obligations on the state to pay the investors but also the US investors could claim tax credit at home thanks to the adoption of the PRT rules.

Consequently, it can be stated that the proposed new regime would certainly be aligned to deliver a 'fair return' to the government and satisfy the objectives set out in the Fiscal Review. If the UKCS fiscal regime is required to adapt to the 'changing economics of the UKCS, create fiscal stability, help the UKCS compete for investment, simplify the regime and ultimately use the regime to help'[14] with the MER UK strategy, then the proposed fiscal regime is the reform that is sorely needed.

Notes

1 HM Treasury, 'Driving Investment: a plan to reform the oil and gas fiscal regime' (Report, HM Treasury December 2014) Box 4.A
2 HM Treasury (n 1) Box 4.A
3 HM Treasury (n 1) Box 4.A
4 As has been argued in Section 2.1.4, the second principle was more of a platitude than a guiding principle and as such would not be focussed on in this work
5 HM Treasury (n 1) 4.6
6 Oil & Gas UK, '*Oil & Gas UK meeting with Chancellor George Osborne*' (Press Release, Oil & Gas UK 25 February 2015)
7 Oil & Gas Authority, '*Call to Action: The Oil and Gas Authority Commission 2015*' (Report, the OGA Commission 25 February 2015)
8 Finance Act 2015 s 48
9 Finance Act 2016 s 58
10 Finance Act 2015 s 49 and Schs 12 and 14
11 Finance Act 2015 s 50 and Sch 13
12 Finance Act 2015 s 52
13 Finance Act 2016 s 140
14 HM Treasury (n 1) and George Osborne, *'Chancellor George Osborne's Budget 2014 Speech'* (Speech, HM Treasury, 2014)

Appendix

Chart A.1 Historical Brent spot FOB prices

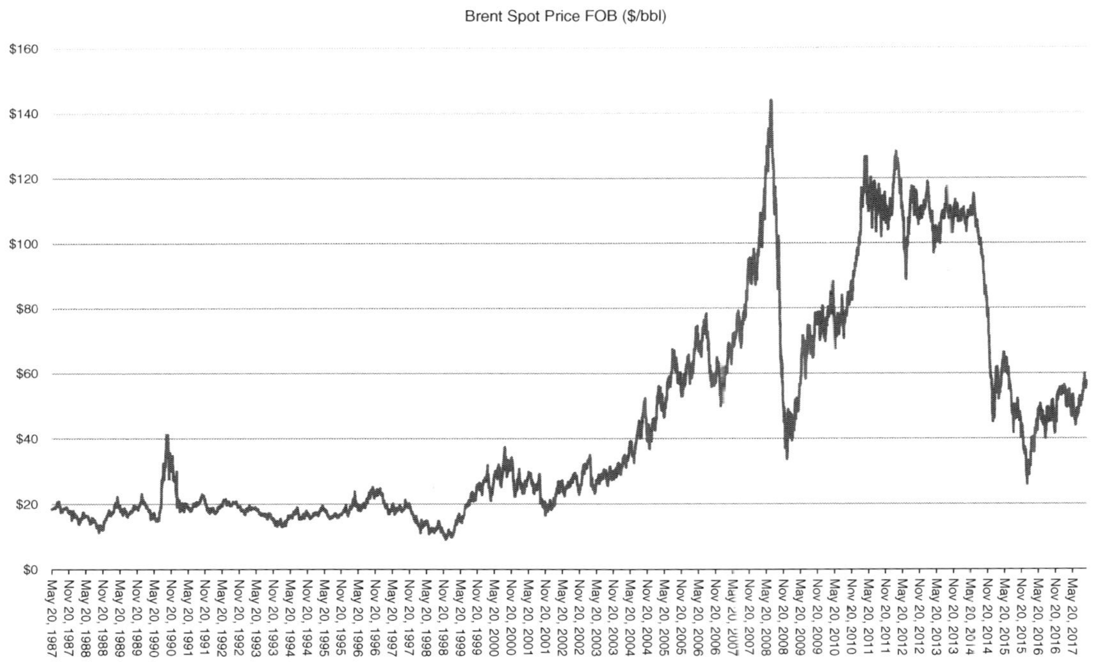

Source: US Energy Information Agency, *'Petroleum & Other Liquids: Europe Brent Spot Price FOB'* (US EIA, 13 December 2015)

Bibliography

Al-Emadi T A Q, 'Stabilisation Clauses in International Joint Venture Agreements' (2010) 3 International Energy Law Review 54.

Allen and Overy, Guide to Extractive Industries Documents: Oil and Gas (Report, World Bank Institute Governance for Extractive Industries Programme, September 2013).

Allen R J and Pardo M S, 'The Myth of the Law – Fact Distinction' (2003) 97 Northwestern University Law Review 1769.

Al-Mazeedi W, 'Privatizing the National Oil Companies in the Gulf' (1992) 20 Energy Policy 983–994.

Australian Financial Review, Rio Joins BHP in Suspending RSPT Ads (Article, AFR 24 June 2010).

Babadagli T, 'Development of Mature Oil Fields – A Review' (2007) 57 Journal of Petroleum Science and Engineering 221.

Baunsgaard T, A Primer on Mineral Taxation (IMF Working Paper No. 01/139, IMF, 2001).

Bird R, Taxation and Development (October 2010 The World Bank Economic Premise 34).

Berk J and DeMarzo P, Corporate Finance: Global Edition (3rd Ed, Pearson, 2014).

Bittker B I, Equity, Efficiency, and Income Tax Theory: Do Misallocations Drive Out Inequities (1979) Yale Law School Faculty Scholarship Series 2301.

Black J, 'Talking about Regulation' (1998) PL 77, and I Lianos, 'Lost in Translation?' (2009) Towards a Theory of Economic Transplants', vol. 62 (CLP) 346.

Boadway R and Bruce N, 'A General Proposition on the Design of A Neutral Business Tax' (1984) 24 Journal of Public Economics 2, 231–239.

Boadway R and Keen M, 'Theoretical Perspectives on Resource Tax Design', in P Daniel, M Keen, and C McPherson (eds) The Taxation of Petroleum and Minerals: Principles, Problems and Practice (Routledge, 2010).

Boadway R and Keen M, Theoretical Perspectives on Resource Tax Design (Queen's Economics Department Working Paper No. 1206, Queen's University, 2009).

Bond S and Devereux M P, Generalised R-Based and S-Based Taxes under Uncertainty (IFS Working Paper W99/9, Institute of Fiscal Studies, 1999).

Bradley A and Ewing K, Constitutional and Administrative Law (13th Ed, Pearson, 2013).

Brealey R A, Myers S C, and Allen F, Principles of Corporate Finance: Global Edition (10th Ed, McGraw-Hill, 2011).

Brown E C, 'Business-Income Taxation and Investment Incentives', in L A Metzler (ed) Income, Employment and Public Policy: Essay in Honor of Alvin H. Hansen (W W Norton & Co, Inc, 1948).

Brown R, 'Some Policy and Legal Issues Affecting Mining Legislation and Agreements in African Commonwealth Countries' (1977) Commonwealth Secretariat and Institute of Development Studies 70.

Cnossen S, 'Taxing Capital Income in the Nordic Countries: A Model for the European Union?', in S Cnossen (ed) Taxing Capital Income in the European Union – Issues and Options for Reform (OUP, 2000).

Combs S, 2014 Property Value Study: Discount Range for Oil and Gas Properties (Texas Comptroller of Public Account August 2014).

Cordes J, 'An Introduction to the Taxation of Mineral Rents', in J Otto (ed) The Taxation of Mineral Enterprises (Graham & Trotman, 1995), 26.

Cramton P, 'How Best to Auction Natural Resources', in P Daniel, M Keen and C McPherson (eds) The Taxation of Petroleum and Minerals: Principles, Problems and Practice (Routledge, 2010).

Delaume G R, The Proper Law of State Contracts Revisited (Spring 1997) 12 ICSID Review-FILJ 25.

Devereux M P and Freeman H, 'A General Neutral Profits Tax' (1991) 12(3) Fiscal Studies 1.

Dixit A and Pindyck R, Investment Under Uncertainty (1994).

Edens J, Extracting Maximum Value from a Maturing Basin: Case for Fiscal Incentives (CNR International presentation, 28 Feb 2012).

Emhjellen M and Alaouze C, The Discounted Net Cashflow Method and a Modern Asset Pricing Method – Implications for Project Selection and Government Policy (2001, The University of New South Wales).

Faber M and Brown R, 'Changing the Rules of the Game: Political Risk, Instability and Fairplay in Mineral Concession Contracts' (1980) 2 Third World Quarterly 100.

Fane G, 'Neutral Taxation Under Uncertainty' (1987) 33 Journal of Public Economics 1, 95–105.

Farley A and Wilson M, 'Capital Allowances', in N Lee (ed) Revenue Law: Principles and Practice (21st Ed, Bloomsbury Professional Ltd, 2013).

Fraser R, 'On the Neutrality of the Resource Rent Tax' (1993) 69 The Economic Record 56–60.

Gammie M, Equity for Companies: A Corporation Tax for the 1990s: A Report of the IFS Capital Taxes Group Chaired by Malcolm Gammie (The Institute for Fiscal Studies, 1991).

Garnaut R and Ross A C, Taxation of Mineral Rents (Clarendon Press, 1983).

Garnaut R and Ross A C, 'The Neutrality of the Resource Rent Tax' (September 1979) The Economic Record 193.

Garnaut R and Ross A C, 'Uncertainty, Risk Aversion and the Taxing of Natural Resource Projects' (1975) 85 The Economic Journal 338, 272–287.

Gordon G and Paterson J, 'Mature Province Initiatives', in G Gordon, J Paterson and E Usenmez (eds) Oil and Gas Law: Current Practice and Emerging Trends (2nd Ed, DUP, 2011).

Gordon G, 'Petroleum Licensing', in G Gordon, J Paterson and E Usenmez (eds) Oil and Gas Law: Current Practice and Emerging Trends (2nd Ed, DUP, 2011).

Graham J and Harvey C, 'The Theory and Practice of Corporate Finance: Evidence from the Field' (2001) 60 Journal of Financial Economics 187.

Haig M, 'Corporation Tax', in N Lee (ed) Revenue Law: Principles and Practice (21st Edition, Bloomsbury Professional Ltd, 2013) 41.91.

Hansen T B, 'The Legal Effect Given Stabilization Clauses in Economic Development Agreements' (1987–1988) 28 Virginia Journal of International Law 1015.

Harden C, Discount Rate Development in Oil and Gas Valuation (Society of Petorleum Engineers Hydrocarbon Economics and Evaluation Symposium SPE-169862-MS 19–20 May 2014).

Hasseldine J, 'The Administration of Tax Systems', in E Albi and J Martinez-Vazquez (eds) The Elgar Guide to Tax Systems (Edward Elgar, 2011).

Hayllar R F and Pleasance R T, UK Taxation of Offshore Oil and Gas (Butterworths, 1977).

Henry K, Harmer J, Piggott J, Ridout H and Smith G, Australia's Future Tax System: Report to the Treasurer (Commonwealth of Australia The Treasury, December 2009).

Herfindahl O C, 'The Value of Mineral Surveys to Economic Development', in D M Brooks (ed) Resource Economics: Selected Works of Orvis C Herfindahl (Johns Hopkins University Press, 1974).

Hotelling H, 'The Economics of Exhaustible Resources' (April 1931) 39 The Journal of Political Economy 2, 137–175.

Infanti A C and Crawford B J, Critical Tax Theory: An Introduction (CUP, June 2009).

Isaac J, 'A Comment on the Viability of the Allowance for Corporate Equity' (1997) 18 Fiscal Studies 3, 303–318.

Jacoby H and Laughton D, 'Project Evaluation: A Practical Asset Pricing Model' (1992) 13 Energy Journal 19.

Jahn F, Cook M and Graham M, Hydrocarbon Exploration and Production (2nd Ed, Elsevier, 2008).

Jaidah A M, Problems and Prospects of State Petroleum Enterprises in OPEC Countries (United Nations Integral Symposium on State Petroleum Enterprises in Developing Countries, Vienna, Austria (7–16 March 1978).

Johnston D and Johnston D, Introduction to Oil Company Financial Analysis (PenWell, 2006).

Kaplow L, Horizontal Equity: Measures in Search of Principle (1985) Harvard Law School Program of Law and Economics Discussion Paper No. 8, 5/85.

Kemp A G and Jones P D A, Progressive Petroleum Taxes and the 'Gold Plating' Problem (1996) North Sea Study Occasional Paper No. 59.

Kemp A G and Macdonald B, The UK and Norwegian Fiscal Systems: A Comparative Study of Their Impacts on New Field Investments (1992) North Sea Occasional Papers No. 38.

Kemp A G and Masson K, Oil and Gas Exploration and Development in the UKCS: A Monte Carlo Analysis of the Risks and Returns (1998) North Sea Study Occasional Paper No. 69.

Kemp A G and Masson K, Taxation and Project Risk Sharing with Special Reference to the UKCS (1998) North Sea Study Occasional Paper No. 66.

Kemp A G and Reading D, A Comparative Analysis of the Impact of the UK and Norwegian Petroleum Tax Regimes on Different Oil Fields (1990) North Sea Study Occasional Paper No. 31.

Kemp A G and Reading D, Economic and Fiscal Aspects of Field Abandonment with Special Reference to the UK Continental Shelf (1991) North Sea Study Occasional Paper No. 34.

Kemp A G and Reading D, The Economics of Incremental Investments in Mature Oil Fields in the UK Continental Shelf (1991) North Sea Study Occasional Paper No. 36.

Kemp A G and Reading D, The Impact of Petroleum Fiscal Systems in Mature Field Life: A Comparative Study of the UK (Norway, Indonesia, China, Egypt, Nigeria, and United States Federal Offshore, 1991, North Sea Study Occasional Paper No. 32).

Kemp A G and Rose D, Fiscal Aspects of Investment Opportunities in the UKCS and Norway, Denmark, the Netherlands, Australia, China, Alaska (North and South) and the US Outer Continental Shelf (1993) North Sea Occasional Paper No. 43.

Kemp A G and Stephen L, Price Sensitivity, Capital Rationing and Future Activity in the UK Continental Shelf after the Wood Review (November 2014 North Sea Study Occasional Paper 130).

Kemp A G and Stephen L, Prospective Activity Levels in the Regions of the UKCS under Different Oil and Gas Prices: An Application of the Monte Carlo Technique (1999) North Sea Study Occasional Paper No. 71.

Kemp A G and Stephen L, 'The Investment Allowance in the Wider Context of the UK Continental Shelf in 2015: A Response to the Treasury Consultation (February 2015 North Sea Occasional Paper No. 132).

Kemp A G, Maximising Economic Recovery from the UK Continental Shelf: A Response to the Draft DECC Consulting Strategy (January 2016 North Sea Occasional Paper No. 135).

Kemp A G, Petroleum Exploitation in North West Europe and the Atlantic Margin: Tax and Government Takes and Investor Returns (August 2012 Unpublished work).

Kemp A G, Petroleum Rent Collection around the World (The Institute for Research on Public Policy 1987).

Kemp A G, Rose D and Kellas G K, Petroleum Exploration Risks and Fiscal and State Participation Systems: A Monte Carlo Study of the UK, Norway, Denmark and the Netherlands (1988) North Sea Occasional Paper No. 27.

Kemp A G, Rose D and Stephen L, Petroleum Investment and Taxation: The North Sea and the Far East (1995) North Sea Study Occasional Paper No. 49.

Kemp A G, The Official History of North Sea Oil and Gas (Routledge, 2012).

Klemm, A, 'Allowances for Corporate Equity in Practice' (2007) 53 CESifo Economic Studies 2, 229.

Knull W H III, Jones S T, Tyler T J and Deutsch R D, Accounting for Uncertainty in Discounted Cash Flow Valuation of Upstream Oil and Gas Investments (August 2007) 25 Journal of Energy and Natural Resources Law 3.

KPMG, 'Corporate Tax Rates Available' (2015) <http://www.kpmg.com/global/en/services/tax/tax-tools-and-resources/pages/corporate-tax-rates-table.aspx> accessed 02 March 2015

KPMG, The Treasury: CGE Analysis of Part of the Government's AFTSR Response (Report, KPMG 2010).

KPMG, A Guide to UK Oil and Gas Taxation: 2012 Edition (Report, KPMG 2012).

Lagarde C, Revenue Mobilization and International Taxation: Key Ingredients of 21st-Century Economies by IMF Managing Director Christine Lagarde (22 February 2016 IMF Communication Department, the Arab Fiscal Forum Speech Transcript).

Land B C, 'Resource Rent Taxes: A Re-Appraisal', in P Daniel, M Keen, and C McPherson (eds) The Taxation of Petroleum and Minerals: Principles, Problems and Practice (Routledge, 2010).

Laughton D, Sagi J and Samis M, Modern Asset Pricing and Project Evaluation in the Energy Industry (Sept 2000) Vol. 56 Western Centre for Economic Research, University of Alberta Bulletin.

Lewis W, The Power of Productivity: Health, Poverty and the Threat to Global Stability (University of Chicago Press, 2004).

Lianos I, "Lost in Translation?' (2009) Towards a Theory of Economic Transplants' 62 (CLP) 346.

Lund D, 'Petroleum Tax Reform Proposals in Norway and Denmark' 23(4) Energy Journal 37.

Maniruzzaman A F M, 'Some Reflections on Stabilisation Techniques in International Petroleum, Gas and Mineral Agreements' (2005) 4 International Energy Law & Taxation Review 96–100.

Mantzari D, 'Economic Evidence in Regulatory Disputes: Revisiting the Court-Regulatory Agency Relationship in the US and the UK' (2016) 36(3) Oxford Journal of Legal Studies 569.

McAfee R P and McMillan J, 'Auctions and Bidding' (1987) 25 Journal of Economic Literature 669.

McCray W A, Petroleum Evaluations and Economic Decisions (Prentice-Hall Inc, 1975).

McLure C E Jr, Mintz J, Zodrow G R, US Supreme Court Unanimously Chooses Substance over Form in Foreign Tax Credit Case: Implications of the PPL Decision for the Creditability of Cash-Flow Taxes (Centre for Business Taxation WP 14/11, Oxford University, August 2014).

Meade J E, The Structure and Reform of Direct Taxation (Report of a Committee chaired by Professor J. E. Meade, The Institute for Fiscal Studies, George Allen & Unwin Ltd, 1978).

Mommer B, Private Landlord-Tenant Relationship in British Coal and American Oil: A Theory of Mineral Leases' (1997) Oxford Institute for Energy Studies Paper EE20.

Mommer, B, Oil Prices and Fiscal Regimes (1999) Oxford Institute for Energy Studies Paper WPM24.

Montembault B, 'The Stabilisation of State Contracts Using the Example of Oil Contracts. A Return of the Gods of Olympia?' (2003) 6 International Business Law Journal 593–643.

Musgrave R A and Musgrave P B, Public Finance in Theory and Practice (5th Ed, McGraw-Hill, 1989).

Nakhle C, Petroleum Taxation: A Critical Evaluation with Special Application to the UK Continental Shelf (July 2004 University of Surrey Unpublished PhD Thesis).

Nakhle C, Petroleum Taxation: Sharing the Oil Wealth: A Study of Petroleum Taxation Yesterday, Today and Tomorrow (Routledge, 2008).

Newendrop P, Decision Analysis for Petroleum Exploration (Planning Press, 1975).

Nore P, 'The Transfer of Technology: The Norwegian Case', in R El Mallakh and D H El Mallakh(eds) New Policy Imperatives for Energy Producers (International Centre for Energy and Economic Development, 1980).

Osmundsen P, Emhjellen M, Jensen T, Kemp A G, and Riis C, Petroleum Taxation Contingent on Counter-Factual Investment Behaviour (September2015) 36 The Energy Journal 1.

Otman W, The Petroleum Development Investment Risks and Returns in Libya: A Monte Carlo Study of the Current Contractual Terms (EPSA IV) (2004) North Sea Study Occasional Paper No. 94.

Otto J, Andrews C, Cawood F, Doggett M, Guj P, Stermole F, Stermole J, and Tilton J, Mining Royalties (World Bank, 2006).

Palmade V, Industry Level Analysis: The Way to Identify the Binding Constraints to Economic Growth (World Bank Policy Research Paper No. 3551, The World Bank, 2005).

Paterson J, 'Decommissioning of Offshore Installations', in G Gordon, J Paterson and E Usenmez (eds) Oil and Gas Law: Current Practice and Emerging Trends (2nd Ed, DUP, 2011).

Peat, Marwick, Mitchell & Co, A Guide to UK Oil & Gas Taxation (Peat, Marwick, Mitchell & Co, 1986).

Peter W, 'Stabilization Clauses in State Contracts' (1998) 8 International Business Law Journal 875.

Platts, 'Dated Brent' (McGraw Hill Financial 2015) < http://www.platts.com/price-assessments/oil/dated-brent > accessed 17 August 2015

Platts, 'Glossary' (McGraw Hill Financial) <http://www.platts.com/glossary> accessed 16 November 2015

Radulescu M D and Stimmelmayr M, 'ACE versus CBIT: Which Is Better for Investment and Welfare?' (2007) 53 CESifo Economic Studies 2, 294–328.

Rahman M, 'Forecast of the World Oil and Gas Market Development' (Speech at the 4th Russian Oil and Gas Week, OPEC, Moscow, Russia, 26–28 October 2004)

Research Excellence Framework, 'About the REF' <www.ref.ac.uk/about> (15 December 2014) accessed 18 July 2017

Ricardo D, Principles of Political Economy and Taxation (1817).

Rosengard J K, Property Tax Reform in Developing Countries Harvard Institute for International Development and International Tax Program (Harvard University, Kluwer Academic Publishers, and Springer Science + Business Media, 1998).

Rutledge I and Wright P, 'Profitability and Taxation in the UKCS Oil and Gas Industry: Analysing the Distribution of Rewards between Company and Country' (1998) 26 Energy Policy 10.

Schumann C P P C, 'Oil & Gas Royalty Interest Valuations' (2015) <http://www.cpschumannco.com/business.asp?subject=11> accessed 24 February 2015

Shanahan D, Kevin Rudd to Backflip on Mining Tax Rate (The Australian, 27 May 2010).

Siew W, Financial Evaluation Techniques Used to Evaluate Risk and Appraise Projects in the Oil Industry (2001) University of Dundee Unpublished Thesis.

Slemrof J and Yitzhaki S, 'The Costs of Taxation and the Marginal Efficiency Cost of Of Funds' (March 1996) 43 IMF Staff Papers 1, 172.

Smith A, An Inquiry into the Nature and Causes of the Wealth of Nations (1776).

Smith J E and McCardle K F, 'Options in the Real World: Lessons Learned in Evaluating Oil and Gas Investments' (January-February 1999) 47 Operations Research 1, 1.

Snyder C and Nicholson W, Microeconomic Theory: Basic Principles and Extensions (11th International Ed, South-Western, Cengage Learning, 2012).

Stevens P, 'National Oil Companies: Good or Bad? A Literature Survey' (2004) CEPMLP Research Network 14(10).

Stiglitz J E and Walsh C E, Principles of Microeconomics (WW Norton, 4th Ed, 2006) 298.

Styles S, 'Joint Operating Agreements', in G Gordon, J Paterson and E Usenmez (eds) Oil and Gas Law: Current Practice and Emerging Trends (2nd Ed, DUP, 2011).

Swierzbinski J, 'Chapter 162: The Economics of Exploration for and Production of Exhaustible Resources' in J Shogren (ed) Encyclopedia of Energy and Natural Resource and Environmental Economics (Vol. 3, Elsevier Press, 2013).

Tordo S, Fiscal Systems for Hydrocarbons: Design Issues (World Bank Working Paper No. 123, 2007).

Tordo S, Tracy B S, and Arfaa N, National Oil Companies and Value Creation (World Bank Working Paper No. 218, The World Bank, 2011).

Turpin C and Tomkins A, British Government and the Constitution (7th ed, Cambridge University Press, 2011).

University College London Faculty of Law, 3rd Annual Bentham House Conference on the Philosophical Foundations for Tax Law (UCL, 8–9May2015).

Usenmez E, Formation of Oil Prices: The Commodity Futures Markets, the Role of Reporting Agencies and the Potential Ways Forward (unpublished, 2018).

Usenmez E, 'Optimising Offshore Health and Safety Inspections: How the Markets Could Help', in M Baram, P Lindoe and O Renn (eds) Risk Governance of Offshore Oil and Gas Operations (Cambridge University Press, 2014).

Usenmez E, The Stability of the UK Tax Regime for Offshore Oil and Gas: Positive Developments and Potential Threats (2010) ICCLR 16.

Usenmez E, 'The UKCS Fiscal Regime', in G Gordon, J Paterson and E Usenmez (eds) Oil and Gas Law: Current Practice and Emerging Trends (2nd Ed, DUP, 2011).

Vass U, 'Access to Infrastructure', in G Gordon, J Paterson and E Usenmez (eds) Oil and Gas Law: Current Practice and Emerging Trends (2nd Ed, DUP, 2011).

Waelde T W and Ndi G, 'Stabilizing International Investment Commitments: International Law Versus Contract Interpretation' (1996) 31 Texas International Law Journal 215.

Waelde T W, The Current Status of International Petroleum Investment: Regulating, Licensing, Taxing, and Contracting (1994) CEPMLP 1 (5).

Walton P and Aerts W, Global Financial Accounting, And Reporting: Principles and Analysis (2nd ED, Cengage Learning, 2009).

Woodside Petroleum, 'North West Shelf Project' (Woodside Petroleum) <http://www.woodside.com.au/Our-Business/Producing/Pages/North-West-Shelf.aspx> accessed 26 March 2017

Wright C J and Gallun R, International Petroleum Accounting (PenWell, 2005).

Yergin D, The Prize: The Epic Quest for Oil, Money and Power (Simon & Schuster, 1991).

Index